COACH'S GUIDE

to

THE MEMORY JOGGER™ II

The easy-to-use, complete reference
for working with
improvement & planning tools
in teams

GOAL/QPC
Methuen, MA

Editor: Francine Oddo
Cover design: Lori Champney
Illustrations: Deborah Crovo, Michele Kierstead and Jim Pinto
Book design and production: Michele Kierstead

Manufactured in the United States of America.

First Edition
10 9 8 7 6 5 4 3 2 1

For information call or write:

GOAL/QPC
P.O. Box 329, Lawrence, MA 01842-0629
Toll free 1-800-643-4316
978-685-3900   FAX 978-685-6151

GOAL/QPC is a nonprofit organization striving to help companies continually improve
their Quality, Productivity, and Competitiveness. (Hence, the "QPC" in our name.)

Printed on 50% recycled paper with 10% post-consumer and 40% pre-consumer waste.

ISBN 1–879364–47–6

Contents

Acknowledgments

Thanks go to many, many people for contributing to this endeavor.

▶ **To the wacky, intrepid, and supremely competent core project team:**

Michael Brassard, Michele Kierstead, Francine Oddo, Dorie Overhoff, and Lisa Boisvert. Especially to Michael for inspiring the creation of this book, to Francine for her steady and discerning eye for language and detail and for her wisdom and balance in times of stress, and to Michele for her ability to build the bridge between her creative and artistic gifts and the practical needs of a business.

▶ **Individuals who contributed valuable insight in the market research and prototype review stages of the Coach's Guide development:**

These people were instrumental in making the *Coach's Guide* a publication that helps meet the needs and relieve the fears of our real heroes—the just-in-time coaches and facilitators called on to guide their teams through the use of the tools. They are listed below in alphabetical order by last name.

Anthony Borgen, Hamilton Standard
Donald Botto, Goodyear Tire & Rubber Company
Robert Brodeur, Bell Canada
Liane Dolezar, Waukesha County Technical College
Clydie Douglass, 3M Corporation
Steve Fischer, Holy Family Hospital
Nicholas Governale, Pendleton Productivity Center
Hollis Hohensee, Deere & Company
George Lejbjuk, Town of Coaldale, Alberta, Canada
Ann McManus, Consultant
Susan Murphy, SRM
Delia O'Connor, Holy Family Hospital
Brian Sesack, University of Pittsburgh Medical Center
Janet Shepperd, AT&T
Larry Smith, Ford Motor Company
Capt. T.C. Splitgerber, U.S. Navy, Naval Dental Center
Gary Starcher, Goodyear Tire & Rubber Company
Karen Tate, BGP
Pat Trout, Chandler Regional Hospital
Debra Walker, Goodyear Tire & Rubber Company
Jeanette Wallace, Rhode Island Hospital

Continued next page

▶ Company Teams Who Generously Told Their Stories for the Mini Case Studies (listed in alphabetical order):

> Bell Canada
> BGP
> Georgia State Department of Human Resources, Division of Rehabilitation Services
> Goodyear Tire & Rubber Company
> Hamilton Standard
> Millcreek Township School District, Millcreek Township, PA
> Novacor Chemicals (Canada) Ltd.
> Parkview Episcopal Medical Center
> Town of Andover, MA
> U.S. Air Force, Air Combat Command
> U.S. Navy, Naval Dental Center, San Diego

▶ Individuals and organizations that contributed additional examples to illustrate the real-life application of the tools:

Marshall W. Bond, Greater Pittsburgh Chamber of Commerce (Q-NET), Pittsburgh, PA; and Cindy Gentile, Sewickley Valley Hospital, Sewickley, PA.

▶ The individuals who made the time to apply their particular expertise to technically reviewing chapters in this publication:

David Ginder, I-Tech Group Ltd., for the Histogram and Process Capability chapters; Karen Tate, BGP, for the Prioritization Matrices and Scatter Diagram chapters; and Ledi Trutna, Advanced Microsystems, for the Control Chart chapter.

▶ The many individuals who contributed to the technical production of the book:

Editing support from Karen Jamrog Martel for these chapters: Brainstorming, Check Sheet, Interrelationship Digraph, Matrix Diagram, Nominal Group Technique, Pareto Chart, Radar Chart, Run Chart, and Tree Diagram; *Illustration design and support from:* Deborah Crovo and Jim Pinto; Steve Boudreau for patiently and skillfully supporting the project team's way through the printing and packaging processes of this project; *Word processing support from* Georgette Beaulieu; and Susan Griebel and Laurie Watkins for their willingness to interrupt their own work to help out the project team.

▶ Ellen Domb, Ph.D., President of The PQR Group, for sharing some lessons from her experience training adults to help enhance parts of the Nominal Group Technique chapter.

▶ Susan Ferraro-Leger, Judi Glidden, and Bill Montgomery for offering some helpful input early in the development process.

▶ Richard Morrison for the quotes we never used.

Contributors to "A Team's Experience . . . Using the (Tool)" (A Mini Case Study)

Continued next page

Introduction

What is The Memory Jogger™ II?

The Memory Jogger™ II, which was introduced in July of 1994, was designed to pick up where *The Memory Jogger™* left off. The original *Memory Jogger™*, published in 1985, included the basic quality control (QC) tools. The current generation Jogger, *The Memory Jogger™ II*, still features the QC tools, *and* adds the Seven Management & Planning Tools, *and* a chapter on teams, *and* a start-to-finish, problem-solving case study. *The Memory Jogger™ II* has a new cover and layout design, is twice the number of pages of *The Memory Jogger™*, is spiral-bound, is just about the same size as *The Memory Jogger™*, and is arranged alphabetically by tool name.

The main purpose of both versions of *The Memory Jogger™* has always been to increase the likelihood that all of the helpful methods for improvement, planning, and problem solving, are used frequently, appropriately and effectively by all people, regardless of their knowledge level or position in the organization. The key to progress is not acquired knowledge but *applied* knowledge!

Why a Coach's Guide? Who Needs It?

The *Coach's Guide* is intended to make it easier to use *The Memory Jogger™ II* as a key resource in planning and problem-solving efforts by:

- Providing advice, in-depth information and examples to get the most out of every step of each tool.

- Providing all of the material in a quick reference format that allows you to easily use it in both planned, formal training situations as well as impromptu learning opportunities.

- Providing high-quality overheads of all of the illustrations and organization examples in the book. (The set of overheads is part of the *Coach's Guide to The Memory Jogger™ II* **Package**; the set is not available separately.)

Who is a "Coach"?

Adults present an interesting learning challenge in that we seek and absorb new knowledge on an "as-needed" basis. Therefore, adult learning happens in many ways, whether it be in the classroom, the shop floor, a staff meeting, or a hallway. Who is the "teacher" in these different situations? It could be a professional trainer, a manager, or a team leader/member. Each type of person should share at least one common aim: to help others use methods effectively to tackle and improve the tough problems facing their organizations. In fact, each person may not see themselves as "trainers" per se, but they are all in the business of coaching for the resolution of problems and for effective planning. This role requires that coaches feel as confident as possible in their knowledge and ability to communicate it to others. This guide is designed to bolster confidence in both of these arenas.

How to Get Around in the Coach's Guide

The chapters of the *Coach's Guide* are organized in the same alphabetical order as *The Memory Jogger™ II*, except for three chapters—Data Points, Problem-Solving/Process-Improvement Model, and Team Guidelines—because they do not deal directly with any one specific tool. These chapters appear at the end of the book in Part III. All the tool chapters in Part II have the same general organization and include the following standard sections:

OVERVIEW

This section is the "Cliff Notes" for the already abridged *Memory Jogger™ II*. The Overview includes the essentials of why and when to use the tool (purpose), what questions and group challenges to expect in the process of constructing and using the tool, and (sprinkled throughout the book), a real-life team's experience in using the tool, with an illustration of what the tool looked like when they completed it. (These illustrations first appeared in *The Memory Jogger™ II*.)

The Overview can be used as a refresher for the coach or a very brief introduction for participants and team members. The Overview breaks down into these parts:

IS THIS THE RIGHT TOOL? ASK . . .

This section includes up to six guiding questions for the coach and team to answer in choosing the appropriate tool.

▶ **Purpose:** The most frequently cited problem in the use of improvement methods is choosing the right tool for the right situation. The questions are designed so that every "yes" response increases your confidence that this is the most effective tool choice.

▶ **Best Use:** As the coach, present the questions as a simple checklist for team members to use when the Tool Selector Chart (page xvi) indicates that a specific tool or method may be appropriate. The questions can also be used as a final check before you and the team begin to use the tool, to choose another tool or method, or to opt for an unstructured discussion (sometimes the best choice).

STEPS AT A GLANCE

People process information differently; we all have our own best mode for learning and taking in information. Some people learn best by listening and discussing, some by reading and visualizing, and others by doing, or using their body to complete a task. The "Steps at a Glance," with the exception of the Data Points chapter, is always a flowchart. This form will strongly appeal to visual learners. The flowchart is intended to provide a simplified and condensed version of the construction steps of the tool.

▶ **Purpose:** Provides a single visual representation of the process while still showing the decision points that actually occur during the construction steps.

▶ **Best Use:** Use the overhead transparency of the flowchart as a visual representation of the process and as a summary after either the presentation or the practice of that tool.

COMMONLY ASKED QUESTIONS

When helping others learn, it is natural for "teachers" to feel that they should know more than the learner. At minimum, this section will help you to avoid too many surprises. This section includes the most frequently asked, (and most-critical-for-the-success-of-the-tool), questions, from both team members and coaches. (We provide the answers too.)

▶ **Purpose:** Helps both the experienced and novice coaches feel that the major "sticking points" have been anticipated and that they will not be immobilized by a basic question. Also included are those nitty gritty questions that are very simple (and sometimes even trivial) which can distract you from the essential points you need to make. For example, the question of how Nominal Group Technique got its name sometimes comes up. The answer, find it on page 124, is not of earth-shattering importance but coaches sometimes get flustered when they don't know how to respond. When you have both the significant and trivial answers in your "back pocket," you can feel more prepared for tackling a variety of questions from the team. You can also include these questions in your lesson plan.

▶ **Best Use:** Only use the responses as needed—don't review them as typical questions. Those people who are inexperienced with the tools won't normally understand the context of the questions. Neither the question nor the answer will make sense. These tidbits are just for the coach.

FACILITATION ESSENTIALS

The tools and methods in *The Memory Jogger™ II* may fail for reasons that have little or nothing to do with the execution of the steps. Often, interpersonal problems exist within a team that show up in the team's poor use of a tool. This section includes techniques that will help coaches help teams to use the tools to their maximum benefit and deal with typical behaviors among team members that tend to surface when a particular tool is being used.

▶ **Purpose:** To help the coach anticipate the types of challenging behaviors that a particular tool tends to bring out in a team, and also the behaviors that should be encouraged to get maximum benefit from the use of a tool.

▶ **Best Use:** These facilitation essentials should not be reviewed with the team. Draw upon these facilitation tips as they are required. Rest assured that each team will exhibit some or all of these behaviors naturally (and invent some of their own).

Read This First

Team members frequently need a simple exercise to illustrate the major components of a process. The learning activities are generally flexible enough to accommodate either organizational or "life" examples. The learning activities are not intended to be all-inclusive of the steps of constructing a tool, they are really to help the team understand the very basic and core essence of the tool.

▶ **Purpose:** To provide an all-occasion exercise that can fit into virtually any training design. This is helpful when working with teams or classes at various levels of the organization. It is also intended to give team members just enough experience with the tool or method to see its benefits and to contrast it with current practices.

▶ **Best Use:** Simple illustrative activities are effective as ways to both "break the ice" and reduce "tool anxiety." Use these activities as early in the process as possible once the tool purpose and broad steps of tool construction have been defined. Ask team members how this tool or method is the same as or different from current methods being used in the department or other departments in the organization. Keep the discussion broad by emphasizing the simplicity of the tool or method, *not* its complexity.

This section is called "A Team's Experience . . . Using the [name of tool]." Not all the chapters have this section; the mini case study is included only in these chapters: AND, Affinity, Check Sheet, Control Chart, Flowchart, ID, Matrix, Pareto, Run, and Scatter. The case study page consists of eight questions about the use of the tool, which have been answered by the team leader or a team member who helped create the completed tool. An illustration of the completed tool appears on the page opposite the case study questions. If some of these tool graphics look familiar to you, that may be because you saw them in *The Memory Jogger*™ *II*. We asked those people who had contributed to *The Memory Jogger*™ *II* to give us their story behind the tool graphic. As you can see, many of them did!

▶ **Purpose:** At times there are team members who say: "Why should I bother with this?" or "What is the value for me, or for us?" or "Why is this a good investment of time?" The real stories help lend a sense that others have found value in these methods and tools. The mini case studies in this book describe the people who were involved with using a tool, and the team's process and results; the members of your team will get a glimpse into the context and logic of the real team, and see pictures of the real people. In addition, your team will see the flexibility and diversity of tool applications. While the specifics of the mini case studies are different, a common theme supports them all: each team had a need to find the real problem and deal with it effectively.

▶ **Best Use:** Using the overhead transparency of the completed tool example from the mini case study, (or simply pointing it out in the book), is an effective way to introduce the team to the steps of constructing the tool. As you talk to the team about the tool example, it will help you to establish credibility if you share insights from your own experience that may not be apparent in the graphic.

Each chapter has the same straightforward organization and design. (This introduction is designed the same way.) At the top of each page there is a bold banner that has the name and number of the construction step under discussion. On the same banner are the corresponding page numbers from the *The Memory Jogger™ II*, which is abbreviated "MJII." Each page in the *Coach's Guide* contains the kind of detailed construction advice that was not possible in *The Memory Jogger™ II*. There is plenty of white space and a dedicated column for notes.

▶ **Purpose:** The main advantage of *The Memory Jogger™ II* is its convenient size combined with essential information and comprehensive details. However, its size has created an enormous challenge in describing what IS essential and in deciding how comprehensive it CAN be. This section is intended to give a coach the detailed information that will help the team get the most from each step. Once again, only *essential* information has been included—otherwise, this book could have easily become a 500+ page tome instead of a manageable resource that is as approachable as the book it supports, *The Memory Jogger™ II*.

▶ **Best Use:** Every coach should become thoroughly familiar with the details in this section. Make note of additional information you learn that you find adds significantly to your understanding of the tool, and include it with your instruction as the team moves through each step. Be selective and make it personal by highlighting comments in the notes column of each page.

NEW TOOL EXAMPLES

All of the tool chapters, except Brainstorming, include a graphic example of the completed tool. Also, depending on the complexity of the tool, an interpretation of the completed tool is included as well.

▶ **Why Are These Examples New?**

These tool examples are "new" because they are different than the examples shown in the mini case studies, and they are not in *The Memory Jogger™ II*. The new tool example may be a single, simple tool graphic, or it may be more in-depth, such as a series of building graphics that illustrate each step in the process, and a descriptive analysis of what the completed tool shows. For the chapters that require mathematical calculations, the example may show how to figure the calculations, and show the diagram that results from the calculations. (For example, Control Chart, Data Points, Histogram, Process Capability.)

▶ **Where Can I Find These Examples?**

You can find the new tool example in the "Example" section at the back of the chapter, (just before the "Coach's Answer Key" for the Learning Activity, if there is one). The one exception is the Control Chart chapter, in which the example builds step by step throughout the chapter.

▶ **Purpose:** These new examples are designed to give you one more look at the diverse possibilities of each tool. These examples represent a variety of topics and industry divisions. Since these examples are generally not cited from real companies, they may be simpler (than is really the case), or on the "lighter" side to help demystify the tool. These examples are intended to inform both the team and the coach and reduce the general anxiety many people experience in trying something new.

▶ **Best Use:** The examples can be most effectively used in combination with the tool examples in *The Memory Jogger™ II*, or other examples you may have of your own. You can use the example before or after using the real company example, depending on the character of the team. If the team is willing but nervous, it may help to show the "lighter" example first. If team members are more confident in their abilities but skeptical about the usefulness of the tool or method, show the real company example first to enhance the credibility of the tool or method.

COACH'S GUIDE PACKAGE

Clearly, *The Memory Jogger™ II* is the key product that the *Coach's Guide* supports. The *Coach's Guide to The Memory Jogger™ II* **Package** is also available to support both this guide and *The Memory Jogger™ II*. It includes:

▶ The *Coach's Guide*

▶ *The Memory Jogger™ II*

▶ High quality overhead transparencies that are arranged alphabetically by chapter name, separated into individual folders, and divided by clearly labeled tabs. The types of overheads include:

  – Summary of the steps in constructing the tool

  – Key success behaviors in using the tool

  – Flowchart summary of the steps in constructing the tool

  – Illustrations of the tool in progress

  – Finished tool illustrations from *The Memory Jogger™ II*

  – New tool examples from the *Coach's Guide*

The *Coach's Guide* **Package** is organized to provide any coach with the ability to quickly find, easily organize, and take along ALL of the necessary graphical support for training and coaching a team in the use of the tools. The *Coach's Guide* **Package** will support both structured training events as well as impromptu, "just in time" learning opportunities. The *Coach's Guide* **Package** is intended to meet the varied and evolving needs of all coaches.

▶ **Using the Coach's Guide with Other GOAL/QPC Products**

GOAL/QPC has also developed software and videotape packages that fully support the teaching and practice of the basic QC Tools and the Seven Management and Planning Tools.

Tool Selector Chart

This chart organizes the tools by typical improvement situations, such as working with numbers, with ideas, or in teams.

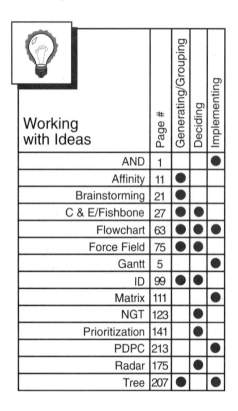

Working with Ideas	Page #	Generating/Grouping	Deciding	Implementing
AND	1			●
Affinity	11	●		
Brainstorming	21	●		
C & E/Fishbone	27	●	●	
Flowchart	63	●	●	●
Force Field	75	●	●	
Gantt	5			●
ID	99	●	●	
Matrix	111			●
NGT	123		●	
Prioritization	141		●	
PDPC	213			●
Radar	175		●	
Tree	207	●		●

Working with Numbers	Page #	Counting	Measures
Check Sheet	35	●	
Control Chart	45	●	●
Data Points	217	●	●
Histogram	83		●
Pareto	129	●	
Process Capability	159	●	●
Run	183	●	●
Scatter	191	●	●

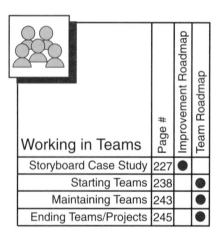

Working in Teams	Page #	Improvement Roadmap	Team Roadmap
Storyboard Case Study	227	●	
Starting Teams	238		●
Maintaining Teams	243		●
Ending Teams/Projects	245		●

PDPC Tool Selector Chart

This chart organizes the tools by the steps of the PDCA cycle described in the Problem-Solving/Process-Improvement Model chapter of this book.

Page #	Tools (Improvement Storyboard)	Plan				Do	Check	Act
		1. Select & Describe Opportunity	2. Describe Current Process	3. Describe Root Causes	4. Develop Solution	5. Implement Solution or Change	6. Review Evaluation Results	7. Reflect & Act on Learnings
1	AND				●	●		
11	Affinity	●		●	●			●
21	Brainstorming	●	●	●	●			●
27	C & E/Fishbone			●				○
35	Checksheet	●		●		○	●	○
45	Control Chart	●				●	●	●
217	Data Points	●						
63	Flowchart		●	○	●	●	●	●
75	Force Field			●	●		○	●
5	Gantt				●	○	●	
83	Histogram	●				●	●	●
99	ID	●		●	○		○	●
111	Matrix				●	●	○	○
123	Consensus Tools (NGT & Multivoting)	●		●	●			●
129	Pareto	●		●		○	●	●
141	Prioritization Matrices	●		○	●			●
159	Process Capability	●				●	●	●
213	PDPC				●	○	○	○
175	Radar	●				○	○	●
183	Run	●		●		○	●	●
191	Scatter			●		○	●	○
207	Tree		●		●	○	○	●

● = Typical use

○ = Possible use/referenced from previous step

OVERVIEW

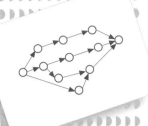

Activity Network Diagram (AND)

*Scheduling sequential
& simultaneous tasks*

IS THIS THE RIGHT TOOL? ASK . . .

▶ Are the risks of failure high enough that any slippage in the project schedule will have serious consequences?

▶ Are there a significant number of tasks that can be done simultaneously to make the plan more efficient?

▶ Is it important that people know throughout the project how the timely completion of their particular task affects the overall project?

▶ Are team members familiar enough with the majority of the tasks of the project to be able to provide accurate time estimates for each task?

STEPS AT A GLANCE

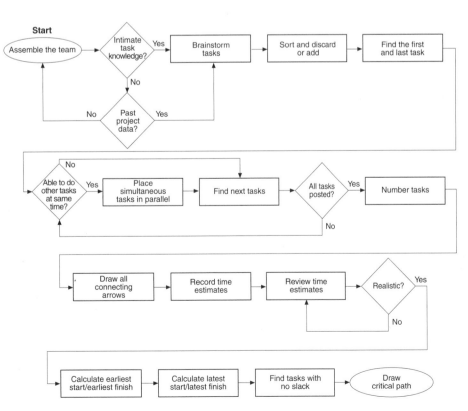

ACTIVITY NETWORK DIAGRAM

Q. How is this different from a process flowchart?

A. First, the AND records the time for each task. While the process flowchart can include this information, it generally does not. Secondly, the tasks in the AND are sequenced and connected based upon what must be done before other tasks can be started. It doesn't represent the ideal flow, as does a flowchart, but rather it deals with what is possible.

Q. How do you guarantee that the time estimates are accurate?

A. There are two approaches to increasing the accuracy of estimates. (There are no guarantees in life, except at L.L. Bean.) First, rely on previous project documentation whenever possible. If there are tasks that have been completed as part of other projects, find the actual completion time and use it where appropriate. Secondly, create a planning team that has people as close to the implementation effort as possible. The team will provide everyone with a healthy dose of reality.

Q. How long should it take to do a "typical" AND?

A. This is nearly impossible to answer since the applications of the AND range from a project that may include 12–15 tasks to the construction of a space shuttle. With the right team in place, a small- to medium-size project of 25–50 tasks should be completed in about a 2–3 hour session. This assumes that team members have been asked to come prepared with input on specific portions of the project. Even this can vary widely depending on whether the process is done manually or using dedicated software. (See the next question.)

Q. Should the process be done manually or should a software program be used?

A. Either way or a combination of both ways is possible. The AND, as described in this chapter and *The Memory Jogger™ II*, does not require teams to use a software program. As a general recommendation, try using the manual method first if people have never constructed an AND before.

Manual AND: When significant participation and consensus are necessary for the success of the project, the manual process of using Post-it™ Notes is a great way to create a dynamic diagram that will take its final form only when the team agrees to the "final picture." Another reason for manually constructing the AND is that many people can't read or understand a computer printout of an AND and won't admit it—manually creating the schedule can therefore increase understanding as well as commitment.

AND with software: There are many software programs available to support the AND, (usually under the name PERT or CPM), including the program from GOAL/QPC that features all of the Management and Planning Tools. Using a software package to create an AND is an excellent and efficient way to construct the diagram and the accompanying calculations.

Manual AND Combined with Software: Even very large projects can be broken down into smaller parts and assigned to small groups. Each small group can create an AND manually to reflect one piece of the project, then the output from all the ANDs can be fed into a software program to get one large AND that is a combination of all the pieces of the project.

If: **A member of the team is slowing progress by insisting that tasks will take either more or less time than is felt by the rest of the team . . .**

Then: ▶ Suggest ending the meeting and scheduling another meeting at which documentation from previous projects can be reviewed.

▶ Continue the meeting and ask the team to reconstruct a quick case study of similar projects, including a range of completion times for each task.

▶ Don't "turn-off" the person who is in the minority. He or she may indeed be right. Instead, ask for examples to support that person's differing views.

If: **The overall spirit of the team is negative, leading to unrealistically long completion times for tasks . . .**

Then: ▶ Take a break from the process and review the purpose and implications of the project. The team may have lost sight of the importance of the project and the accompanying tasks. There also might be fundamental disagreement over the wisdom of the effort. In either case, the negative atmosphere around the specifics may be a mask for disagreement on the overall direction.

▶ End the meeting, and review the composition of the team. The skepticism may reflect that the team is overloaded with "planners" and short on "doers." The solution is to balance the team.

LEARNING ACTIVITY

1. Have the group agree on a topic. Some suggested topics are:

   Work-related: buying a copy machine, producing a department/company newsletter, hiring a new department manager, finding a new job

   Non-work: buying a car, moving to another city, planning a wedding/reunion, buying or building a house

2. Form teams of 4–6 people. Form teams randomly if a non-work example is used. If a work example is chosen, form teams that represent as much of a cross section of the operation as possible.

3. Follow the instructions in this section for constructing the AND—with this addition: ask team members to individually estimate and record a realistic completion time for the topic project, however, ask them to keep their time estimates to themselves until the AND is complete.

4. When the AND is complete, compare the computed total project time to the individual estimates made before the exercise.

> 66 *The AND helped us to explain what activities we would do with the department managers through the auditing process.* 99
>
> *Karen Tate*

Written by Karen Tate, BGP

What was the problem?

The charter of the ISO 9000 Audit Team was to assess the current situation and to determine the amount and type of work that would be required to achieve ISO 9000 registration. Management would continue to evaluate the benefits of registration so that the decision to become certified could be made once the audit reports were published and the corrective actions had been completed. Regardless of the decision, the company would benefit from documentation of processes and compliance to the documentation.

Who was on the team?

The team had 15–20 members and was composed of representatives from every department in the company.

How long did the process take?

Since the ideal team size is 4–6 people, we decided that a small group would develop the schedule for the larger group to review. This group had experience in what needed to be done and in what sequence. They completed the draft AND in 2 hours. The AND was reviewed and approved by the larger team in less than 1 hour.

What did we learn?

The auditing, training, and corrective actions would involve coordination of many people in the company and timing of the activities was critical. Due to the nature of this work and the need to communicate the activities and timing to all department managers, the AND was chosen to develop the schedule.

How was the team affected?

Everyone on the team knew what they were supposed to do when and with whom. It gave all the team members as well as the other people involved a perspective of the big picture.

What else did we use?

In order to share this information with the rest of the company, a Gantt Chart was drawn to display the activities on a time line. Although the Gantt method does not show interdependencies, predecessors, and successors, it clearly shows when the activities will occur and was easier to communicate with people outside the team. The team needed to have the AND to test the feasibility of their plans.

KAREN TATE, MEMBER OF THE ISO 9000 TEAM

What was the conclusion?

The developers used the AND process to give credibility to their target end date for themselves and with others, and to "sanity check" their plan before forging ahead.

What were the results?

A schedule that we could manage to and the confidence of management that we could pull it off as planned.

Gantt Chart

ISO 9000 Audit Schedule

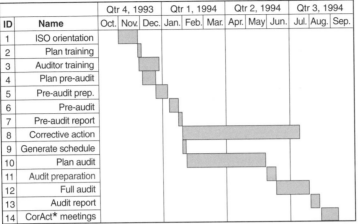

ID	Name	Qtr 4, 1993			Qtr 1, 1994			Qtr 2, 1994			Qtr 3, 1994		
		Oct.	Nov.	Dec.	Jan.	Feb.	Mar.	Apr.	May	Jun.	Jul.	Aug.	Sep.
1	ISO orientation												
2	Plan training												
3	Auditor training												
4	Plan pre-audit												
5	Pre-audit prep.												
6	Pre-audit												
7	Pre-audit report												
8	Corrective action												
9	Generate schedule												
10	Plan audit												
11	Audit preparation												
12	Full audit												
13	Audit report												
14	CorAct* meetings												

*CorAct = Corrective action

Key Dates

1/3	Release documentation request for pre-audit	2/25	Release full audit schedule
1/21	All documentation for pre-audit collected	6/13	Commence full audit
		7/29	Finish full audit
1/28	Hold pre-audit orientation meeting	8/12	Hold full audit orientation meeting

Activity Network Diagram

Phase I ISO 9000 Certification Audit Schedule

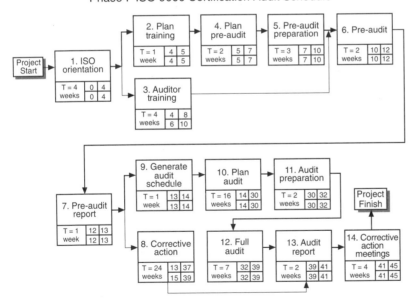

Earliest Start (ES)	Earliest Finish (EF)
Latest Start (LS)	Latest Finish (LF)

ES = The *largest* EF of any *previous* connected task

EF = ES + the time to complete that task

LS = LF - the time to complete that task

LF = The *smallest* LS of any connected *following* task

When ES = LS AND EF = LF, that task is on the critical path, and therefore there is no schedule flexibility in this task.

Information provided courtesy of BGP

Note: The AND shows that the certification process will take 45 weeks. The bold arrow, indicating the critical path, clearly shows those tasks that must be completed as scheduled. The tasks off the critical path will also require careful monitoring since there is only two weeks of slack time in the schedule.

5

STEP 1 ASSEMBLING THE TEAM

MJII p. 3

▶ **Composition of the Team**

Traditionally, the largest obstacle to the day-to-day use of the AND has been its lack of credibility. It has often been prepared by individuals or teams that are far removed from the reality of implementation. Therefore, the time estimates may be seen as "wishful thinking," based on either budgetary or scheduling pressures rather than the actual tasks at hand. The people who are expected to execute the plan often feel shut out of the process. They also don't see how their contribution fits into the success of the overall project. As a result of these perceptions, they feel much less commited to the outcome.

What are three methods to increase the level of team participation and commitment?

– Expand the initial team to include representative "doers." Involve them at least through the brainstorming and time estimate steps. The actual contruction of the chart can be done by a smaller team.

– Include the "doers" as reviewers *early* in the process. For example, invite them to review the list of tasks and time estimates rather than waiting until the final version is produced.

– Have the team to form subgroups for the purpose of producing different ANDs that represent increasing levels of detail. For example: a top-level team could form and build an AND that includes only major milestones. A second team could take this information and focus on identifying the places where tasks are handed off from one department or unit to another. Finally, teams at the unit level can break down their tasks into assignable jobs.

▶ **Individual and Team Accountability:** Another major reason for the lack of credibility of the AND is the perception by the people who will implement the tasks that other team members will not be held accountable for ensuring the tasks are completed as scheduled. In the traditional management model, managers hold individuals accountable, however, team accountability can be more powerful. In team accountability, team members are accountable to each other, and it's unlikely that any team member will fail to recognize the mutual dependence each member has on another. If there is no consequence for the lack of participation and commitment, no scheduling tool will help.

STEP 2 BRAINSTORMING ALL TASKS

MJII p. 3

▶ **Supplementing Brainstorming**

Brainstorming is a very powerful tool but it does have limitations. It represents the knowledge of a specific group of people at a particular moment. It's possible that some key tasks may be omitted because no one remembers them or a key person is not present. At this critical stage of project planning, a few facts won't hurt. Turn to work records from past projects for review to make sure that nothing critical was missed. These records may also provide information on the actual schedule of similar past projects.

MJII p. 4

STEP 3 FINDING THE FIRST TASK

▶ **Necessary + Possible = The First Task**

The first necessary task is a bit deceiving. It doesn't matter if the task the team chooses as the first is the most important task to complete first. What is important is that the task is possible. The team should ask, "*What is the most important task that can be carried out independently of all the other tasks?*"

MJII p. 4

STEP 4 FINDING SIMULTANEOUS TASKS

▶ **Could Do vs. Would Do**

When looking for those tasks that could be done simultaneously, teams often confuse this with what would normally be done in a typical plan. For example, when planning a vacation anywhere in the United States, it's possible to buy postcard stamps at the same time that the budget is being developed (the first thing to do). This is true only because buying stamps doesn't depend on any of the other tasks in the plan, and it may actually be one of the *last* tasks done in the process. By identifying stamp buying as a task that could be done simultaneously with another task, efficiencies can be gained. Instead of buying stamps at the hotel, the person could buy the stamps while at the pharmacy waiting for a prescription to be filled. This is a trivial example, but for large projects that typically use ANDs, tremendous efficiencies can be gained by identifying such parallel tasks, which can then be assigned to various teams or team members. Don't let traditional practices get in the way of new possibilities.

▶ **Creating More Tasks**

New tasks can be created at any time during the process and added as appropriate. Watch out though, these creations can take on lives of their own. Always ask, "*Are the possible additions to the chart at the same level of detail as the original tasks?*" Otherwise, the plan could sink to the level of planning the trivial rather than the vital. Such tasks can be broken out in sub-schedules done by individuals or teams.

MJII p. 4

STEP 5 FINDING THE NEXT TASKS

▶ **Repeat After Me**

The tips described in Steps 3 and 4 also apply in this step. The team should use either Post-it™ Notes or a software program because both methods make everything "portable" rather than permanent. Encourage a team member to propose a next task . . . put it up . . . get consensus . . . move on. The AND can always be changed at this step in the process so *don't draw any connecting lines yet!* The lines will be drawn in the next step. Patience.

STEP 6 DETAILING THE CHART

MJII p. 5

▶ Making Sound Connections

When drawing the arrows between tasks, ask of each task card, "*What are the next tasks that cannot start until this task is completed*?" The arrow can lead to any of the tasks that follow. This connection can exist with just one task or several task cards. Remember that the arrow must reconnect with *some* task that follows, even if it only connects with the very last task in the diagram. Otherwise, an "unconnected" task is not necessary and should be eliminated.

▶ Base Time Estimates on Facts

The team must never start with the required completion date and work backwards to estimate each job task. This can be an exercise in creative math. Don't be afraid to blow the desired completion date out of the water. When the project cycle is clearly too slow, the team can either reexamine the reality of the original date or begin to change how the project gets executed. Always ask, "*If the time estimate is shortened, what will be done to modify the task or the logic to account for the change*?" This may prevent the team from simply engaging in "wishful thinking."

STEP 7 FINDING THE CRITICAL PATH

MJII p. 5–8

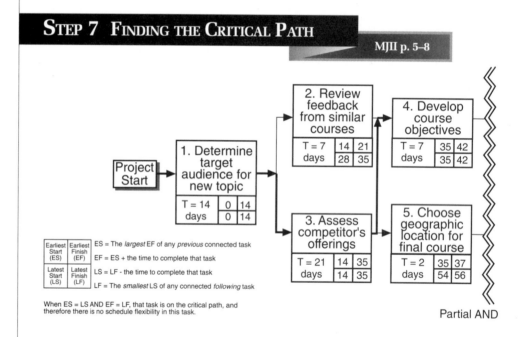

Partial AND

▶ Calculating Slack Time

Calculating the slack time for each task is easier than it looks! Slack time is how much a task can deviate from the schedule before it delays the remainder of the project, including the end date. The reason why the team needs to determine slack times is to in turn determine the critical path, which is the shortest possible time to complete the project.

Earliest Start

Notice in the graphic at the beginning of this step that Task 4 has two tasks feeding into it. This is not unusual. The completion of one task is often directly dependent on as many as 4–5 previous tasks. It is vital to remember that *a task cannot start until the slowest previous task is finished*. This means that Task 4 cannot start before Task 3 is completed. Why? Because Task 3 has the latest possible completion time of all the tasks that lead up to Task 4. Notice that Task 2 can be finished by the 21st day. However, since Task 4 depends on *both* Tasks 2 and 3, the later completion time dictates the start time for this task.

Latest Finish/Latest Start

Referring to the graphic at the beginning of this step, notice again that Task 4 depends on the completion of both Tasks 2 and 3. Since the Latest Finish (LF) of Task 4 is 42 days, the Latest Start of that task is 35 days (42–7=35). The Latest Start of Task 4 therefore becomes the Latest Finish of all of the tasks feeding into it (Tasks 2 and 3). In this example, Early Start and Late Start for Task 4 are the same because this activity is on the critical path.

▶ Forward Pass/Backward Pass

At the bottom of the graphic in Step 7 (and MJII page 6) are the definitions and formulas for calculating the Earliest Start, Earliest Finish, Latest Start, and Latest Finish. The process of calculating the Earliest Start and Latest Finish is called the *Forward Pass* because it is a rolling calculation that begins with the first task and works its way through the diagram to the last task in the project. The process of calculating the Latest Start and Latest Finish is called the *Backward Pass* since it is also a rolling calculation that starts instead with the last task and works its way through the diagram to the first task in the project. Generally, teams start with the Forward Pass and then do the Backward Pass.

▶ Drawing the Finished Diagram

Once the Forward and Backward Passes are completed, the team will be able to identify the tasks that are on the critical path. When the numbers in the boxes for the Earliest Finish/Latest Finish (top quadrants) are identical to the numbers in the boxes of the Earliest Start/Latest Start (lower quadrants), these tasks are on the *critical path*. Connect all such tasks with a bold arrow to indicate they are the most time-sensitive tasks, and also to represent the flow of events as the shortest possible time to complete the entire project.

▶ So What If the Critical Path is Identified?

Knowing the critical path should help any team do three things: 1) Go back to the drawing board when the total project time exceeds the available time for completion, 2) Closely monitor the tasks on the critical path to make sure that the team has as much notice as possible about potential delays in the schedule, and 3) Shift people and resources as needed from tasks that are not on the critical path to the tasks on the path that have exceeded the time estimate or seem likely to do so.

INCIDENTALLY

The Activity Network Diagram (AND) is equivalent to the Program Evaluation Review Technique (PERT) and the Arrow Diagram, and similar to the Critical Path Method (CPM). The similarity of these tools lies in their roots to post-World War II operations research. During the 1950s, as new weapons were developed, so were a series of cost and schedule overruns. Along came the Polaris Missile System, which would become a project planning milestone, in that it was the largest integrated weapons system development in history. Since the completion of this project, virtually every major construction project has used PERT and CPM. Most project planners have excellent software available to do the calculations and physical production of the final chart.

EXAMPLE

Pulling Off a Surprise Anniversary Party

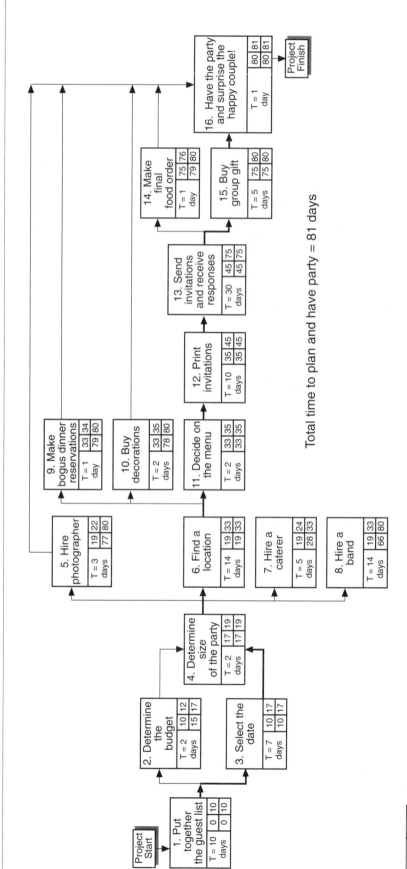

OVERVIEW

Affinity Diagram
*Gathering &
Grouping of Ideas*

Affinity Diagram

IS THIS THE RIGHT TOOL? ASK . . .

▶ Does your team need to find a starting point for discussion after it has brainstormed a large number of ideas?

▶ Is your team "stuck" and unable to break out of old ways of thinking?

▶ Do you need to create a positive atmosphere for everyone to think creatively about a tough problem?

▶ Has your team just generated lots of ideas and is asking "So what?"

▶ Does your team need to prevent individuals from dominating an important discussion?

STEPS AT A GLANCE

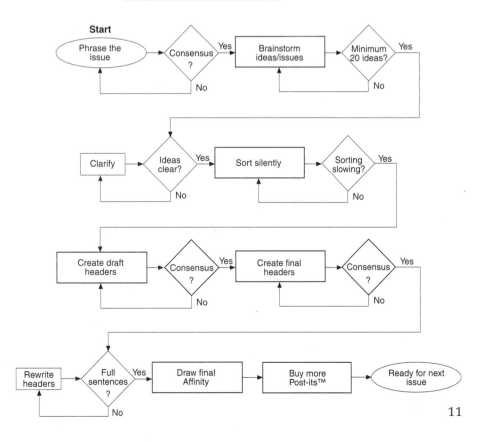

11

Affinity Diagram

Q. How is this tool better than traditional brainstorming?

A. The point of brainstorming is to create a high volume of unfiltered ideas, but brainstorming won't help team members identify important patterns within the ideas. The Affinity preserves the creativity of brainstorming while enabling the team to focus on a few common themes that emerge.

Q. Why use Post-its™?

A. Four reasons: It's easy to stick them on a surface; it's different from using notepads or slips of paper, and this encourages a more creative environment; it makes one idea stand apart from another because ideas are written down on separate pieces of note paper; and team members can move and regroup similar ideas freely because the note paper is portable.

Q. Do we own stock in 3M?

A. No, but we wish we did.

Q. How big is a typical Affinity?

A. 40–60 ideas, although 100–200 ideas are not unusual. 6–10 groupings is typical, with 15–17 groupings as a maximum.

Q. Is sorting in silence important? Why?

A. Silent sorting has proven to be invaluable for these reasons: it forces people to focus on the content of the idea, not on the originator; it allows people the freedom to see new combinations of ideas since they don't have to defend their ideas or convince others; people tend to avoid old semantic battles; and working together as a group in silence is different and therefore fosters new ideas and solutions.

Q. How do I know when to stop moving a particular Post-it™ back and forth? And when to stop overall sorting?

A. Common sense. If an idea goes back and forth between two groupings at least 3–4 times, stop to talk about interpretation, and if needed, create a duplicate and put it in both groupings. Stop overall sorting when the sorting slows down dramatically and when it's almost a struggle to move things. Test this by asking: Are we comfortable with the way this looks?

Q. Why work so hard at creating header cards?

A. Value and meaning are added in the headers. The objective *is not* to state the lowest common denominator within groupings. The objective is to capture the combined meanings of ideas that may never be grouped exactly the same again. Every header has the *potential* of being a breakthrough concept, but it won't be clear ahead of time which groupings will produce a breakthrough header.

Q. How do we know we have a good header card?

A. Ask two questions: If our team only had the header and with no detail beneath, would someone else understand what was unique about that grouping? Does it tell us the common theme and what all the ideas in the grouping add to that theme?

If: **There's a need to prevent a senior person or a personally powerful member of the team from dominating the process . . .**

Then: ▶ Ask someone else to lead the brainstorming and write down the headers.

▶ Listen for and identify when there is a wide consensus on the problem statement.

▶ Encourage everyone to sort simultaneously, not in subgroups.

▶ Make sure the team leader or facilitator is recording and posting suggested headers from which the team can choose the final version.

If: **A team is afraid to honestly share ideas or is unaccustomed to participating . . .**

Then: ▶ Have the team brainstorm in silence with each person writing his or her own Post-it™ anonymously and then combine and post them.

If: **The team produces "weak" header cards and resists working harder to improve them . . .**

Then: ▶ Ask them to imagine that all of the detailed Post-its™ have disappeared (or cover them up with a sheet of flipchart paper) and ask:

"Would the header cards communicate the full breadth and depth of the ideas generated to someone who was not at the session?"

LEARNING ACTIVITY

To "loosen up" the team:

1. Work in groups of 4–6 people.

2. Ask everyone to place 5 different personal items in a single pile in the center of a table. For example: pictures, keys, credit cards.

3. Ask each group to simultaneously sort the items into piles of like items.

4. Have each person list, in full sentences, what ties each pile of items together.

5. Ask each person to share and compare their versions. Note differences and similarities.

Suggested issues for generating Affinity Diagrams:

1. What must an effective supervisor do?

2. What are some barriers to effective training?

3. What are some features of an excellent hotel?

4. How can creativity in the workplace be encouraged?

5. How can planning be improved?

13

> "This tool took a very complex situation and boiled it down into manageable pieces that could be discussed intelligently, clearly, and objectively."
>
> Debra Walker

Written by Debra Walker, Goodyear Tire & Rubber Co.

What was the problem?

The team was a tactical business unit (TBU) that had made great progress in the writing of business plans but had difficulty using them to guide day-to-day activity.

Who was on the team?

It was a cross-functional team including marketing, development, sales, production, and physical distribution.

How long did the process take?

Because the group was large, four subgroups worked together for about 2 hours. It took another 2 hours to consolidate each subgroup's work into one Affinity Diagram.

What did we learn?

The tool took a very complex situation and boiled it down into manageable pieces that could be discussed intelligently, clearly, and objectively.

How was the team affected?

The team enjoyed the Affinity process. The silent sorting "evens out" team members, giving the quieter ones an even chance against the more vocal ones. We would assign header creation to all members and thus get full participation. Final header wording was reached by consensus, requiring a lot of discussion, but ultimately agreement was reached through some give-and-take effort.

What else did we use?

We went from the Affinity to an Interrelationship Digraph and finally a Tree Diagram.

What was the conclusion?

The Affinity showed us that our business plans were not as effective as they could be because of problems in three areas: 1) in the steps of our current planning process (in its multiple forms), 2) in how the planning team worked together, and 3) in the resources that supported whatever plan was produced. The question that remained was, "Which of these should we focus on in order to have the greatest impact?"

What were the results?

We defined as a group the basic nature of our business planning challenges, but the Affinity did not help us to prioritize among them. We agreed that we needed to work on the most practical improvement plan, and therefore committed to using the Interrelationship Digraph and Tree Diagram to reach this consensus.

**Issues Surrounding
Implementation of the Business Plan**

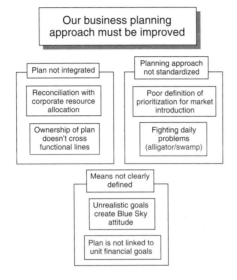

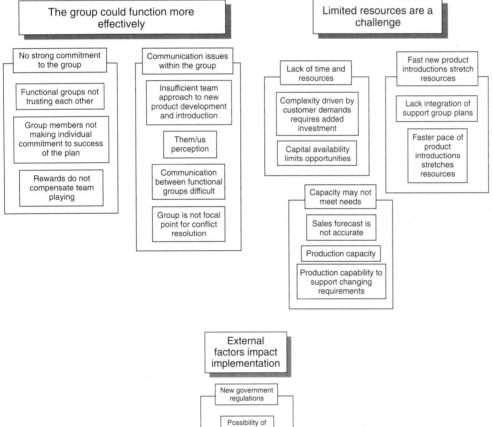

Information provided courtesy of Goodyear

Note: The Affinity helped the team bring focus to the *many* opinions on business planning. The headers that surfaced became the key issues in the ID example (shown in the ID tool section of *The Memory Jogger*™ *II* page 82.)

STEP 1 PHRASING THE ISSUE

MJII pp. 12–13

▶ Types of Statements

Neutral statements are often preferable to positive, negative or solution-oriented statements because they encourage wide-open thinking. Team members may be thinking of problems, solutions, important data, and so on. Great ideas come in many forms and should be encouraged to emerge naturally. While the format of the statement or question is important, getting consensus and clarity is far more critical.

Here are examples of the different formats that can be used to phrase an issue statement:

Neutral

"What are the issues involved in expanding our market share?"

Positive

"What advantages does our company have that we can use to expand our market share?"

Negative

"What is stopping us from expanding our market share?"

Solution-Oriented

"What can we do, or must we do, to expand our market share?"

INCIDENTALLY

How the Affinity Came to Be: The Affinity process was developed during the 1960s by a Japanese anthropologist named Jiro Kawakita, (the name KJ was coined from his initials), who was frustrated by the difficulty in picking out the critical patterns among large volumes of observations. He would make hundreds of observations within a particular study and know intuitively that he was seeing some new and interesting things, but he found himself categorizing them using old concepts. His thinking was "stuck." For Kawakita to see new patterns emerge in the information, he needed a fresh outlook. He created the Affinity Diagram to capture his knowledge while not limiting his thinking. He began sorting all of his observations so that his "right brain" could more clearly see important new patterns.

When the Affinity was discovered, it was combined with the other Management & Planning (MP) Tools, and applied to Total Quality in Japan in the 1970s. It was introduced to the United States by GOAL/QPC in 1983. It has become the most widely used of the MP Tools.

▶ **Traditional Brainstorming**

Try to Do

- Encourage everyone to participate.

- Record everything exactly as stated.

- Think fast. More is better.

- Keep the process moving quickly.

- Encourage people to build on each other's ideas.

- Do it in short bursts, 5–15 minutes.

- Record all ideas for everyone to see.

Don't Do

- Don't criticize ideas.

- Don't discuss ideas. Clarify only the *meaning* of ideas, not their merits.

▶ **When Building an Affinity**

Also Do

- Play a more active role than you usually take in pushing for clear meaning (without editing ideas). Undefined words and phrases greatly complicate the later steps in the process.

- Ask people to rephrase their ideas if they don't include a minimum of a noun and a verb. Full, *brief* sentences are even better. Use a maximum of 10 words.

Brainstorming best done in silence or out loud?

Positives of brainstorming **in silence:**

- Allows for "thinking time."

- Allows even the quietest person to participate.

Positives of brainstorming **out loud:**

- Allows people to build on each other's ideas.

- Helps people avoid creating duplicates and preventing the Affinity from getting bigger and more cluttered than it needs to be.

- Helps to create "team energy" and identity.

STEP 3 SORTING IDEAS IN SILENCE

MJII pp. 13–14

▶ **Sorting Space:** Allow about a flipchart page for every 25 Post-its™ generated. This provides enough space for several people to read, sort, and review the Affinity at the same time.

▶ **Reasonable Sort Times:** Depending on the number and complexity of the ideas and the size of the team, the sorting time can range from 5–25 minutes. 15 minutes is the average time needed.

▶ **Enforcing the Silent Sort:** Silent sorting was introduced because early attempts at mixing discussion and sorting led to prolonged debates about the merits of individual ideas, the logic of certain groupings, and a revisiting of past discussions. Creative connections were often stifled. Silence has four advantages:

— It establishes a clearly different atmosphere (creative, non-judgmental).

— It focuses on the idea, not the generator.

— It speeds up the process.

— It lessens the effect of hierarchy within the team.

Exception to the silence rule: Teams review all of the ideas before sorting so they can clarify the *meaning* (not the merits) of each idea. This can also be done during sorting as long as the discussion centers on increasing the team's understanding of an idea.

▶ **When to Stop Sorting:** When the team reaches "consensus." Consensus occurs when team members are comfortable enough with a proposal or conclusion to support it. In open discussions, it's often difficult to know when consensus has been reached. During an Affinity, people express consensus by moving fewer and fewer Post-its™. Through actions, (or lack of action), team members don't feel compelled to change where ideas have been placed.

If you can answer "yes" to these two questions, you have consensus!

— "Do these groupings make sense?"

— "Does anyone feel the need to continue sorting in order to support the Affinity?

STEP 4 CREATING HEADER CARDS

MJII pp. 14–16

▶ **Draft Headers:** Agreeing on a quick consensus word or phrase helps to focus the team on the theme of each grouping. The team then revisits every draft header to create a "richer" final header.

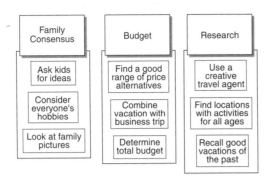

▶ **Good Final Headers:** Header cards have evolved over the years from single words or phrases that described the theme of each grouping, (more like today's draft headers), to "rich" sentences. Each "enriched" header card builds on the theme from the draft word or phrase to capture the full meaning in the column.

If you can answer "yes" to these two questions, you have a good header!

– Does the header answer fully the question: "What are *all* of the Post-its™ within the column saying about the central theme (draft header)?"

– Can the header card stand alone? If all of the individual Post-its™ were removed, would the final header make sense and communicate clearly the breadth and depth of all the ideas?

▶ **Header Length:** The power of an effective header card is not determined by length alone. Powerful headers have ranged from 3–4 words to 15 words. *The ideal range is between 6–10 words.* This allows for a truly "full" sentence, but forces the team to distill and blend ideas into concise, creative thoughts.

▶ **Creating Subheaders:** Subheaders are a very helpful way to further refine the team's thinking and increase the opportunity for breakthrough headers.

When should a team create subheaders? When:

– A column is at least 2 times larger than average. For example: The average number of ideas per column is 4, except for one column, which has 8.

– A final header has two or more major thoughts in it.

▶ **Using an Existing Post-it™ in the Column as a Header:** Sometimes one idea in a column has all the characteristics of a good header. Use this approach sparingly since this could replace good, hard thinking and consensus. Opt for creativity and clarity, NOT just convenience.

EXAMPLE

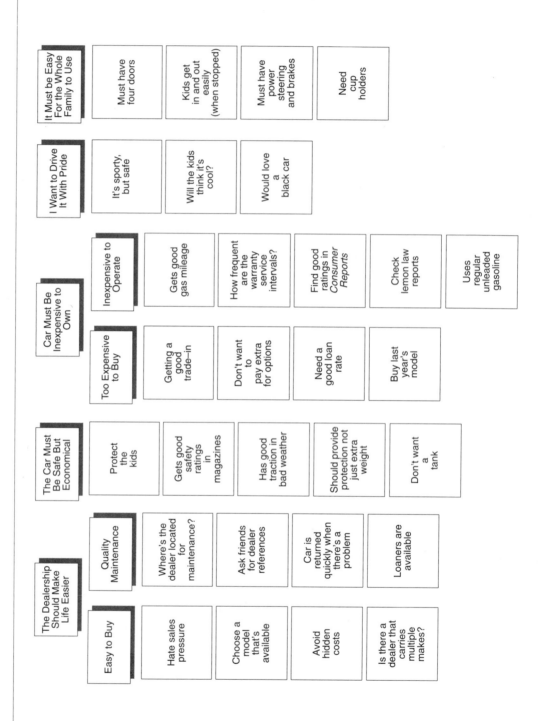

Issues in Buying a Car

It Must be Easy For the Whole Family to Use
- Must have four doors
- Kids get in and out easily (when stopped)
- Must have power steering and brakes
- Need cup holders

I Want to Drive It With Pride
- It's sporty, but safe
- Will the kids think it's cool?
- Would love a black car

Car Must Be Inexpensive to Own

Inexpensive to Operate
- Gets good gas mileage
- How frequent are the warranty service intervals?
- Find good ratings in *Consumer Reports*
- Check lemon law reports
- Uses regular unleaded gasoline

Too Expensive to Buy
- Getting a good trade-in
- Don't want to pay extra for options
- Need a good loan rate
- Buy last year's model

The Car Must Be Safe But Economical
- Protect the kids
- Gets good safety ratings in magazines
- Has good traction in bad weather
- Should provide protection not just extra weight
- Don't want a tank

The Dealership Should Make Life Easier

Quality Maintenance
- Where's the dealer located for maintenance?
- Ask friends for dealer references
- Car is returned quickly when there's a problem
- Loaners are available

Easy to Buy
- Hate sales pressure
- Choose a model that's available
- Avoid hidden costs
- Is there a dealer that carries multiple makes?

Brainstorming
Creating bigger
& better ideas

▶ Do you need a way to help a team broaden their focus and open the range of options they consider?

▶ Is the team bored or tired of the analytical process? Do members need a creative break?

▶ Do you need a way to maximize one of the key benefits of teamwork: team members use the ideas of others as springboards for their own contributions?

▶ Has the team discussion become circular and stuck?

STEPS AT A GLANCE

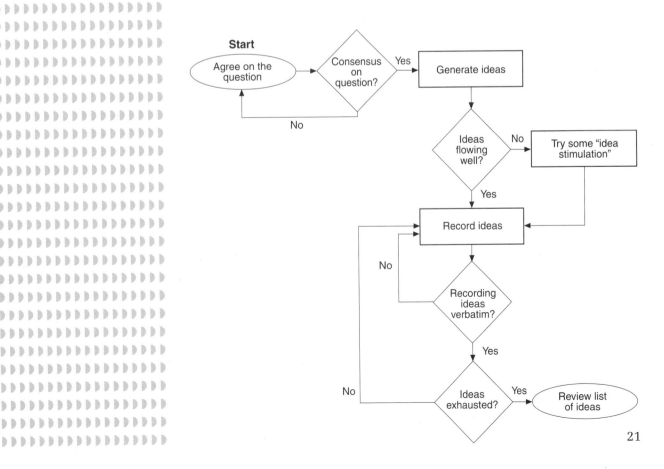

Brainstorming

BRAINSTORMING

Brainstorming

Q. **What if the brainstorm starts and no one says anything?**

A. Use humor and fun to loosen the team up. Use exercises that will perform like the intellectual equivalent of WD40, unclogging any rusty hinges of the mind. These visual stimuli, unusual juxtapositions, and fun games can help the team feel more confident and excited about brainstorming. (See the Learning Activity section in this chapter for a few ideas.)

Q. **What are the advantages and disadvantages of structured vs. unstructured brainstorming?**

A. Here they are:

Structured Brainstorming (Each team member gives ideas in turn.)

Advantages

- Ensures that everyone will have the opportunity to give input.

- Helps diffuse the effect of a dominant team member.

- Adds a science to the process that can set more logical, analytical people at ease.

Disadvantages

- Can make timid team members feel put on the spot.

Unstructured Brainstorming (Team members give ideas as they come to mind.)

Advantages

- Creates a free flowing, positively chaotic environment.

- May create more spontaneous and unusual connections.

Disadvantages

- Requires more vigilant facilitation to make sure contributions are balanced.

Q. **Isn't it better to evaluate and discuss ideas as they are generated to help "weed" them out early?**

A. Every idea is potentially a good one. In order to encourage people to share their ideas, you need to create an environment where they know what they say will not be criticized. Commenting on ideas, beyond simple requests for clarification, will slow the pace of the brainstorm and inhibit the free exchange of ideas. There will be time for evaluation of ideas later.

If: **There is a lag in the number of ideas being offered . . .**

Then: Remember that silence is okay. Sometimes a little quiet space is just what people need to gather up more mental energy and present new ideas. If after some silence, ideas are still not flowing, try stating the question slowly a couple of times. Ask some non-leading questions, like *"What else should we consider when planning for this new area of our business/resolving this problem/developing this new product?"* After these attempts to get every last idea from the team, end the brainstorm with the reminder that members can always come back later and add things that they didn't think of during the brainstorm. It's important to keep the avenue for ideas open.

If: **A person with authority begins to "take over" the process . . .**

Then: Try saying things like *"Does anyone else have any ideas?"* or *"Thank you (name). That's useful input. Does that trigger anything for anyone else?"* If the situation reaches the point where other team members are inhibited to speak or the tension in the room is too high, this is a good time to use the structured methodology, if you are not already. It's okay to switch from unstructured to structured part way through the process, as long as you transition smoothly.

LEARNING ACTIVITY

Here are some potential warm-up brainstorm topics. Experiment with visual aids and hands-on methods to get team members' thoughts loosened up.

▶ You're standing in the express lane at the supermarket behind a person who has more than 12 items. What are all the ways to get that person out of your lane?

▶ What are all the things you could do with the junk mail you receive?

▶ A meteorite lands on your front lawn one night. What are all the ways you could use the resulting crater and debris?

▶ Take something from your pocket or briefcase (such as a pen, lighter, tissue, or key). Think of 20 to 30 new ways you could use that item.

Brainstorming

STEP 1   AGREEING ON THE QUESTION

MJII p. 20

▶ All Aboard

In all variations of brainstorming, a high-quality framing question is pivotal to the success of the exercise. Ways to test the team's comfort with the framing question include:

— Asking one or two team members to paraphrase the question before committing it to paper.

— Having the team underline the words of the question that they want emphasized.

— Doing a mini brainstorm to test the question. Check in after one minute and ask *"Does this still make sense to us?"*

▶ The Champions of Brainstorming

The real heroes and heroines of the brainstorming process are those free thinkers who make unusual, flexible connections between things. They raise the energy level in the group and are committed to finding solutions. They are independent thinkers who are not afraid to say something that people might laugh at. **Tip:** Fill the team with as many of these bright stars as possible.

Caution: As with all participative tools, watch out for dominating authority figures. As the team's coach, you need to make sure that the opinions of people in organizational leadership roles are not overemphasized simply because they are "in charge." Reinforce the fact that everyone has something to contribute to the issue.

STEP 2   GENERATING IDEAS

MJII p. 20

▶ "More is Better" or "Quantity Begets Quality"

No matter what the title, the story remains the same. The more ideas the team generates, the higher the probability they will find a breakthrough idea that will help them succeed in their aim. Your role as coach is to use all means possible to help team members free their minds, make serendipitous connections, and generate a bounty of ideas.

In addition to the proven and reliable "structured" and "unstructured" methods of brainstorming, and the 6-3-5 method offered in *The Memory Jogger™ II*, here are just a couple of the fun and powerful options for brainstorming ideas.

Brutethink

This is a method described by Michael Michalko in *Thinkertoys: A Handbook of Business Creativity for the 90s* (Ten Speed Press, 1991). Brutethink challenges the team to force unusual relationships between things as a means for surfacing new ideas and patterns. Michalko suggests using things like random words, (which he provides a thought provoking list of), new noun and verb relationships, magazines, and shapes to stimulate ideas. Such methods help break up old paradigms and mental prisons and can move the team into a higher and freer level of thought.

Crawford Slip Method (CSM)

In 1925, C.C. Crawford of the University of Southern California used an innovative method of generating new ideas as part of his Slip Method. There is a good summary and a list of references on this method in "The Crawford Slip Method," *Quality Progress*, May 1992. Crawford's brainstorming process, generally involving approximately 20 people, starts by preparing "targets" (or framing statements) and writing individual ideas on small slips of paper. The slips are then sorted and grouped by the facilitators. Once they have offered their ideas, participants usually don't have any more involvement in processing the combined data. Also, unlike methods that rely on piggybacking ideas on each other, the ideas in the CSM are generated individually, anonymously, and without group exchange. Team members will experience a noteworthy loss with this method: the opportunity to free associate with everyone's ideas. However, it may be a good option for a team that is diverse in terms of authority or has a few members who are particularly dominating.

MJII p. 20

STEP 3 RECORDING IDEAS

▶ **Rules of the Game**

- Make sure all ideas are recorded as spoken. The power of the pen is a heady one. It's tempting to edit and interpret ideas as they are spoken, but this practice will eventually demoralize the group and discourage members from contributing. Everyone wants to feel that their idea, as they state it, is of value.

- Keep all ideas visible at all times. Try recording ideas on flipchart paper and posting the sheets of paper to the wall as they are filled or finding a large surface that you can write on and that will hold all of the ideas at once. Be creative about how to achieve this end.

▶ **Variation: Mindmapping**

This tool for recording brainstorming is gaining in popularity and earning a good track record. Mindmapping was developed by Tony Buzan, and you can find a user-friendly guide to the method in *Mindmapping: Your Personal Guide to Exploring Creativity and Problem-Solving* by Joyce Wycoff, Berkley Books, 1991.

Using the same behavioral brainstorming principles as outlined here and in *The Memory Jogger™ II*, mindmapping can lead the team members through the development of a graphical depiction of their ideas. The basic construction guidelines, as outlined in Wycoff's book, are:

- Place a focusing image or statement in the center of a page.

- Use key words to represent ideas.

- Print one key word per line.

- Connect key word ideas to the central focus with lines.

- Use color to highlight and emphasize ideas.

- Use images and symbols to highlights ideas and stimulate other connections.

STEP 4 CHECKING: IDEAS EXHAUSTED?

MJII p. 20

▶ Pace

Keep the pace fast. Quick generation of ideas and connections does at least two good things. It makes it more likely that good ideas will be recorded before they are lost, and it keeps the energy and excitement meter on high.

Just as a popcorn popper will start out with a pop or two, build to a wild melee of rapid popping, and gradually descend to just the occasional pop, so too will the team's brainstorming. Keep drawing out new ideas with neutral questions, and allow free air space for people to think of new ideas. But when your team is too pooped to pop, it's time to stop.

STEP 5 REVIEWING LIST OF IDEAS

MJII p. 20

▶ What Stays and What Goes?

Here is where the team might begin to evaluate and separate the ideas. Purge the list of only the ideas that are virtually identical to another.

One way to help your group move forward with the information they generated is to separate the ideas into lists like "Things we can do easily and immediately" and "Things that require more attention or research." Help the team decide what the categories should be, and encourage them to make the categories action-oriented. This will help the team feel that they have made a productive end to their brainstorming effort.

▶ Where to Now?

Brainstorming is the primary input for the Activity Network Diagram (AND), Affinity Diagram, Process Decision Program Chart (PDPC), and Tree Diagram. Brainstorming is also critical in the effective use of the Cause & Effect/Fishbone Diagram and the process Flowchart.

Reprinted with permission of Neatly Chiseled Features

Cause & Effect/Fishbone Diagram

Find & cure causes,
NOT symptoms

▶ Does the team need to intensively study a problem condition or improvement opportunity to identify its root cause(s)?

▶ Do you want to be sure you have studied all of the possible reasons why a process has begun to "wobble" or go out of control?

▶ Would it be helpful to blend creative thinking with data collection/analysis in the problem-solving process?

▶ Do you need to increase motivation and commitment for solving a problem?

STEPS AT A GLANCE

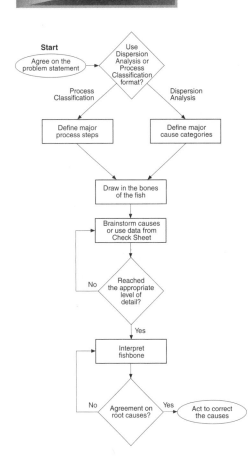

C&E/FISHBONE

Q. How detailed does the Cause and Effect/Fishbone Diagram have to be?

A. The answer is "It depends." As a rule of thumb you should ask "Why" for between three and six levels of each cause that is listed under each major cause "bone." Avoid both of the following extremes: One, "analysis paralysis," where the team just keeps digging and surfaces possible, but not plausible, causes. The other, superficiality, where only the obvious possible causes are examined.

Q. What happens if a possible cause doesn't fit comfortably under any of the major headings?

A. Don't force a cause into a category where it doesn't fit. On the other hand, if you created a new major cause category for each "oddball" cause, the diagram may end up with 10 major cause categories, which is unwieldy at best. Instead, record these unusual causes on a flipchart and look for emerging categories among them. If nothing emerges, group them under the ever popular "Other." The team could also decide that an entire developed branch should be relocated to another category. It is difficult to manually make major changes while doing the diagram. As a reminder for the team, visually highlight, (by underlining, applying a sticker, referencing with an asterisk, and so on), the section to be changed and make the changes as the final version is committed to paper. This is a case in which a software program such as *The Memory Jogger™ Software* (for Windows) is invaluable.

Q. What major cause categories should the team start with?

A. The traditional categories used in the Dispersion Analysis Type are referred to as the 4 M's: Machines, Methods, Materials, and Manpower/People. Another option is the 4 P's: Plant/Equipment, Policies, Procedures, and People. However, with the increasing popularity of the Affinity Diagram, the Affinity has often been used for grouping causes to allow the major cause categories to emerge naturally. The Affinity process both spurs good initial brainstorming as well as team consensus on the structure of the Cause & Effect Diagram. In a Process Classification Type diagram, these cause categories would be replaced by the steps that make up the production or service process.

Q. What's the most important step in using the Cause and Effect Diagram?

A. *Forming the problem statement! Forming the problem statement! Forming the problem statement!* The more information the team has about the problem, the more opportunities its members have to connect important data and ideas to possible causes, and the better the problem statement will be. The team should understand the extent of the problem, its impact on the customer, when the problem began, and performance from the time the problem first appeared. Ensure that the problem statement includes information on what is discrepant and where the discrepancy is occurring.

When beginning the diagram, it is helpful to include charts and graphs to further explain the dimensions of the problem. By visually communicating the problem, it becomes more vivid and compelling to the team, and sets up the process for monitoring progress.

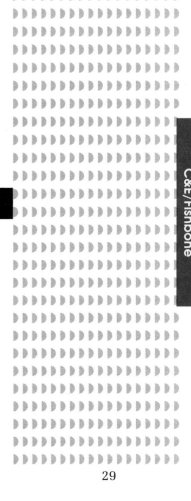

If: **You believe that the output from your supplier might be a possible cause of your problem . . .**

Then: If everyone agrees that a significant piece of the problem depends on supplier input and cooperation, invite the supplier to temporarily join the team. If this isn't possible, the team should specifiy on the diagram the impact of the supplier on the problem. However, stop the team from digging too deeply into supplier-related causes. Instead, meet with the supplier to get this input and then share this information with the rest of the team.

If: **The problem is complex and the team feels that the process workers can supplement the team's development of the diagram . . .**

Then: Post a large and highly visible Cause and Effect Diagram in the work area where the problem is being experienced. Encourage process workers to use Post-it™ Notes to add to, comment on, suggest solutions, or ask questions about the diagram that was developed by the team. This option is fully explored in the book *CEDAC: A Tool for Continuous Systematic Improvement* by Ryuji Fukuda, distributed by Productivity Press.

If: **The team is going too far in its search for root causes or staying at a superficial level . . .**

Then: *When the search for root causes seems endless,* **STOP** *and try the follow*ing:

▶ Ask the team to eliminate any "deep" cause that is controlled more than one organizational level above or below the team. This will prevent the team from blaming "them."

▶ Eliminate any lowest level cause for which the team can't generate practical improvement activity within 90 days. This can limit statements like "If only we could someday . . ."

When the search for root causes is superficial, **STOP** *and try this:*

▶ Simply ask "Have we identified everything within our control that is related to the problem?"

LEARNING ACTIVITY

1. Keep the team to a manageable number (4–6).

2. Select a real problem in which everyone has energy, interest, and knowledge. Take no more than 20 minutes to select and frame the issue.

3. Videotape a team discussing a problem without a C & E Diagram. Be sure to capture the dynamics of the team as the discussion progresses, or fails to. About a 10-minute video segment works well.

4. Now videotape the same team discussing the same problem, but using a fishbone diagram. View both video clips as a team. Team members are sure to notice the dramatic contrast in team behavior between using and not using the C & E Diagram.

5. Discuss and record the impact that the C & E Diagram had on the quality of the team's behavior and the output or product of the discussion.

STEP 1 CREATING A PROBLEM STATEMENT

▶ **A Picture is Worth a Thousand Words**

Orient the team to the nature of the problem or process improvement opportunity and the importance of solving it. This can be effectively accomplished by presenting the problem in a storyboard. For example, you might use a Control Chart to show a process that has been unstable recently or has gone out of control. Next, you might show a series of Pareto Charts that compare the patterns of customer complaints before and after the problem began.

Using a picture to tell the story does the following:

– Helps the team fully understand the scope and impact of the problem or opportunity.

– Promotes group cohesion and focus.

– Motivates the team to act.

▶ **Select Appropriate Format**

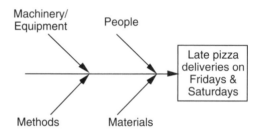

Illustration Note: In a Process Classification Type format, replace the major "bone" categories with: "Order Taking," "Preparation," "Cooking," and "Delivery."

▶ **Dispersion Analysis Type:** Using this format, the diagram is constructed by placing major possible cause categories at the ends of the major "bones" of the diagram, which are then connected to the "backbone" of the diagram, as depicted above.

Use the Dispersion Analysis Type format when you want to get maximum creativity in exploring possible causes, since this format allows the team complete freedom in the selection of the cause categories.

▶ **Process Classification Type:** There are two common formats: the Sequential Process version, and the Arrayed Process version.

Sequential Process Version

The bones that branch directly from the process step relate to causes within that step. Those bones that branch off the connecting arrows, e.g., the bones shown between "Assembling pizza," and "Baking pizza," relate to causes that are found in the transition from finishing one step and starting the next in the sequence of steps leading to the delivery of the pizza.

Sequential Process Version

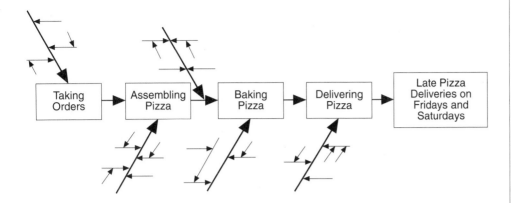

Use the Sequential Process version format when it's important to keep the team focused on both the process steps and the "hand-offs" between the steps.

Arrayed Process Version

This version of the Process Classification format of a Cause & Effect Diagram does not show the branches of causes created by progressing from one step to a sequential step in the process. What the Arrayed Process version does show are the major steps required in the process and the causes that are found within each step.

Arrayed Process Version

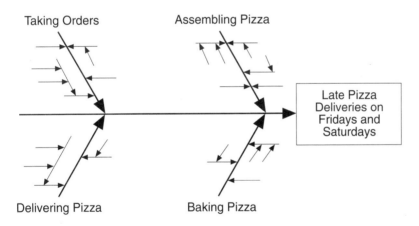

Use the Arrayed Process version format when you want the team to stay focused on only the process steps, not on the transition between the steps.

STEP 2   GENERATING THE CAUSES

MJII p. 24

The two most common ways of generating possible causes are through brainstorming and by using data collected from Check Sheets, Pareto Charts, and other data collection/analysis tools.

▶ **Brainstorming:** The team freely explores possible causes and, if the Dispersion Analysis Type is used, places the brainstormed ideas under the appropriate cause category. (See pages 19–22 of *The Memory Jogger™ II* for Brainstorming.) To get maximum creativity and freedom from the group in generating causes, brainstorm first and then place each idea in the appropriate cause category. If the team is "stuck" and needs to be "prompted," use the cause categories as a stimulating question. For example: *"What in 'People' causes the problem?"* *"What in 'Policies' causes the problem?"*

▶ **Data Sources:** The team might examine things like Flowcharts, procedure manuals, and Check Sheets for clues as to possible causes. The team might also seek supplier data, such as inspection reports for incoming goods and visual inspection of the process, for additional ideas.

STEP 3 CONSTRUCTING THE DIAGRAM

MJII pp. 24–28

▶ **Writing Space**

Use flipchart paper or butcher paper or white board, which offers plenty of space as the beginning point for the diagram. Place the problem statement/ problem storyboard at the righthand side of the writing space. If it becomes difficult to fit all of the ideas, try using individual flipchart sheets for each major cause category. Remember to keep all of these sheets visible, (posting them), for the team to focus on.

▶ **Placing Causes in the Right Category**

Place the brainstormed or data-based ideas on the "bones" under each major heading. You may find that some ideas fit under sub-categories. For example, in *The Memory Jogger™ II*, page 29, find that under the Timing heading, the main reason a patient waits for a bed is because a discharged patient did not leave. Several causes, such as "Wait for ride," fit under that sub-category.

Bed Assignment Delay

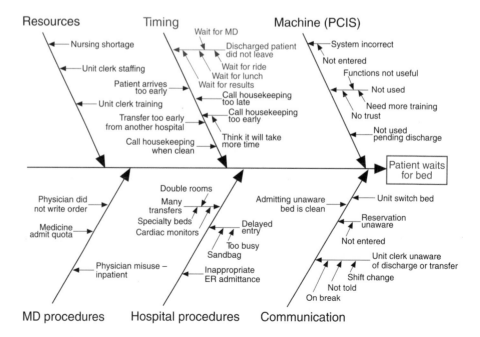

C&E/Fishbone

Hints on completing the diagram:

— If a cause seems to fit in more than one category, enter it in both categories and see how the logic works out as you question and progress through the levels of each cause. For example: "**Why** didn't the discharged patient leave?" The patient is: 1) Waiting for results. "**Why?**" 2) Waiting for a ride. "**Why?**" And so on for each cause level.

— Use the power of the total group to help make the diagram robust. It is often helpful for the workers in the process that is being improved to examine the diagram to see if it has any gaps. They might see a need to ask "Why?" several more times in one or more areas to "root out" what's really going on.

▶ Interpreting the Diagram

Get at the Root Cause

If the process that is being studied has been stable and suddenly has shown signs of instability, you will want to look for items in your diagram that have undergone a recent change. Scan the completed diagram to isolate those items that are known to have undergone some change and circle them. Select the one(s) that have the highest probability of being the root cause of the problem. Also, look for causes that appear repeatedly within or across major cause categories. *Note: Always look for a change in the supplier relationship as a possible contributing cause.*

Use Supplementary Data

Use supplementary data from Control Charts, Run Charts, Check Sheets, and Pareto Charts to validate probable causes that are selected through consensus methods such as Nominal Group Technique or Multivoting. For example: in the Problem-Solving/Process-Improvement Model chapter (MJII pages 115–131), the team used two Run Charts to confirm its opinion that high turnover was caused by a lack of training, and this turnover had a strong effect on late deliveries (MJII page 121). Each Run Chart showed statistically significant trends in turnover rates and training hours per new employee over the last 12 months.

EXAMPLE

Process Classification Method

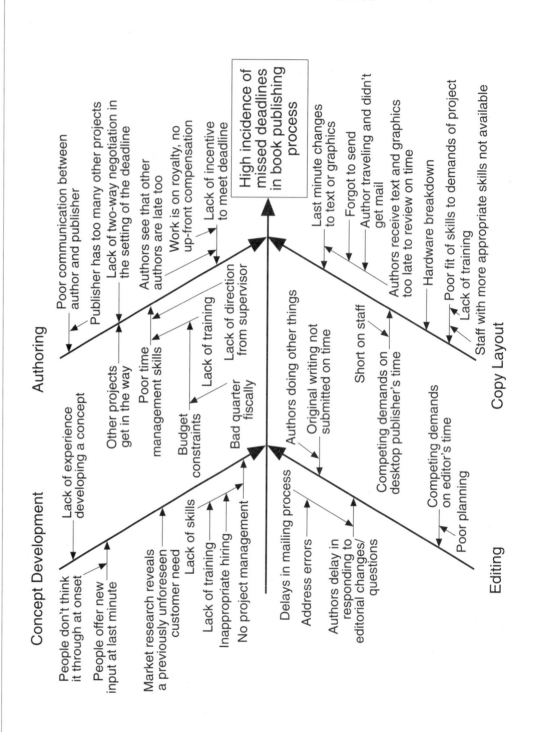

High incidence of missed deadlines in book publishing process

Authoring

- Poor communication between author and publisher
- Publisher has too many other projects
- Lack of two-way negotiation in the setting of the deadline
- Authors see that other authors are late too
- Work is on royalty, no up-front compensation
- Lack of incentive to meet deadline
- Lack of experience developing a concept
- Other projects get in the way
- Poor time management skills
- Budget constraints
- Lack of training
- Bad quarter fiscally
- Lack of direction from supervisor

Concept Development

- People don't think it through at onset
- People offer new input at last minute
- Market research reveals a previously unforeseen customer need
- Lack of skills
- Lack of training
- Inappropriate hiring
- No project management

Copy Layout

- Last minute changes to text or graphics
- Forgot to send
- Author traveling and didn't get mail
- Authors receive text and graphics too late to review on time
- Hardware breakdown
- Poor fit of skills to demands of project
- Lack of training
- Staff with more appropriate skills not available

Editing

- Authors doing other things
- Original writing not submitted on time
- Short on staff
- Competing demands on desktop publisher's time
- Competing demands on editor's time
- Poor planning
- Delays in mailing process
- Address errors
- Authors delay in responding to editorial changes/questions

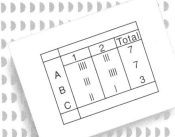

Check Sheet

*Counting &
accumulating data*

▶ Are trends and patterns unclear?

▶ Is a simple process for data collection needed?

▶ Does the team need a method for data collection that can be easily used by people not on the team?

▶ Is the data based on observing and counting rather than sampling and measuring?

▶ Does the team need to leave a clear "data trail" for its records?

▶ Is the team in need of a flexible data collection tool that can be tailored to the project requirements?

STEPS AT A GLANCE

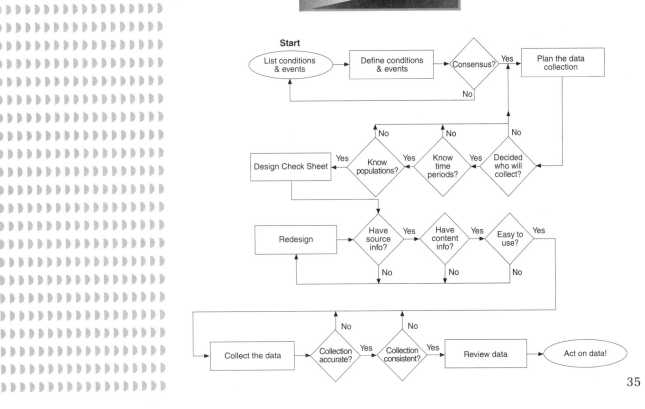

Check Sheet

Q. **How do you make sure that the data is collected correctly?**

A. The key to the success of a Check Sheet is to create one that is self-explanatory. No one wants to make an error on, say, recording errors. Two ways that can help ensure correct data collection are: 1) enlist the help of the people who will be collecting the data in creating the worksheet; and 2) have a brief training session on the use of the Check Sheet.

Q. **Who should collect the data using the Check Sheets?**

A. If possible, people who are closest to the "facts" of the events or the conditions should record the data.

Q. **What if the person is afraid that he/she will be blamed for the cause of the defect or event that is being recorded on the Check Sheet?**

A. The team needs to disconnect the collection of the data from any placement of blame. It should be explained that the reason for collecting data is to improve the process and not "point the finger" at anyone. In fact, people should be encouraged to conduct their work as they normally would, so that the process is not be falsely optimized.

Q. **How do I know that my definition of an event or a defect is the same as those of my fellow team members and the people who are using the Check Sheet?**

A. Too often, everyone assumes that because the same word is being used, each person understands the same thing. Not only is it a good idea to involve the people who collect the data in the actual design of the Check Sheet, but it's also a great idea to have them involved in specifying what those events/defects really mean. If the team creates a list of operational definitions for all the events/defects and attach it to the Check Sheet, there's less chance of misinterpretation. If the team members are not the ones who are collecting the data, this involvement is a great opportunity for them to learn from the people closest to the data.

Another way to ensure that everyone who will use the Check Sheet has the same definition of an event or defect is to actually test it out, on a small scale. The test will help identify any differences in the way people are interpreting the Check Sheet, and will indicate which parts, if any, need to be redesigned or reworded.

Q. **Won't using a Check Sheet interfere with the performance of the person trying to collect the data?**

A. It would be optimistic to say that data collection will never interfere with someone's work. If the person collecting data is involved in the design of the Check Sheet, and if that design has taken into account the ease of use in completing the Check Sheet, then time, effort, and confusion in collecting the data can be kept to a minimum.

Q. **What is the time period, or how long should we collect the data?**

A. The team should select a time period that reflects a "typical" slice of the process being examined. Is the operation cyclical? Has only one shift been included, when in fact, all shifts should be included? Does the process behave the same on Friday as it does on Tuesday? Is the end of the month the same as one week into the month? In some cases, some data are so vital that a team may want to continuously maintain a Check Sheet to detect a change in performance.

If: **Team members cannot reach an agreement on the design of the Check Sheet . . .**

Then: Try two or three possible designs. Run through a simulation and compare the results of each against two criteria: ease of use and the consistency with which two people look at the same events and record the data in the same way.

If: **The team is "jumping to conclusions" that are not supported by the Check Sheet . . .**

Then: Ask simple questions that the Check Sheet *is* answering. Then start asking more complex questions that require stronger analysis. It will become more clear to the team what conclusions can be supported and not supported by the Check Sheet.

LEARNING ACTIVITY

To help the team understand that they may perceive things differently:

1. Get a five-minute video clip from any speech. A speech by a President or a Presidential candidate will work well.

2. Instruct the team that they will be viewing a five-minute segment of a speech. They will be viewing it one minute at a time. The team will be watching for the number of "gestures" that the speaker uses during that minute.

3. Have the team agree on a quick method for recording data.

4. Run the first one-minute segment.

5. After the first one-minute viewing, ask the team members to debrief among themselves, and invite them to refine definitions or data-collecting strategies.

6. Complete the cycle two more times.

7. Ask the team to share its lessons. Questions on agreement of what defines a "gesture" should arise and the need to come to consensus on what is a condition or an event will also surface.

Check Sheet

> "*Check Sheets are effective tools on the road toward customer satisfaction and continuous improvement.*"
>
> Dr. Verel R. Salmon

Written by Dr. Verel R. Salmon, Millcreek Township School District

What was the problem?

McDowell High School business teachers wanted to get keyboarding students to focus on their errors. In the elementary school in Millcreek, students use Check Sheets daily as a quality assurance method in evaluating their own work before turning it in to their chief customer, the teacher.

Who was on the team?

Business students and teachers who were interested in improving customer satisfaction. Since the customer is the next person to receive your work, the teachers were the students' customers and the students were the teachers' customers. The students' goal was to satisfy the teachers by submitting error-free work; the teachers' goal was to provide students with appropriate instructional materials and guidance so this could happen.

How long did the process take?

Not long. Preliminary data collection will indicate which mistake categories should be listed. Tallying errors can then be a group effort by taking a few minutes of class time after assignments are returned for a show of hands to indicate frequency of errors in each category.

What did we learn?

The Check Sheet enabled us to see areas of weakness at a glance. Therefore, teachers could focus instruction and remediation where it was most needed. Just by looking at the Check Sheet tallies, students could understand the purpose for this instruction and remediation. The tool also helped us establish a benchmark so we could actually see that we were improving.

How was the team affected?

The process of tallying mistakes on the Check Sheet made us more aware of those areas needing attention. Reinforcement came as fewer mistakes were made in each area. We could *see* our improvement!

MILLCREEK ELEMENTARY SCHOOL STUDENTS IN CLASS

What else did we use?

We used Brainstorming and the Affinity to help us target problems to work on or discuss throughout the year.

What was the conclusion?

The Check Sheet became an important tool toward customer satisfaction in the McDowell Business Department.

What were the results?

Because the Check Sheet let us see how we were doing, we were able to focus our efforts on areas of weakness and work toward continuous improvement.

Keyboard Errors
in Class Assignment

Mistakes	March			Total
	1	2	3	
Centering	II	III	III	8
Spelling	ЈНТ II	ЈНТ ЈНТ I	ЈНТ	23
Punctuation	ЈНТ ЈНТ ЈНТ	ЈНТ ЈНТ	ЈНТ ЈНТ ЈНТ	40
Missed paragraph	II	I	I	4
Wrong numbers	III	IIII	III	10
Wrong page numbers	I	I	II	4
Tables	IIII	ЈНТ	IIII	13
Total	34	35	33	102

Information provided courtesy of Millcreek Township School District,
Millcreek Township, Pennsylvania

STEP 1 AGREEING ON DEFINITIONS

MJII pp. 31–32

▶ **Project Definition for Data Collection**

It's possible that a team can become so action-oriented that they forget to discuss the overall purpose of their data collection efforts. For example, if the team is trying to reduce the time it takes for a customer to check out of a hotel, then their efforts should focus on "tracking the delays in the customer checkout process." Having that purpose in place helps the team to define events and conditions in terms of "delays."

▶ **Events and Conditions for Data Collection**

Once the team has its project definition for data collection efforts, it's easier to determine what events and conditions should be considered. The sources for compiling such a list can be:

— Team members themselves

— People involved in the process

— Existing standards or documentation that specify these events and conditions

Having everyone agree on *definitions* for these events and conditions may be more difficult than generating the list of events and conditions. Everyone on the team may be using the same words, but does everyone agree on the same meanings? And again, team members may all agree on the same definition, but use different terminology. This situation has potential for becoming what is known as "violent agreement." Team members are really saying the same thing, but don't realize it!

It is extremely important for all team members to come to consensus on definitions. A valuable tool in this effort is to use one of the following stimuli to help shape the definition:

— A picture, graphic, or diagram

— A physical example of the condition to be observed, such as a monitor casing with self-adhesive dots indicating where there is casing damage

— A reenactment or simulation of the event

The breakthroughs in understanding that are generated by doing one or all of the above can often bring about a stronger consensus on the definitions.

STEP 2 PLANNING THE DATA COLLECTION

MJII p. 32

The key to the planning stage is to find a way to collect data about the process without changing the process. This is why determining who collects the data, what the data is, the collection period, and what populations are to be sampled is important.

▶ **The Integrity of the Data**

Fear Factors: Ideally, it's best to have those who are closest to the data collect it. However, people close to a process sometimes cause a bias by trying to improve their performance while collecting the data. If this happens, they may temporarily eliminate the symptom, and the root cause will never be determined. In most cases, this is not due to deceptive behavior. It's just human to think *"I'm recording a mistake that I must have made. I can't let* *that happen again!"* If there is a strong fear factor present in the department or organization, then one of two things has to be done:

— Explain from the start that the recording of defects or errors will not result in blame, finger pointing, or poor performance reviews, and that there is a sincere effort to find the root cause that will help improve the process.

— Use independent observers to record the data if there is still too strong a possibility for biased data collection.

Time Practicality: It's a good idea, regardless of who collects data, to free up some time from the data collectors' daily responsibilities during the data collection period.

Automation: Sometimes it's possible to automate data collection. One caution here: the team should focus on collecting the information that's truly needed for the project. Just because automating data collection makes it possible to collect a large volume of data, this doesn't mean it's worthwhile to do. The data may be meaningless!

▶ What is the Data Collection Period?

The most important question here is *"What time period is representative of the process?"* Will a week reflect all significant cycles? Should all shifts be observed, or just first shift? Is end of the month activity very different from mid-month activity? Some of these questions become apparent while defining conditions and events for the data collection. Here's an example. The location is a hospital emergency room. The data being collected are the types of emergencies coming into the emergency room. What's the best period for collecting this data? If the data is collected just on a Monday, Tuesday, and Wednesday, rather than a full week, the team could miss some vital data. A Friday or Saturday night in a hospital emergency room can get pretty hectic!

▶ What Populations are Being Sampled?

Where are these events and conditions occurring? In all types of circuit boards? Or just one class of circuit boards? On the first floor or all floors in the clinic? Should grades one through six be observed, or are we just concerned with the second graders?

It's important to note that these questions are asking for the *sources* of an event or condition. There is no need here to discuss sample size in formal statistical terms! See page 52 in *The Memory Jogger™ II* for a brief description of population sampling methods. For a more in-depth explanation of sampling and sampling methods, see Chapter 11 of Kaoru Ishikawa's book *Guide to Quality Control*, (Asian Productivity Organization, 1986), or any other statistics reference book you have handy.

MJII p. 33	**STEP 3 DESIGNING THE CHECK SHEET**

The great thing about the Check Sheet is that it's a data collection tool that can be tailored for the team's purpose. Results can be interpreted directly from the Check Sheet itself, without additional analysis tools.

▶ Include All Significant Source Information

No matter how the team designs the Check Sheet, information about the sources of the data should always head up the form. Show when, where, who from, and for which project this data was collected. Was this the third collection out of five? How do we know we have all the Check Sheets for that particular data collection effort?

▶ **Be Flexible and Clear in Displaying Content Information**

The most common format for capturing content information is a "column and row" format that contains the following:

– Columns with collection days/dates

– Totals for each column

– Totals for each row

– Grand total for both the columns and rows

Flexibility

If the team is showing just one type of defect in a general environment or product, a simple graphic where the defect is indicated with an "x" at the site of the defect would be far more effective than a "column and row" format. If there are different types of failures in a circuit board, it may still be more meaningful to code each type of failure and note its location by code on a modified diagram of the circuit board. If the team is tracking crime occurrences, it may be more useful to indicate the frequency of these events on a city map and code the types of crimes according to their nature.

Clarity

The actual form should be as self-explanatory as possible. It should allow data recording to be easy. The Check Sheet should capture data in way that ensures error-free recording and unambiguous interpretation. While Check Sheets that are typed or printed are much easier to use than handwritten forms, don't waste too much time trying to make the form look fancy or overly sophisticated. After all, the objective is to make the form neat and easy to use, not elaborate or perfect.

Although the Check Sheet should be self-explanatory, include simple written instructions for the recording of data. Is data to be collected at intervals or at exact times? When taking measurements, should the numbers be rounded to the nearest whole number? Even if the team plans on providing some training on how to use the Check Sheet, team members' memories can be short, and simple written instructions help trigger what they may have forgotten, half-listened to, or replaced with a more interesting daydream.

▶ **Take a "Test Drive"**

The "rubber meets the road" when the team takes the Check Sheet out for a "test drive." This trial can test the form and the instructions that go with it. Do people have difficulty seeing the connection between a condition and what's represented on the form? Does the event get recorded in the wrong column because it's unclear where to record the data?

The ideal "test drive" is to have the data collectors watch the same event at the same time, and using the proposed Check Sheet, compare the consistency of the results between them.

Testing the design of the Check Sheet is a good opportunity to see if it captures the data the way the team intended. It's also a way to get valuable feedback from the people who will be using the Check Sheet.

MJII p. 34

By now the Check Sheets have been tested. The data collectors have been trained. The simple, effective instructions for the Check Sheets are literary gems. What else is there left to do but collect the data?

▶ Key Questions and Answers to Help Make Data Collection Successful

Q. **At what points in the process will it be appropriate to place the data collectors?**

A. A Flowchart, and possibly a map of the area will help in strategic data collection. It may sound obvious but data collectors should be in the place where they are most likely to see the events or defects occur.

Q. **How often and how soon do data collectors or data collector coordinators need to get the Check Sheets back to the team?**

A. Preferably, after the completion of a single Check Sheet, especially when there's to be a series of data collection trials. This way, if there are unexpected results or mistakes in the data collection, they can be addressed quickly.

EXAMPLE

Carmen's World Famous Whoopie Pies

Project: Types of defects in finished pies	Data collected by: *Carl* Location: *Heavenly, Maine plant*		Dates: *June 20-26* Lot size: *200*				
Defect	**June 20**	**June 21**	**June 22**	**June 23**	**June 24**	**June 25**	**June 26**	**Total**
Too much cream	卌	|||	卌	||	||||	||	|||	24
Too little cream	– –	||			||	|||	– –			9
Too crumbly	|||	卌	|||	||	||||	|||			21
Too big	||||			||	|||			– –	||	13
Too small	||	||	– –			||||	|||	||	14
Not sweet enough	– –	||			||	|||	– –			9
Not chocolaty enough	– –	– –			– –	– –	– –	– –	1
Has a bite in it									||	– –	– –	6

OVERVIEW

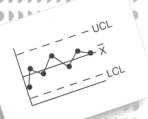

Control Chart

Recognizing sources of variation

IS THIS THE RIGHT TOOL? ASK . . .

▶ Does the team need to monitor the performance of a process over time?

▶ Does the team need help in recognizing, understanding, and controlling variation in a process?

▶ Is it important for the team to determine whether a process is stable?

▶ Does the team need a real-time method of centering and controlling a process to minimize variation and prevent defects?

▶ Is it necessary for the team to separate out special causes of variation from common causes to find out who has responsibility to correct the problem?

▶ Does the team need to know when to leave a process alone and when to adjust or improve it?

STEPS AT A GLANCE

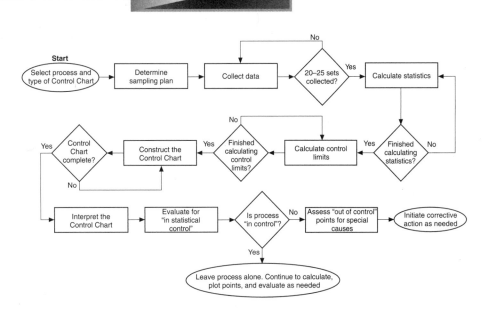

45

Q. **Why use a Control Chart?**

A. A Control Chart will show whether a process is out of control or in control, statistically speaking. In this world, no two events or products are precisely alike. They are characterized by some amount of variation. Variation is the inevitable difference that exists among individual outputs of a repeatable process. Variation is attributable to the combination of different people, methods, materials, machines, policies, procedures, environments, and so on, that come together to produce a product or service. A Control Chart is a useful graphic tool that allows teams to visibly track variation in a process over time. It is important to monitor changes in process variation in order to control the process. Subsequently, a process must be in statistical control before a team can improve it.

Q. **What is meant by "in statistical control"?**

A. A process is said to be in a state of statistical control, or "in control," when measurements from the process vary randomly within statistically calculated limits. That is, there are no points outside the limits or no points forming trend lines, shifts, cycles, or other patterns. Over time, the variation present is consistent and predictable.

A process that consistently and predictably produces product or service within three standard deviations (the statistically calculated "control limits") of the mean is considered to be in a state of statistical control. This means that all special causes of variation within the process have been removed.

Note that a process "in control" may not be producing good product or service, however, only that it is consistent and predictable. It could be consistent and predictably bad!

Q. **What is common cause versus special cause?**

A. Sources of variation can be grouped into two major classes: *common cause* and *special cause. Common cause* is a source of variation that is always present; part of the random variation inherent in the process itself. Its origin can usually be traced to an element of the process that only management can correct. *Special cause* is a source of variation that is intermittent, unpredictable, unstable. Its origin can usually be traced to an element of the system that can be corrected locally, that is, an employee or operator can correct a special cause.

Q. **Is there only one type of Control Chart?**

A. No, there are several different types. The type of chart a team decides to use will depend on the circumstances and the type of data they have. The most widely used charts include the four variables charts: 1) $\bar{X}$ & R for averages and ranges, 2) $\bar{X}$ & s for averages and standard deviations, 3) $\tilde{X}$ & R for medians and ranges, and 4) individuals and moving range; and the four attributes charts: 1) p, 2) np, 3) c, and 4) u. There are also Cusum, Hotelling-T, and Geometric Moving Average charts, and others. Check a good statistics book on these, or refer to "Other Resources" at the back of this book.

Q. **Should the team start a new chart and calculate control limits when they finish the old one?**

A. As long as nothing major has changed in the process, do not recalculate the control limits. When you have reached the end of a chart, start a new one, but draw the same mean line(s) and control limits.

FACILITATION ESSENTIALS

If: **The team is unsure in choosing between Variables and Attributes Control Charts . . .**

Then: ▸ Use the Tree Diagram on page 37 of *The Memory Jogger*™ *II* to help guide their decision, based on the type of data they have.

▸ Brainstorm, use the Cause and Effect Diagram or Pareto Chart to come to agreement on a "key" characteristic of the product, service or process, then determine some measure of it. The type of measure (data) will help clue in the team to the appropriate chart to use.

The table below categorizes the types of Control Charts that are appropriate to use with the data a team has available, either variable or attribute data.

	Variable Data	**Attribute Data**
Type of Chart:	$\bar{X}$ **and R** (minimum measured data, usually subgroup size of 3–5) $\bar{X}$ **and s** (to chart large subgroup sizes, as well as a more efficient measure of subgroup variability) **Median** (minimum calculations required, plot all subgroup values) **Individuals** (subgroup size of one)	**p-chart** (to chart *fraction defective* with subgroup size constant or variable) **np-chart** (to chart *number of defective units* with constant subgroup size) **c-chart** (to chart *defects per unit* with *constant* subgroup size) **u-chart** (to chart *defects per unit* with *constant or variable* subgroup size)
Characteristics:	Measurable Continuous	Countable Discrete
Types of Data:	machine downtime, dollar losses, accounting figures, temperature, pressure, volume, pH levels, humidity, tension, time duration, speed, weight, voltage, length, meal deliveries, transport time or turnaround time, time to register students or patients	# or % machines down daily, # flaws per unit of fabric, # of reported failures per month, # or % absent, typing mistakes, shipping errors, # bugs per unit software coding, % defective in the work of a person or machine, defects per hotel room, # of complaints

Purpose: To guide a group through the basics of constructing a Control Chart, specifically an $\bar{X}$ & R Chart, from a normal distribution. (Variable data is needed to construct an $\bar{X}$ & R Chart.) The group, in doing this activity, should also notice how the chart quickly identifies a change in a process. (This change will be a result of the coach's dexterity in the *bait and switch* method. You'll see, keep reading.)

Preparation: Make up two bowls of 200 numbered chips each (bingo chips work well). The two bowls should look identical. The chips are marked with one number according to the following normal distributions:

# on Chip	1	2	3	4	5	6	7	8	9	10	11	12	13	Total
Frequency Bowl A	1	3	10	23	39	48	39	23	10	3	1	–	–	200 chips
Frequency Bowl B	–	–	1	3	10	23	39	48	39	23	10	3	1	200 chips

For Bowl A, mark one tag with "1," mark three tags with "2," ten tags with "3," and so on up to tag number 11. This bowl will have a mean value of 6. For Bowl B, mark one tag with "3," mark three tags with "4," ten tags with "5," and so on up to tag number 13. This bowl will have a mean value of 8. Discretely identify the two bowls for your own knowledge. *Hide one bowl from the team.*

Start Activity: Mix the chips well in a bowl, then have participants draw 20 samples of 5, replacing the chips after each sample is drawn. Ask the group to record all data points. Then together as one group or as teams, have participants work through developing an $\bar{X}$ & R Chart. This is the appropriate chart since the data is variable and the sample size is small, n = 5. *Without telling the group, switch the bowls (bait and switch) and let everyone continue to sample and record data on the Control Chart.* Don't tell anyone what you've done; they should quickly recognize that something has changed. Tell them about the switch and how the chart quickly picks up a change in a process (in this case, a higher mean value).

Benefit of the $\bar{X}$ & R Chart: The calculations are fairly easy—only the sum, mean, and range are necessary for each sample.

Simple calculation of the mean: For a sample size of 5, double the sum and move the decimal one digit to the left, as shown on the next page.

One sample of 5: (5, 3, 7, 4, 6)

Standard calculation of mean:

$$\frac{5 + 3 + 7 + 4 + 6}{5} = \frac{25}{5} = 5.0$$

Quick calculation of mean:

Sum = 25.0

Double the sum = 50.0

Move decimal one digit to the left = 5.0 (It's the same!)

INCIDENTALLY

Dr. Walter Shewhart, while studying process data at Bell Labs in the 1920s, first made the distinction between controlled and uncontrolled variation. Today, we distinguish between *common* and *special* causes of variation. It was in 1924 that Dr. Shewhart developed the Control Chart, a simple but powerful tool to separate the two causes of variation. (This chart is also referred to as the Shewhart Chart.) A Control Chart directs attention toward two types of causes of variation: 1) special causes, which can be controlled by an employee or operator, and 2) common causes, which must be reduced by the actions of management, not a specific employee or operator.

> "The Control Chart is an extremely valuable tool that enables us to objectively visualize and understand process control and capability, as well as any changes resulting from quality improvement efforts."
>
> Eric Watson, R.N.

Written by Eric Watson R.N., Parkview Episcopal Medical Center

What was the problem?

The open heart admission team worked on the process of decreasing the complexity of admitting open heart surgery patients into the intensive care unit (ICU).

Who was on the team?

A multidisciplinary team of nurses, physicians, anesthesiologists, and directors.

How long did the process take?

Our team began in the fall of 1991 and continues today with team meetings and strategies that continue to improve the admission process.

What did we learn?

The team learned a "new" way of working together by focusing on processes that affect the quality of the work we do. We also learned by application that the quality improvement methodology (FOCUS-PDCA) really does work.

How was the team affected?

The team was affected the most by how well the methodology worked and especially enjoyed using all the tools and seeing the results of objective data and not falling for the "I know what's wrong" approach to problems.

What else did we use?

We used many of the tools—Micro- and Macro-flow Diagrams, Brainstorming, Fishbone Diagrams, Pareto Charts, Histograms, and Run Charts—both to improve the process and as a learning experience for everyone on the team.

FRONT ROW (L TO R): KAY HOBBS, DR. OTERO, DENISE BACICH, STANDING: ERIC WATSON, R.N.

What was the conclusion?

The tools helped us to identify and verify what the true causes of variation in our admitting process were, which then led us to develop and implement appropriate strategies for improvement. The Control Chart helped us understand the effects of IV line connections on the overall admission times.

What were the results?

By using the FOCUS-PDCA methodology and a team approach, we were able to implement strategies that decreased our mean admission time from 25 minutes to our current 4 minutes, as well as indirectly decrease costs for our hospital by about $500 per patient for an overall savings of $100,000 over the last three years. More importantly, we found that we exceeded in meeting the needs of all the customers of our open heart surgery admission process.

Individuals & Moving Range Chart

IV Lines Connection Time

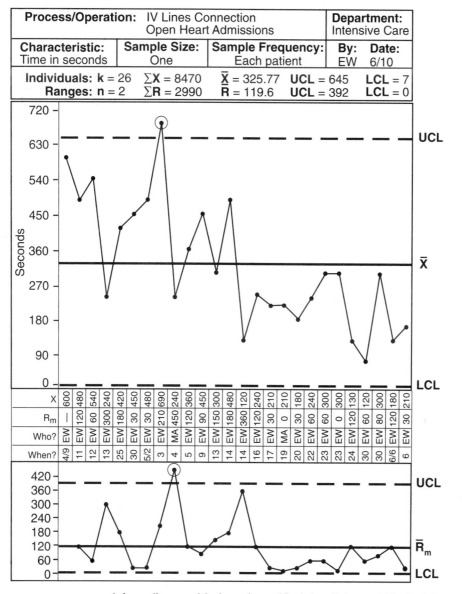

Process/Operation:	IV Lines Connection Open Heart Admissions		Department: Intensive Care	
Characteristic: Time in seconds	**Sample Size:** One	**Sample Frequency:** Each patient	**By:** EW	**Date:** 6/10
Individuals: k = 26 **Ranges: n** = 2	$\sum X$ = 8470 $\sum R$ = 2990	$\bar{X}$ = 325.77 $\bar{R}$ = 119.6	UCL = 645 UCL = 392	LCL = 7 LCL = 0

X	600	480	540	240	420	450	480	690	240	360	450	300	480	120	240	210	210	180	240	300	300	130	120	300	180	210
Rm	—	120	60	300	180	30	30	210	450	120	90	150	180	360	120	30	0	30	60	60	0	120	10	80	120	30
Who?	EW	EW	EW	EW	EW	EW	EW	EW	MA	EW	EW	EW	EW	EW	EW	EW	MA	EW	EW	EW	EW	EW	EW	EW	EW	EW
When?	4/9	11	12	13	25	30	5/2	3	4	5	9	13	14	14	16	17	19	20	22	23	23	24	30	30	6/6	6

Information provided courtesy of Parkview Episcopal Medical Center

Note: Something in the process changed, and now it takes less time to make IV connections for patients being admitted for open heart surgery.

> "The team was enlightened by the fact that if you monitor the "goings on" within a process by using the Control Chart you can see if a process is in control and improve it."
>
> Robert McMahon

Written by Robert McMahon, U.S. Navy, Naval Dental Center

What was the problem?

The patient appointment system was not conducive to the needs of the patients who could not receive instant attention.

Who was on the team?

The team was comprised of members who worked in every facet of the patient appointing process.

How long did the process take?

The actual historical statistics were acquired manually from the reception desk appointment books, which took approximately 2 months. This tallying took place prior to the formation of the process action team. Because the data collection is now an ongoing process, the actual formulation of the chart takes only 5 minutes.

What did we learn?

The team learned that by using a Control Chart effectively we could determine if our processes were out of control.

How was the team affected?

The team members were enlightened by the fact that if you monitor the "goings on" within a process by using a Control Chart, you can see if a process is in control and improve the process.

What else did we use?

We went from the Control Chart to Brainstorming and creating a Cause and Effect Diagram to see what we could do to improve the appointing process, and formulate a customer survey to see what ideas we could receive from the patients.

FRONT ROW (L TO R): ROGER HUNTER, KELLY MILLER, DR. DAVID KATZER. BACK ROW (L TO R): ERVIN BORJA, TONY PRESTRIDGE, ROBERT MCMAHON (FACILITATOR), DR. MARK WATERMAN. NOT PRESENT: DAWN PRADIA

What was the conclusion?

We learned that due to the preset hours worked within the command, the patient failures could be reduced by adjusting the work hours to better suit the customers' needs. With this same tool we learned that the majority of patient failures were on Friday afternoons and Mondays.

What were the results?

We found out that for us to continue on our journey of continuous process improvement, we must look at historical data with Control Charts to help us better foresee the next paradigm shift.

Control Chart

p Chart

**General Dentistry: Percent of
Patients Who Failed to Keep Appointments**

Historical Statistics:

$\overline{p}$ = 39   **UCL** = 47   **LCL** = 31

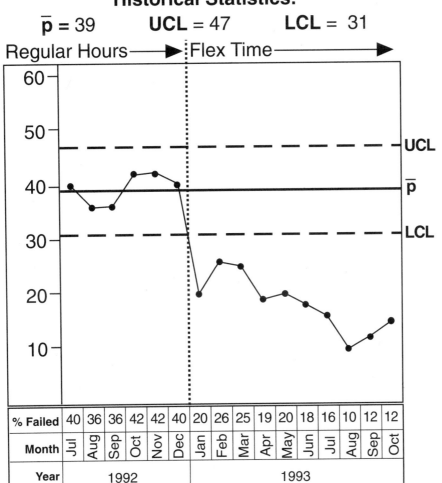

% Failed	40	36	36	42	42	40	20	26	25	19	20	18	16	10	12	12
Month	Jul	Aug	Sep	Oct	Nov	Dec	Jan	Feb	Mar	Apr	May	Jun	Jul	Aug	Sep	Oct
Year	1992						1993									

*Information provided courtesy of U.S. Navy,
Naval Dental Center, San Diego*

Note: Providing flex time for patients resulted in fewer appointments missed.

53

> "If you don't know if your process is in control, not only will you not know what to fix, you won't even know that you need to fix something."
>
> Paul Hearn

Written by Paul Hearn, Hamilton Standard

What was the problem?

The continuous improvement training team knew that the approval rating of the attendees at the weekly total quality training sessions needed to be consistently high in order to maximize the benefits of the quality effort. They needed a way to measure and determine if they had consistently high ratings from the participants.

Who was on the team?

The team was made up of four trainers who were experienced in presenting the training sessions.

How long did the process take?

The training was to be carried out over a five-year period and was conducted for 50 employees a week. Data was gathered at the end of each week from the training session for 26 weeks and the data was assembled into $\bar{X}$ and R charts. This effort took approximately 1 hour each week.

What did we learn?

Although the average perception of the training was acceptable, there were some data points (training weeks) that were "OUT OF CONTROL." This implied that some training weeks were not being perceived as well as others due to some unknown factors.

How was the team affected?

After creating the Control Chart, the team was motivated to investigate why there wasn't consistency in our training. Although we had casually discussed improving the consistency of training delivery, the data showed us that we really had a problem. It was the Control Chart that drove us into action.

PAUL HEARN,
TEAM MEMBER

What else did we use?

The above learning caused the team to investigate the out of control data points further through the use of brainstorming possible causes and the Scatter Diagram.

What was the conclusion?

The team decided to investigate causes for the out of control data points. (See the Scatter Diagram Case Study in this book or page 146 of *The Memory Jogger™ II*.)

What were the results?

The team determined that the training process needed to be investigated further because it was not in control.

X̄ & R Chart
Overall Course Evaluations

n = 10 evaluations randomly sampled each week
1-Not at all   2-Not very   3-Moderately   4-Very   5-Extremely

Wk #	1	2	3	4	5	6	7	8	9	10	11	12	13	14	15	16	17	18	19	20	21	22	23	24	25	Ave.
X̄	3.76	4.21	4.29	4.36	4.13	3.77	4.17	4.21	4.22	4.00	4.30	4.20	4.32	4.18	4.02	3.71	4.08	4.23	3.98	4.46	3.96	3.63	4.48	4.30	4.29	4.13
R	1.01	1.27	0.48	1.32	1.52	1.03	1.15	1.07	0.70	2.05	0.95	0.99	1.06	1.21	1.33	0.78	1.21	1.23	1.08	1.64	1.20	0.98	0.91	1.19	1.03	1.14

Information provided courtesy of Hamilton Standard

Note: Weeks 1, 10 (from bottom chart), 16, and 22 should be reviewed to understand why the ratings are outside the control limits.

STEP 1 SELECTING THE PROCESS

MJII p. 38

Selection of what is to be charted is the important first step. Each chart will present only one characteristic at a time. Rather than make charts on everything and then try to figure out which one is influencing your system, (an expensive, time-consuming procedure), have the team decide first on what the biggest problem is. Identify the biggest problem by using Brainstorming, Pareto Charts, or Cause and Effect Diagrams. Once the problem is identified, the group should define its process. Work on this process only.

For Example

Let's look at the quality of copies made by a copier. A team, self-named the BCD team, must determine if all the copiers in house are consistently producing good black images. (BCD stands for Black Copy Density.) They have determined that the most important "key" copy quality measurement is black density. Only this characteristic will be plotted using the $\overline{X}$ & R Chart since they have a variable measure, that is, black density as recorded by a "MacBeth Black Density" machine. The team wants to collect a minimum of data. If it was thought necessary to track background density, the team would then set up readings and a chart for that characteristic only.

STEP 2 DETERMINING THE SAMPLING PLAN

MJII p. 38

Use these guidelines in determining the sampling method and plan the team should use:

— Using variable data (measurable and continuous) is preferable to attribute data (countable and discrete) because variable data provides more information. Attribute data just tells you whether a product or service passed or failed, it doesn't tell why or by how much.

— Obtain data under the same conditions: same machine, lot, operator, vendor, class, student, and so on.

— Collect at least 20–25 subgroups to start up a new chart. A subgroup is a subset of the population of data points. Subgroups should be obtained at small enough intervals to identify cycles, changes in temperatures, shifts, changes in materials, lots, and so on. For example: in an $\overline{X}$ & R Chart, a subgroup might consist of four or five samples of product or service drawn from the process under study. Or, for a p chart, it might be a sample of 200 units. Subgroups might be drawn hourly, daily, weekly, by each shift, and so on.

— Samples (units collected to form a subgroup) should not be based on picking the best or the worst from the process.

— Once the process is "in control," the team can probably reduce the frequency of their data collection efforts.

For Example

The BCD team, mentioned in the previous "For Example," decided to randomly select four machines each day and take copies from them using a test master. The average black density from each sheet would be recorded.

STEP 3 INITIATING DATA COLLECTION

MJII p. 38

Use these guidelines for collecting data:

– Keep an "events log." In it record anything observed that was special or different, e.g., different worker, increased humidity, using a new supplier.

– **On startup, don't touch the process.** Don't adjust any knobs or change any procedure. Don't tamper with the process in any way.

For Example

The BCD team collected the following data on black density readings:

MacBeth Black Density Readings

		Randomly Chosen Machines			
		1	2	3	4
April	20	0.88	1.36	1.01	1.33
	21	1.25	1.06	0.83	1.05
	22	1.14	1.29	0.96	1.10
	23	0.74	1.26	0.62	0.96
	24	0.90	1.18	1.17	1.03
April	27	Holiday			
	28	1.21	0.82	0.89	0.92
	29	0.95	1.19	1.01	--
	30	0.77	1.04	0.95	0.83
May	1	1.19	1.15	0.67	0.98
	4	1.06	1.33	0.82	0.80
	5	1.04	1.12	1.12	1.21
	6	0.94	1.13	1.28	0.85
	7	1.34	0.95	1.02	1.00
	8	1.02	1.14	1.18	1.13
May	11	0.87	1.09	1.30	1.04
	12	1.12	1.32	1.04	0.78
	13	1.32	0.96	1.07	0.93
	14	0.90	1.38	0.86	1.27
	15	1.29	0.99	1.01	1.22

STEP 4 CALCULATING STATISTICS

MJII pp. 39–40

For Example

The BCD team's subgroup size is 4 (four randomly chosen copiers each day). The BCD team began their calculations by figuring out the mean and range for the four readings for each day. Like this:

$$\text{April 20} \quad \overline{X} = \frac{(0.88 + 1.36 + 1.01 + 1.33)}{4}$$

$$= \frac{4.58}{4}$$

$$= \mathbf{1.14}$$

$$\text{Range} = (\text{Highest} - \text{Lowest})$$

$$= (1.36 - 0.88)$$

$$= \mathbf{0.48}$$

For Example Continued

The BCD team recorded this information on a data/graph sheet, and also recorded the dates that data were collected. This type of detailed information is referred to as an "events log." The BCD team continued the calculations for the mean and range for each day and recorded these as well.

The BCD team noticed that April 27 was a holiday, and so no data were collected or recorded here. Also, they noticed that on April 29 there were only 3 observations. One of the machines was not working. In this case, the team summed the density readings for the three working machines and divided by three, the sample size, to obtain that day's average.

Next, The BCD team calculated the process grand average, $\bar{\bar{X}}$, and the average range, $\bar{R}$. Usually, this is done after at least 20 sets (or groups) of data are collected. The BCD team, knowing this, decided to go ahead with the 19 data sets anyway. (One set of data was lost on the holiday.)

$$\bar{\bar{X}} = \frac{\sum \bar{X}}{k}$$

$$= \frac{(1.14 + 1.05 + 1.12 + 0.09 \ldots 1.07 + 1.10 + 1.13)}{19}$$

$$= \frac{20}{19}$$

$$= 1.05$$

$$\bar{R} = \frac{\sum R}{k}$$

$$= \frac{(0.48 + 0.42 + 0.33 + 0.64 \ldots 0.54 + 0.39 + 0.52 + 0.30)}{19}$$

$$= \frac{7.43}{19}$$

$$= 0.391$$

STEP 5 CALCULATING CONTROL LIMITS

MJII p. 41

For Example

The BCD team next calculated the upper and lower control limits for the mean, $\bar{X}$, and the Range, R. From the previous step, they took this information:

$$n = 4$$
$$\bar{\bar{X}} = 1.05$$
$$\bar{R} = 0.391$$

Next, the BCD team looked at the Table of Constants in *The Memory Jogger™ II,* page 42, and found these values, based on the sample size n = 4:

$$A_2 = 0.729$$
$$D_3 = 0.000$$
$$D_4 = 2.282$$

And at last, the BCD team calculated the upper and lower control limits for the mean, $\overline{X}$, and the range, R.

Limits for $\overline{X}$:

$$\text{Upper Control Limit} = UCL_{\overline{X}} = \overline{\overline{X}} + A_2\overline{R}$$

$$= 1.05 + (0.729 \times 0.391)$$

$$= 1.05 + 0.285$$

$$= \mathbf{1.335}$$

$$\text{Lower Control Limit} = LCL_{\overline{X}} = \overline{\overline{X}} - A_2\overline{R}$$

$$= 1.05 - 0.285$$

$$= \mathbf{0.765}$$

Limits for R:

$$\text{Upper Control Limit} = UCL_R = D_4\overline{R}$$

$$= 2.282 \times 0.391$$

$$= \mathbf{0.892}$$

$$\text{Lower Control Limit} = LCL_R = D_3\overline{R}$$

$$= 0 \times 0.391$$

$$= \mathbf{0}$$

Remember, upper and lower control limits are **NOT** specification limits. Control limits describe the amount of variation produced by the process. Specification limits are desired requirements of the customer.

STEP 6 CONSTRUCTING THE CHART

MJII pp. 41–43

Follow these guidelines when constructing the chart:

– Scale the charts for each subgroup's average ($\overline{X}$, R, median or individual value, as well as the p, np, c, or u values), as well as the upper and lower control limits. Make sure the vertical scale for each chart includes all these values. A rule of thumb is to take 1.5 times the difference between the highest and lowest of the calculated subgroup means. For example, in the $\overline{X}$ & R Chart, take half this value and subtract it from the process grand average, $\overline{\overline{X}}$. Make this the lower boundary of the chart. Take half of the value and add it to the process grand average. This becomes the upper boundary of the chart. This usually ensures that the subgroup means and the control limits will fit on the graphic. Do the same for the ranges.

– Plot the points corresponding to each subgroup's mean on the graph(s).

– Draw a solid line corresponding to the process grand average, $\overline{\overline{X}}$.

– Draw a dotted or dashed line for the upper and lower control limits. If a lower control limit is a negative number or zero, set the lower control limit to zero.

For Example

See the BCD team's completed Control Chart in Step 7.

STEP 7 INTERPRETING THE CHART

MJII pp. 43–45

Use these guidelines when interpreting the chart:

- Look at the center (solid) line. Determine if it is where it should be relative to a specification, or where you want it to be relative to your objective.

- Look at the control limits. Look for any of the different "signals" that indicate the process is out of control. Refer to the section called "Determining If Your Process is 'Out of Control'" on pages 45–46 in *The Memory Jogger™ II.* (The source for this information is Lloyd S. Nelson, Director of Statistical Methods, Nashua Corporation, New Hampshire.)

- When the team identifies a signal that indicates the process is out of control, look at the "events log" to identify anything unusual or different at that point.

- Special causes of variation can usually be corrected by the person(s) having direct control over a process. Common causes of variation can only be corrected by a major change in the process.

- A Control Chart does not tell you what's wrong—only that there is something wrong and action is needed. The team should use other tools, such as Brainstorming, the Pareto Chart, Cause and Effect Diagram, or Flowchart, to analyze causes.

For Example

The BCD team interpreted their completed Control Chart, which is shown on the next page, in the following way. When the BCD team examined the averages and ranges charts, they saw that the last nine points were running consecutively above the center line. The BCD team consulted *The Memory Jogger™ II,* page 45, "Determining If Your Process is 'Out of Control.'" According to item 2 c) on page 45, and test 2c on the chart called "Tests for Control" on page 46, the BCD team confirmed their suspicion that the process was out of control; something had changed.

Another piece of information that indicated to the BCD team that the process had changed was that 27 of the 75 sample measurements fell below the specification limit of 1.0. The specification limit, "black density not less than 1.0" is noted at the top of the chart.

After interpreting the chart, the BCD team planned on investigating deeper to understand what was causing the change in the process.

For Example

The BCD's completed $\overline{X}$ & R Chart is shown below.

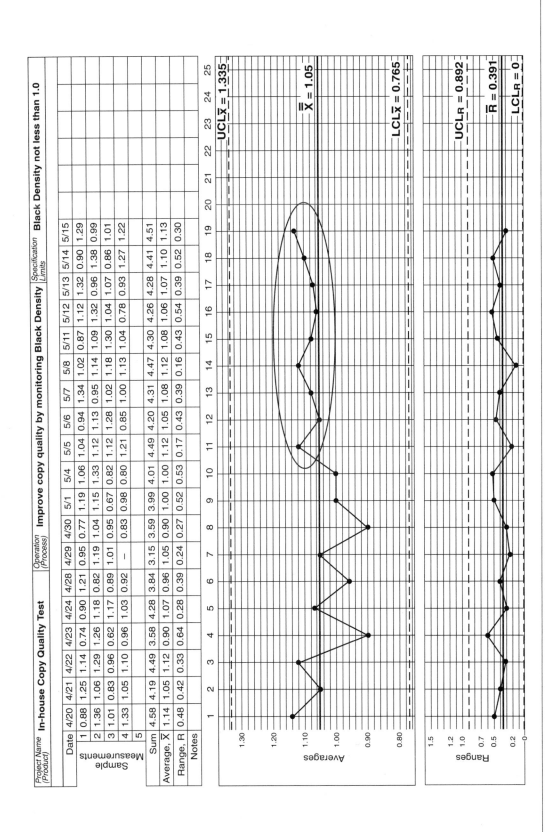

The Control Chart example is shown throughout the seven steps in this chapter. The BCD team, who is featured in the example in this chapter, and the path the BCD team follows in studying their process is *REAL*. (BCD stands for Black Copy Density.)

In this chapter, the BCD team selects a process to study (Step 1), determines a sampling plan (Step 2), initiates data collection (Step 3), calculates the appropriate statistics (Step 4), calculates the control limits (Step 5), constructs a chart (Step 6), and interprets the chart (Step 7).

It all starts one rainy day when the self-named BCD team forms to investigate whether all the copiers in house are consistently producing good black images . . .

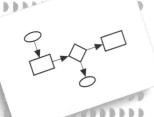

Flowchart
*Picturing
the process*

IS THIS THE RIGHT TOOL? ASK . . .

◗ Does the team need to see how a whole process works?

◗ Do team members need to identify critical points in a process where they might collect data?

◗ Does the team need to locate problem areas, bottlenecks, or instances where non-value-added work is performed?

◗ Do team members need to see how different steps in a process are related?

◗ Do team members need to see a flow of events? Flow of people? Flow of materials?

◗ Is the team looking to identify the "ideal" flow of a process, from start to finish?

STEPS AT A GLANCE

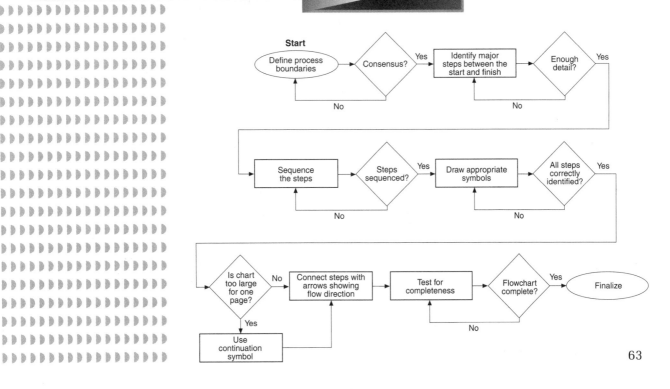

FLOWCHART

Q. **Why should we flowchart our process? Our process seems too complicated and confusing.**

A. That's exactly why you want to flowchart a process. If you take a snapshot of a process, with all its warts and bumps, the Flowchart allows teams to see before them the inefficiencies and complexities within a process. Once a team can really see the warts and bumps and understand what's causing them, a team can then focus its efforts on improving and simplifying a process.

Q. **Are Flowcharts drawn only when there is a problem?**

A. No. Although Flowcharts are commonly used to identify problems in a process, every major process should be flowcharted at some point. The Flowchart can be a valuable teaching aid for showing new employees how a process works or providing a team with the most relevant information on a process so it can be improved.

Q. **How do you know where to start and end a Flowchart?**

A. First, begin by defining what process you are studying. Think about the first thing you do or the first point of this process where some input comes in. This will be the starting point. Next think about the customer of the process. What are customers looking for as an output or outcome? This will be the ending point. The team needs to come to consensus about defining the starting and ending points. For example, take the hiring process: a request to fill a vacancy is the starting point, and a person hired to fill that vacancy is the ending point.

Q. **How big can a Flowchart get?**

A. As big as necessary to show the level of detail the team needs to understand and identify the sources of the problem. But it's best to advise the team to start small, especially if this is the team's first experience in drawing Flowcharts. Grow to the level of detail as needed. The flowcharting process can get overwhelming if the team tries to build too complex a chart at first.

Q. **Is there another way to draw Flowcharts rather than by hand?**

A. Yes. There are several good software packages now on the market that simplify the drawing process and are especially useful when modifications are needed. Some examples are *The Memory Jogger*™ *Software*, *Inspiration*™, and *Intellidraw*.

Q. **What if we really need to understand the relationships of people or departments?**

A. There are various forms of Flowcharts; the one discussed up to this point has been a *process* Flowchart. If your team needs to study the relationships between people or departments, then use a *deployment* Flowchart. (See MJII page 61 and also under Step 6 in this chapter.)

Q. **Can a Flowchart have more than one arrow going in or out of a symbol?**

A. Yes. A diamond-shaped symbol, which indicates a decision is required, will have two arrows coming out of the diamond—one arrow is for a "yes" response, the other for "no." A box- or rectangle-shaped symbol, which indicates an action is required, might branch off in two or more directions. For example, one duplicate of a multi-copy form might need to go to the accounting department and the other to the purchasing department. Any symbol used in a Flowchart might have multiple arrows pointing into it.

If: **A team is confused between flowcharting what *is* and what *should be* . . .**

Then: Have the team ask *"Are we studying a current process to improve it?"* If the answer is yes, then the team should flowchart what is actually happening. If the team is planning a "new" process, then the team should Flowchart what the process should be like. When the team is flowcharting the process as it is currently, the team will likely be able to identify probable causes of the glitches in the process. To be sure, have team members physically walk the process if possible. Ask them to flowchart exactly what is happening as they move through the steps. If it isn't possible to walk through the process, ask the team to invite someone experienced with the process to share his/her knowledge of how the process flows.

After the team has a Flowchart of the "actual" process, team members may want to flowchart how they would ideally like the process to flow. The team can then compare the two flowcharts by looking for the points in the process where the charts deviate from one another. These differences will be the sources of probable causes of problems within the process.

If: **The team is resisting flowcharting a process because it seems too complicated at first . . .**

Then: Have the team look at a macro-level Flowchart first. (MJII pages 57 and 119 and also under Step 6 in this chapter.) This type of chart identifies 5–6 major actions. Then ask the team to take each of these actions, one by one, and break them down into more detail.

LEARNING ACTIVITY

1. Working in groups of 4–6 people, ask each group to create a Flowchart of a process that is familiar to everyone in the group. For example:

   ▶ Getting a cold drink

   ▶ Getting to work in the morning

   ▶ Buying and installing a washing machine

   ▶ Making breakfast

   ▶ Ordering supplies

   ▶ Reimbursing travel expenses

2. To avoid having people redraw or erase their Flowcharts if they want to make a change, simply have the groups use Post-its™ for the elements of the diagram.

3. When the Flowcharts are completed, ask everyone to come back together as one large group, and:

   ▶ Share and compare the Flowcharts;

   ▶ Discuss where the groups had difficulties;

   ▶ Discuss the pros and cons of the tool.

Flow Chart

> " As a group we became open to new ideas for improvement through using the Flowchart. "
>
> Robert McMahon

Written by Robert McMahon, U.S. Navy, Naval Dental Center

What was the problem?

The patient appointment system was not conducive to the needs of the patients who could not receive instant appointments due to the vast amount of patients seen in the building.

Who was on the team?

The team was comprised of members who worked in every facet of the patient appointing process.

How long did the process take?

This process took 4 months of data collection to finalize a proposition for change. It took 1 hour to create the proposed Flowchart.

What did we learn?

The tool can become very complex at times. We found that the Flowchart was necessary to find out not only how things ought to run but also how they actually are running. In doing so you may find your process variation.

How was the team affected?

It affected our team a great deal. A majority of our team was new to the TQL arena and were impressed with what a group of process owners could accomplish when they communicated effectively and worked as a team.

What else did we use?

We went from the Flowchart of "how things are really happening" to the Cause and Effect Diagram to find out all the causes for a missed appointment.

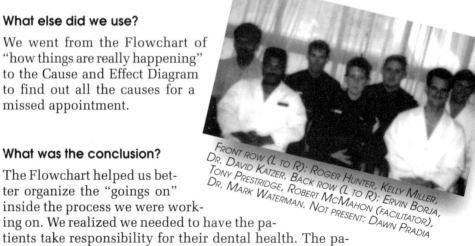

FRONT ROW (L TO R): ROGER HUNTER, KELLY MILLER, DR. DAVID KATZER. BACK ROW (L TO R): ERVIN BORJA, TONY PRESTRIDGE, ROBERT MCMAHON (FACILITATOR), DR. MARK WATERMAN. NOT PRESENT: DAWN PRADIA

What was the conclusion?

The Flowchart helped us better organize the "goings on" inside the process we were working on. We realized we needed to have the patients take responsibility for their dental health. The patients who could not receive appointments due to space availability would now be allowed this access.

What were the results?

As a group we became open to new ideas for improvement through using the Flowchart. Process owners already had ideas of how the process could be improved. Through customer and team interaction these ideas were brought out and helped us come up with a proposal for process improvement.

Proposed Patient Appointment Procedure

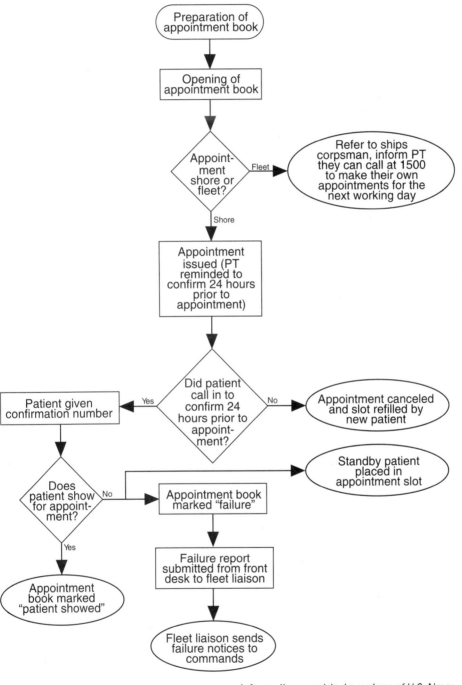

Information provided courtesy of U.S. Navy, Naval Dental Center, San Diego

STEP 1 DETERMINING THE BOUNDARIES

MJII pp. 56–57

▶ **Spend Time To Clarify the Process**

It is important for the team to come to agreement in framing the process under study.

– Examine the mission or charter given to the team. This will often help identify the process as well as what the team has control over studying and improving.

– Discussion will help bring all team members to a common ground, especially if each member understands only his or her part of the process.

– Make sure everyone on the team has ownership in some part of the process or understands what the benefits will be. That way members know why they *all* are there. They will also work aggressively at flowcharting the process—working through the hard parts.

▶ **Define the Starting Point:** Ask *"What activity do I do first?"* or *"What input are we receiving?"* Label this the starting point. Have the team agree on this. For example, in the process of "getting to work in the morning," will the starting point be "the alarm goes off" or "set the alarm"?

▶ **Define the Ending Point:** Ask *"What is the outcome?"* or *"What is the very last thing that happens?"* Label this the ending point. Right now don't be concerned about the activities that fall in between the starting and ending points.

▶ **Work for Team Consensus:** Consensus around the beginning and ending points of the process helps focus the team.

STEP 2 LISTING THE STEPS

MJII p. 57

On flipchart paper or Post-its™, list 6–10 major steps in the process. Use brainstorming. Ask everyone to participate, since everyone should have knowledge of some piece of the process. Make sure the list includes all necessary steps for completing the process flow.

STEP 3 SEQUENCING THE STEPS

MJII p. 57

▶ **Order the Steps From the First Activity or Input to the Last**

– In the team's listing of the major steps, find out what happens after the initial starting point. Place this step under or next to the starting point.

– Find and agree on the second step in the process. Place the step under or next to the previous activity.

– Don't worry about drawing in lines and arrows yet.

– Allow sufficient time for discussion around the steps and their sequencing. This allows team members to learn from each other and better understand the process and its complexities, producing better end results when the team improves the process later.

– If necessary or helpful, have team members physically walk through the process if possible. This can be done just prior to, or after, sequencing the steps. Record everything exactly as it is happening as people move through the steps. Take notes as well; notice who is doing the task or job, how long it takes, the problems that are surfacing, and so on. If the process can't be walked through, talk to the people who perform the work (and are not part of the team) for their ideas and information.

Helpful Hints

Use Post-its™ or index cards. Putting each separate step on individual Post-its™ or index cards allows flexibility. Team members can then arrange and rearrange the Flowchart steps as they go about sequencing them. If team members find they are repeatedly erasing and redrawing the steps, they may become frustrated enough to stop using the Flowchart and not consider using it in the future either.

To represent a starting or ending point, draw an oval on the Post-it™ or index card to differentiate it from the other steps:

Holding the Post-it™ or index card so that it appears as a square or rectangular will work for any task or action:

Task, action, execution step

Rotate the Post-it™ 45° degrees to become a decision point:

STEP 4   DRAWING APPROPRIATE SYMBOLS

MJII pp. 57–59

▶ **Don't Get Hung Up On the Symbols:** First timers should keep it relatively simple. Use the oval, box, and diamond. As confidence and experience grow, add more detailed symbols. See the table of Flowchart Symbols in this step.

▶ **Show the Flow with Arrows:** Don't forget to add arrows after assigning the appropriate symbols. Arrows are better than just lines connecting the symbols because they clearly lead you to the next step; it's especially important when the Flowchart is a complex one.

– If team members have difficulty in flowcharting the process, then maybe they don't clearly understand it.

– Team members should listen to others from outside the team for ideas, changes, or modifications for the Flowchart. Remember though that at this point, the team is not looking for improvements to the process. The team is still trying to chart the process as it currently flows.

Flowchart Symbols

Symbol	Represents	Detail/Example
(oval)	Start/End Input/Output	Request for proposal, request for new hire, raw material
(square)	Task, action, execution point	Hold a meeting, make a phone call, open a box
? No / Yes (diamond)	Decision point	Yes/no Accept/reject Pass/fail Criteria met/not met
(document)	Document	A report or form is filled out, job request, meeting minutes
(shadowed box)	Shadow signifies additional flowchart for this task	A major task has subtasks not needed for this study or subtasks not included due to limited space
(delay)	Delay	Waiting for service, report sitting on a desk
→(A) / (A)→	Continuation	Go to another page, go to another part of the chart
→	Arrow	Shows direction or flow of the process steps

STEP 5 TESTING FOR COMPLETENESS

MJII p. 59

▶ **Allow Sufficient Time for Team Members to Review All the Steps in the Process:** Are the symbols correct? Is the activity being performed clearly understood? Are all the loops closed? For example: Does each arrow point to another step or end in an output? Does every continuation point have a matching point somewhere else on the page or another page?

▶ **Make Sure the Flowchart is at the Depth of Detail Necessary:** If the team views the activity as important, then detail it out. If it is not currently viewed as important or necessary, don't detail it out, but perhaps view it as a shadowed box to remind the team that it involves subtasks and could be detailed out at another time.

▶ **Check for Consistency in the Layout:** There is no hard rule about the direction a "yes" or "no" option should branch out from a decision diamond—to the left, right, or downward—but showing them consistently going in the same direction will facilitate the ease in which people read the chart. Personal preferences and space will often dictate direction. Be open to trying different layouts.

Everyone should participate and agree on the final Flowchart.

▶ Keep An Open Mind

- The team should be open-minded to changes in the process flow.

- If team members have difficulty in flowcharting the process, then maybe they don't clearly understand it.

- Team members should listen to others from outside the team for ideas, changes, or modifications for the Flowchart. Remember though that at this point, the team is not looking for improvements to the process. The team is still trying to chart the process as it currently flows.

Now is the time for the team to look for improvement opportunities.

STEP 6   FINALIZING THE FLOWCHART

MJII p. 59

▶ Look for Problem Areas

Maybe the process can't be flowcharted completely because the process is broken and elements are missing. Compare the current process against the *ideal* process for discrepancies. Find critical areas where more data can be collected to help get at the root cause of the problem.

▶ Listen to Others

As whole or part process owners, emphasize again the need to be open to changes offered up from team members and those outside the team.

▶ Variations

Macro Flowchart

This chart shows the major activities of a process, without including the decision points or loops. Each activity usually represents a part of the process that could be detailed out further.

Taking a Trip

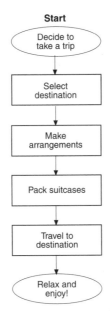

Top-down Flowchart

This chart is an expansion of a macro-level Flowchart that is drawn on its side. More detail is provided in the numbered subtasks to each macro-level task, but the detail does not go to the level of detail in a process Flowchart or Deployment Flowchart by showing decision points or loops, or rework, and so on.

Taking a Trip

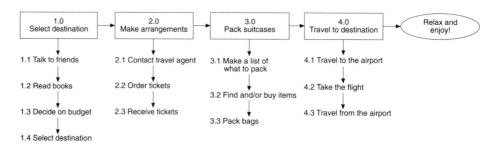

Deployment Flowchart

– Start a Deployment Flowchart by identifying the people or departments involved. Ask who the "players" in the process are. Consider including customers and suppliers as well.

– Write the people, departments, teams, and other players across the top of a sheet of paper as a series of connected boxes—one box per person or department.

– List and sequence the tasks. Assign who has responsibility for each task.

– In column form, working from the top down, place the tasks under the appropriate person or department.

– Draw the connecting arrows showing how the process flows from one person or department to the next.

"Roll Call"

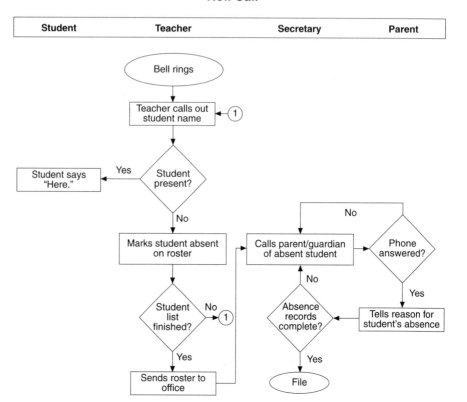

Workflow Flowchart

This type of chart is used to show the flow of people, materials, paperwork, etc., within a work setting. When redundancies, duplications, and unnecessary complexities are identified in a path, people can take action to reduce or eliminate these problems.

Before

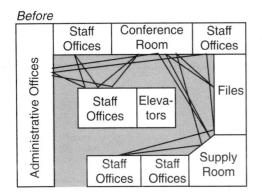

After

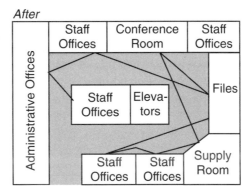

EXAMPLE

Receiving Materials

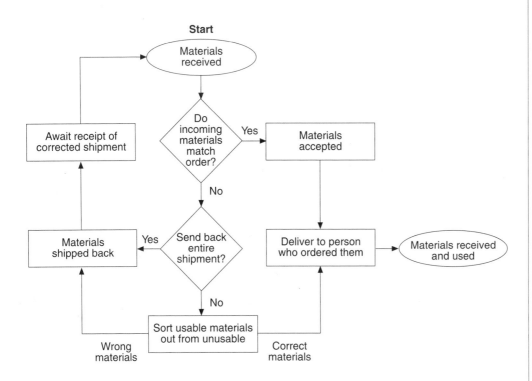

Flow Chart

Flow Chart

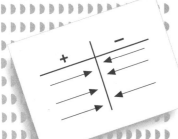

Force Field Analysis

*Positives &
negatives of change*

IS THIS THE RIGHT TOOL? ASK . . .

▶ Does the team need a way to evaluate a situation or available alternatives?

▶ Is there an issue or problem that the team needs to better define?

▶ Is the team working toward a different situation but unsure of what conditions to change, or all the conditions that presently exist?

▶ Does it seem that the situation the team wants to change is static because there are an equal number of positive and negative forces at play?

▶ Does the team need to think about the positive and negative aspects of making a desired change?

▶ Does the team want to know the possible consequences of a proposed change?

STEPS AT A GLANCE

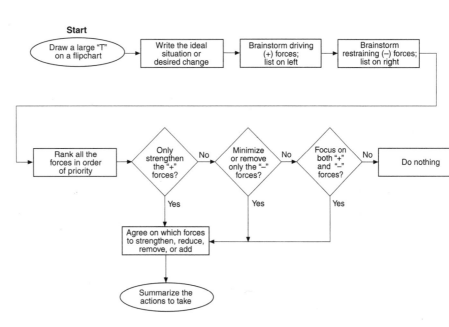

FORCE FIELD

Q. **At what point in the development of a project or proposed change should Force Field Analysis be used?**

A. A team should use Force Field Analysis as one of the first actions during the initial planning stages to generate possible alternatives on which elements of a situation to change. The use of Force Field Analysis can be invaluable as one of the earliest steps; it summarizes a team's "picture" of the dynamics that have created the current situation, makes the problem real, and allows a team to come together around a common understanding. **Caution:** Force Field Analysis can be such a graphic way to illustrate the current situation that it has been known to discourage teams from even proceeding. It is up to the team leader or facilitator to keep the team focused on individual actions that are possible in order to change the status quo.

Q. **What are some other ways to think about opposing "forces?"**

A. Replace the words "driving forces" and "restraining forces" with words like: "advantages" and "disadvantages," "assisting forces" and "hindering forces," "reasons for" and "reasons against," "pros" and "cons," "positives" and "negatives." Oh yes, and "May *The Force* be with you."

Q. **How should the team rank, in order of priority, the driving and restraining forces?**

A. There are several ways. Here are four methods:

▶ The team can use the numbers 1 through 10, with "1" as the lowest and "10" the highest, to rank the impact that each force has on maintaining the current situation. To get a total score for each force, you can consolidate the rankings of each team member by initiating an open discussion, then getting team consensus, or use Nominal Group Technique (MJII pages 91–93).

▶ Each person can be allowed a set number of points, or votes, to distribute among the driving and restraining forces. A good way to represent this visually is to give each person different colored, self-sticking dots that are "worth" one or more points or one vote's worth. (See "Weighted Multivoting," MJII pages 93–94.)

▶ The team can use the numbers 1 through 3, with "1" for small impact, "2" for medium impact, and "3" for large impact.

▶ A variation on the method above: The team can use arrows that point into the center line to indicate the impact of each factor. The thicker and bolder the arrow, or the longer its length, the larger the impact.

Q. **Does every "driving" force require an opposing "restraining" force?**

A. No. However, whether the team brainstorms a restraining force for every driving force or chooses to randomly brainstorm any force, there are advantages and disadvantages to either method. *If the team chooses to brainstorm a restraining force for every driving force*, they have the advantage of keeping a tight focus on the factors that are most relevant to the current situation. However, this method can also force the team to produce an opposite force that could "negatively offset" the positive statement that was created.

If the team chooses to randomly brainstorm any force, the "up" side is that the team's creativity is unrestrained and this allows the team to surface all of the forces that are evident. On the "down" side, using this method can allow a team to get so creative that they generate an unmanageable number of forces, which can be discouraging on later reflection.

A combination of the two methods seems to work best. The team can work first to brainstorm the driving forces, then ask, "Given these forces, what are the *most likely* forces that are stopping, or restraining, the team from achieving the change?" This method will help the team maintain a connection between the two types of forces, while allowing for the possibility that some driving forces will have either no opposing forces or multiple opposing forces.

FACILITATION ESSENTIALS

If: **Members of the team want to accentuate the positive without eliminating the negative . . .**

Then: Select one driving force and one restraining force and brainstorm potential solutions for each. Evaluate the likely lasting impact for each possible solution. Almost invariably, solutions that focus on diminishing the restraining forces are more effective. While driving forces frequently represent all of the good reasons why people should change, the proposed change may never be implemented, or the change may implemented but short-lived, if the fundamental restraining forces that exist in "the system" are not eliminated.

If: **There is a lack of energy around creating the driving and restraining forces . . .**

Then: Return to the original point of the discussion; there is a significant change that the team wants to achieve. The "path of least resistance" is for the team to create, (and agree to by consensus), a statement that summarizes the current situation. **For example:** the team may agree that the current situation is summarized by "We have a significant number of customers who complain and even stop doing business with us," and then come to consensus on the goal they hope to achieve: *"to improve the quality of our customer service."* This is a good goal, however, it is very general. The team will need to be more specific. In the effort to be more specific, the team may decide to gather some data in quantifying the extent of the problem, or they may just continue the discussion. **For example:** the team may have now specified the goal to be: *"to reduce or eliminate customer complaints and for our customers to be our best salespeople."*

In the end, the team must agree that the gap between the current situation and the proposed situation is worth filling. If there is consensus at each step, then the team is more likely to see the value of making a sincere effort to explore *all of the forces* affecting the change. Work worth doing is the greatest motivator of all!

If: **One or more team members are resisting the proposed change . . .**

Then: Perhaps the team needs to discuss why, in general, people find change difficult.

Force Field Analysis

FACILITATION ESSENTIALS

Change is inevitable, but people always resist it on some level, and each person reacts to change differently (because everyone sees the world differently). By understanding why a particular person may resist the proposed change, the coach, and other team members, can better address the issues of change the person is resisting. People resist change for many reasons, some of them perceived and others actual. (Take note: actual and perceived changes are both *real*.) Here are a few examples of why people might resist change: loss of income, inconvenience, loss of status, uncertainty, lack of time, social disruption, loss of control, increased work load.

If you can get the team members who are resisting a change to speak out, you have a better chance to dispel incorrect assumptions and perceptions, and to change the circumstances, if this option is within your capability and if it's desirable. Another good aspect of getting team members to share their thoughts is that once the discussion is opened up, you may help the team discover that either everyone feels the same way, or just one person has a concern. Once each person's concerns are vocalized, the team can work together to address them.

How can you help the team better accept change? Here are several suggestions:

– Explain the change in advance.

– Maintain effective communication about the change.

– Encourage participation in the change.

– Visualize what conditions will be like after the change.

– Reward and recognize those who are living through the change. Reward can take many forms: verbal praise (one-to-one, or in front of other team members, or announced to the company), a bonus, time off, promotion, buying the team breakfast or lunch are just a few examples. Sometimes all it takes to make others feel appreciated is to tell them (sincerely) what a great job you think they are doing, and to recognize that you know the change isn't easy.

LEARNING ACTIVITY

1. Ask the group to agree on a situation in which they would all like to bring about a change. They can get ideas from other tools they've used, from work situations, or personal challenges. For example, here are some proposed changes:

Work	**Personal**	**Social**
▶ Improve time management	▶ Improve fitness level	▶ Reduce litter in community
▶ Truly listen to the customer	▶ Create more time for family and friends	▶ Increase the use of seatbelts
▶ Encourage creativity in solving problems	▶ Acquire a new skill or revive an old interest	▶ Increase the use of public transportation

2. After the group writes the desired change on a flipchart, ask the group to brainstorm the driving forces. Next ask the group to brainstorm the restraining forces. (Driving on the left, restraining on the right.)

3. Ask the group to prioritize the driving forces. Try open discussion first. If people in the group don't agree on the relative importance of each driving force, then try voting as a way to prioritize the forces. Give each person in the group four votes to apply to one or more of the forces. On the flipchart, write in parentheses the total number of votes for each force. The driving force with the highest priority will be the force with the largest number of votes. Ask the group to prioritize the restraining forces, using the same process.

4. Ask the group to decide which side of the Force Field would be the most effective to focus on. Ask team members to explain why. **Optional:** ask the group to list the actions that can be taken to achieve the desired change. This is done by discussing how to strengthen or add driving forces and/or reduce or remove restraining forces.

INCIDENTALLY

Force Field Analyis was invented by Kurt Lewin, a well-known psychologist. (Known well to other psychologists of course.) During World War II, the U.S. government sponsored Lewin to research the meat buying preferences of housewives. Lewin invented Force Field Analysis while he was conducting this research. He found that housewives would rather buy steak and hamburger over liver and tongue. (Probably still the case today!) The bottom line for the government was to have Lewin find out why housewives didn't buy as much liver and tongue, and learn how housewives could be influenced to buy meats that did not require ration stamps. (Source: *Total Quality Transformation*, QIP, Inc./PQ Systems, Inc., Miamisburg, OH, 1992.)

Force Field Analysis

79

STEP 1   BRAINSTORMING THE FORCES

MJII pp. 63–64

▶ **The Forces**

The team should think of two distinct types of forces: driving forces and restraining forces. Some examples of these two types of forces are listed below.

Driving Forces (to learn a new software program)

– It will eventually make some aspects of the job easier

– Pressure from a supervisor

– A coworker already knows how to use the program

– It could be fun

– Acquire a new skill

Restraining Forces (forces against learning a new software program)

– It takes time and effort to learn something new

– There's a similar program that's better and easier to use

– Not much time available during work hours to learn the program

– Will retire in a few months

– After an upcoming project is completed, it isn't clear for what other projects the program will be used

STEP 2   PRIORITIZING THE FORCES

MJII p. 64

▶ **Beware of Team Members Who Carry the Torch for a Cause**

Any list of choices raises the possibility that someone will push hard for a personal favorite. Force Field Analysis exaggerates this tendency because it focuses on the fundamentals of change. Everyone in an organization seems to hold a theory as to why things do or do not happen. This is the ideal forum for people to use phrases such as, "You know, the real problem is that . . ." The possibility that someone will push hard for a personal favorite is strengthened by the fact that Force Field Analysis is often used for major changes. Team members are rarely neutral on such topics. How can such strong feelings be channeled productively? The answer lies in either a gifted leader or facilitator, or in the use of one of the prioritization tools.

Whenever a team is not lucky enough to have a gifted leader or facilitator, (which is frequent), tools such as Nominal Group Technique, Weighted Multivoting, and Prioritization Matrices, will help *diminish,* not eliminate, the possibility that someone will successfully "sell" a cause. Using any of these tools will require the "torch-bearing" team member to repeatedly convince others of the "rightness" of his or her position. If, after using any of these tools, the person "wins," there are really only two conclusions: either this person is right or the entire team has been intimidated. In either case— having a gifted leader or facilitator or using one of the other tools instead— every person will have had an opportunity to fully verbalize his or her position. Discussion is integral to the process of using any of these tools, and as a result of discussion, each person is more likely, than not, to support the decision of the team and work for its successful implementation.

▶ **Use the Simplest Tool First**

A team should use the simplest tool first. When the team is prioritizing the forces, try the weighted multivoting option first. If there are significant implications of the change, and the topic is somewhat, but not highly, controversial, use Nominal Group Technique. However, when the stakes are very high and the associated feelings are running equally high in the team, consider using the Prioritization Matrices method to both diffuse the situation and improve the quality of the final selection.

Desired Change: Quit Smoking

Driving Forces (+)		Restraining Forces (−)	
Clothes & breath smell like smoke	(3)	It's too hard to quit	(10)
Costs money	(8)	Many of your friends smoke	(4)
Getting hackers cough	(6)	Spouse smokes	(9)
Don't want your kids to start smoking	(10)	It's enjoyable	(6)
Know it can adversely affect your health	(9)	Work is too stressful right now to quit	(8)
Can't smoke at work	(5)	Doesn't affect physical activity level	(5)
Support group available in community	(7)	Don't want to gain any weight by quitting	(3)
		You can quit anytime, but you're not ready yet	(2)

Possible Actions

1. Educate yourself, your spouse, and your children on the hazards and drawbacks of smoking. (Strengthen the driving forces "Don't want your kids to start smoking" and "Know it can adversely affect your health.")

2. Figure out what it costs to continue smoking for another year. Another five years, the next decade, and the next twenty years. Think about what you would do with this money if it weren't spent on cigarettes. Write down everything and reread it every day.

3. Join the support group and learn ways to deal with the craving for a cigarette.

4. Talk to your spouse about your desire to quit smoking and ask for support and/or a mutual commitment to quitting.

5. Educate yourself on ways to cope with stress and practice a few of them.

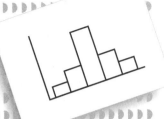

Histogram

*Process centering,
spread, and shape*

Is This the Right Tool? Ask . . .

▶ Is the team overwhelmed by too much data and needs to organize it in some meaningful way?

▶ Would it be helpful for the team to see a process' performance in terms of where it's centered and how much variation it is exhibiting?

▶ Does the team need to see the underlying distribution of a process?

▶ Would it be helpful to the team to monitor process performance by measuring the process before and after an improvement?

Steps at a Glance

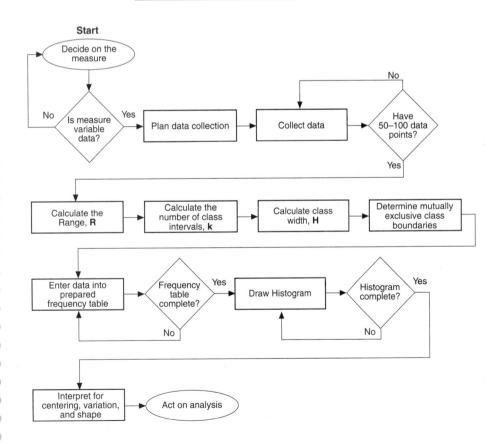

Histogram

Q. **Why use the Histogram?**

A. The theory behind variation is that no two objects or occurrences are exactly alike. If they are, then our measurements are not sensitive enough to find the differences. Thus, variation exists in the world around us. For an organization to be able to ensure that a product or service it provides today will be the same tomorrow, the next day, and the next year, someone must be monitoring and controlling or reducing, as needed, the variation in the process. The Histogram is a useful tool in helping a team gain knowledge about a process by describing the distribution of variable, or measured, data. The Histogram allows a team to visually approximate whether a process is targeted where it should be, determine if there is too much variation, show the relationship of the distribution to customer requirements, specifications, and management targets, and show whether there is mixing of data populations, e.g., different machines, shifts, people, or suppliers. Armed with knowledge about the process from the Histogram and other tools, a team can work towards improving it so that it is stable, reliable, and predictable.

Q. **How is the Histogram different from a Pareto Chart?**

A. Both tools visually appear similar to bar graphs, however, the difference lies in the data that will be used to construct the chart. Use the *Pareto Chart* when it's necessary to arrange the data into categories, which you can *count, rank order, and determine a cumulative percentage line for.* The purpose of the Pareto Chart is to *prioritize* and *focus* attention on what to look at to improve a process or find a problem area. Use the *Histogram* to show the frequency of an occurrence of data that can be *measured on a continuous scale,* e.g., wait times, temperature readings, weights. When the Histogram is drawn, the scale is plotted across the bottom of the chart, and the data *are not* rank ordered. Constructing a Histogram will help you understand process performance by finding the central point (mean) and amount of variation (standard deviation) of the data, and looking at how to improve a process (move the central point or reduce variation), if necessary.

Q. **How much data is needed to construct a Histogram?**

A. A good rule of thumb is between 50 and 100 data points. However, 30–50 data points can be used if there are at least 5–10 in the main (center) bar. The number of intervals should be adjusted to the lower sample size. With too few data points, the Histogram is too crude to yield any meaningful information.

Q. **Is there some relationship between a Histogram and the standard deviation?**

A. Yes. Histograms are created using variable, or continuous, data. Continuous data will take on the shape of a "bell-shaped" or "normal" curve as the sample size increases and the width of the class interval is decreased. The standard deviation is a measure of the average deviation of each data point from the central value. 68% of the data points will fall within $\pm 1s$ from the mean (central value), 95% of the data points will fall within $\pm 2s$, and 99.7% within $\pm 3s$.

Q. **Are there any drawbacks to using the Histogram?**

A. Yes. The Histogram is a snapshot of a process' performance at some point in time. It will not show whether or not the process is changing over time. To do that, construct a Control Chart.

If: **The team is intimidated by the amount of data and work required to construct a Histogram . . .**

Then: The team might elect to:

▶ Draw the frequency table neatly. It can be used in place of the final Histogram.

▶ Use a computer program to display the data, and "key in" the data values.

▶ Find someone who likes to "number crunch."

If: **The team cannot find any patterns in the Histogram . . .**

Then: Don't panic and don't throw out the data! Here are three reasons why:

▶ The number of intervals can influence the pattern within the data. Too many intervals will result in a spread out, flat pattern; too few intervals will result in a tight, high pattern. ***Action***: Go back and recheck the number of intervals based on the data sample size.

▶ There may be multiple populations (different data groups) compiled together. ***Action***: Check to see if the data are comprised of different categories, for example, different people or different machines. Then stratify the data by constructing separate Histograms.

▶ There may not be enough data. ***Action***: Make sure you have at least 50–100 data points.

LEARNING ACTIVITY

Getting Started:

You'll need exactly 200 chips. Choose bingo, poker, tiddleywinks, or similar chips. (Not potato chips!) Mark each chip with one number according to the following normal distribution:

Tag No.	1	2	3	4	5	6	7	8	9	10	11
Frequency	1	3	10	23	39	48	39	23	10	3	1

Begin by marking one tag, or a self-adhesive dot, with "1," three tags with "2," ten tags with "3," and so on up to tag number 11. Attach the tags or self-adhesive dots to the chips. Mix up the chips well in a bowl. Decide whether the group will work together as a whole or split into teams. If the group is larger than six people, it's a good idea to form teams. Ask the group, or each team, to draw a sample of 50, returning each chip to the bowl after the number is recorded. Mix the chips in the bowl well between each draw. When all 50 data points have been recorded, ask the group, or the teams, to develop a frequency table and Histogram. Based on the Histogram, have the group(s) approximate the centering (median and/or mode) and variation (range) of the distribution for their sample. (More next page . . .)

Histogram

The answers for the median/mode, range, and standard deviation are printed in the "Coach's Answer Key" at the end of this chapter.

Follow Up:

Use the following example to expand the group's knowledge into appropriate action.

A company has specified it needs a raw material to be between the percentages of 62 and 72 in moisture content. Sampling from a supplier's shipments over a three-week period, 45 readings were taken. The readings were as follows:

65	71	68	68	70	70	66	68	69
67	68	67	70	71	69	68	70	69
69	69	66	68	65	72	69	67	69
68	69	67	71	66	73	67	68	64
66	71	70	68	69	70	67	67	69

To construct the Histogram, the group needs to answer these questions:

a) Is the supplier meeting the specifications, given the current data? What percentage, if any, of the raw material is not meeting the specifications?

b) What action should be taken?

The answers are printed in the "Coach's Answer Key" at the end of this chapter.

STEP 1 DECIDING ON THE MEASURE
MJII p. 66

Make sure that the team clearly understands continuous data, that is, data that is measured on a continuous scale. Consider:

– **Times**: wait times, delivery times, cycle times, preparation times, time to failure (seconds, minutes, hours, days, weeks, months, years)

– **Weights**: raw material, finished product, additives (ounces, pounds, tons)

– **Dimensions**: length, width, depth, diagonals, volume (inches, feet, yards, miles)

– **Temperatures**: heating or cooling (Fahrenheit, Celsius, Kelvin)

– Also consider, torques, pressure (pounds per square inch), humidity

Note: Data that can be sorted, counted, and prioritized is charted in a Pareto Chart.

STEP 2 GATHERING DATA
MJII p. 67

▶ **Prepare for Data Collection**

Who should be involved?

Who will collect the data? Is it necessary to get permission from a supervisor? Does someone need to be trained how to collect the data?

How will data collectors record the data?

It might be helpful to prepare a simple data collection sheet with the people who will be collecting the information.

What will be the cost of collecting data?

How much data will be collected? Although 50–100 data points is desirable, also consider the cost. Will it take a long time to gather the data? Hours? Days? A month? Longer? Will collecting data destroy the product?

What will be the source of data?

Use historical data initially, if it is available. This data will form a baseline of process performance. Another source is the data from a Control Chart log. If no preexisting data are available, collect current data.

For specific information on data collection—what data to collect, how, and why—see the Data Points and Check Sheet chapters in this book. (MJII pages 32–34, 52–53.)

STEP 3   PREPARING A FREQUENCY TABLE

MJII pp. 67–69

▶ **Determining the Number of Class Intervals**

The two methods for determining the number of class intervals, k, are just rules of thumb to ensure a "nice looking distribution." It's okay to have one more or one less than the number of class intervals calculated. This result is possible whenever the calculation is rounded off.

Too many intervals?

If there are too many intervals in relation to the number of data points, a spread out, flat pattern is produced. Take for example these numbers:

5	3	9	8	1
2	4	8	7	13
5	8	10	7	4
11	9	11	6	5
8	14	6	15	7

which may produce a histogram that looks like this:

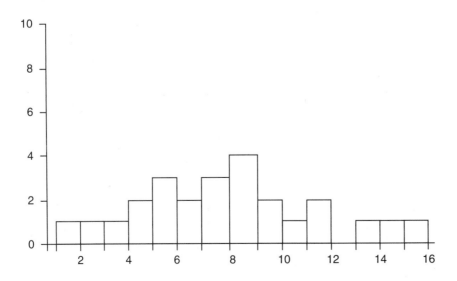

Too few intervals?

If there are too few intervals in relation to the number of data points, a tight, high pattern is produced. Take for example the same numbers that are listed under "Too many intervals?" which may produce a histogram that looks like this:

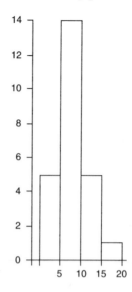

In both cases, the team won't be able to see the natural centering, variation, or shape of the data set

Number of intervals just right?

If there are the right number of intervals in relation to the number of data points, an evenly distributed pattern that forms the shape of a bell curve is produced. Take for example the same numbers that are listed under "Too many intervals?" which may produce a histogram that looks like this:

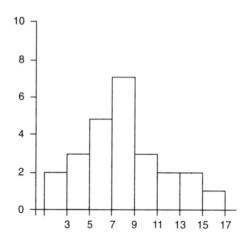

▶ **Constructing the Intervals:** One of the toughest parts for a team is constructing the intervals. Help the team stay focused and moving with these guidelines:

Make sure all class intervals are mutually exclusive: Each class interval must be mutually exclusive, that is, every data point belongs in one, *and only one*, class interval. If the class intervals are not mutually exclusive, then they should be recalculated so that each class interval is different from the others

Work on calculating each of the lower boundaries first: If this is done, then the upper boundaries can be thought of as either:

– Everything up to but not including the lower boundary of the next class.

– Everything less than but not including the lower boundary of the next class.

For example: if the class interval is calculated to be .13, and the first lower boundary is 1.26, then the next lower boundary is 1.26 + .13 = 1.39. The upper boundary for the first class interval would be *everything up to but not including 1.39* or *everything less than 1.39,* whichever way the team wants to state it. It can be written as 1.38 as long as the data does not exceed two decimal places. If it does, round it to two places, then place it in the appropriate class.

Round off numbers: The team should not be afraid to round numbers for the class intervals or class widths Rounding off numbers will more likely help the team avoid making errors.

– Round the class width, **H**, to a even number.

– Start the lowest class boundary with either the lowest value or round down to the next lowest even number of a number divisible by 5 or 10. A team is more likely to make errors when the data points they are placing into class intervals are not familiar multiples.

For example: a lower boundary of 6.23 and class width of .16 would generate the following class intervals:

6.23 – 6.38

6.39 – 6.54

6.55 – 6.70

6.71 – 6.86, and so on

This method will produce more errors when the team places the data points into classes than rounding the lower boundary to 6.20 and class width to .15. Rounding the lower boundary would generate the following class intervals:

6.20 – 6.34

6.35 – 6.49

6.50 – 6.64

6.65 – 6.79, and so on

▶ **Construct a Frequency Table**

Put the first class interval at the top of the table and the highest numbered class interval at the bottom. (As shown above.)

▶ **Neatness of the Table Counts:** Use a "hash" or "tick" mark for each occurrence of a data value within a class interval. If these are neatly recorded, evenly spaced and lined up, the frequency table can be used visually to estimate the centering and variation (MJII page 69 for example).

▶ **Consider this Shortcut:** If the team uses a Stem and Leaf Plot, they will be able to preserve the individual data values, and more quickly and accurately estimate the median and range. (MJII page 74.)

STEP 4   DRAWING A HISTOGRAM

MJII p. 70

For guidance in drawing the Histogram:

– Use the frequency table. Find the highest tally of the class intervals and round this up to the next highest number (an even number or multiples, as appropriate). Draw the vertical line, or y axis, to this number.

- When drawing the horizontal line, or x axis, make sure it includes all the class intervals calculated in the frequency table as well as any data on customer requirements.

- Number each interval. If the graph becomes too crowded with the numbers, number every other interval or every multiple interval for ease of reading.

- If you have the customer requirements, or specifications, draw them and the target value as vertical lines on the Histogram.

- It's a matter of preference, or computer software, as to whether or not to leave space between the bars. However, since these are continuous scales, many people draw the bars placed together. Also, since each class is everything less than some number, but not including the number which is part of the next interval, why leave space? Space could imply that something is being left out.

- Don't draw multiple measures on the same Histogram. It is more appropriate to stratify the data, draw separate Histograms, then compare the two, side-by-side.

STEP 5 INTERPRETING THE HISTOGRAM

MJII pp. 71–74

You can use the Histogram to estimate the centering, spread, and shape of your data (the process' distribution), as well as process capability.

▶ **Center**

The center of the Histogram can be found visually by finding the mode, the most frequently occurring number. If the data forms a normal-shaped curve (bell shape), then this would be the tallest single bar in the center. You can also use the median value to find the center. The median is the middle number of all the numbers when rank ordered.

Ask: *"Is the center where we expected it or is it where it needs to be?"*

If the answer is no, *"How can we change the process average to move it (up or down) to be where it should be?"*

▶ **Spread**

The spread of the Histogram is a rough measure of the process variation. From the Histogram you can quickly calculate this from the range, which is the difference between the highest value and the lowest value.

Ask: *"Is the spread within the limits set by customer requirements (specifications)?"*

If the answer is no, *"How can we change the process to reduce the variation to within the requirements?"*

▶ **Shape**

The shape of the Histogram is important. If the team plans on using statistical calculations (mean, standard variation), they are valid only on distributions that are normal, or shaped like a bell. Don't expect the Histogram to be a perfect bell curve, variations will occur. The number of intervals can also influence the pattern the data will take. (See Step 3.)

- If the Histogram has no discernible shape, with all the bars about the same height, it provides little information. This is called uniform distribution. Sometimes a uniform distribution indicates that too few classes are included in the Histogram.

- A Histogram with random distribution (perhaps having several peaks) has no apparent pattern. A random distribution may indicate too many classes. Or, it might indicate distributions from multiple sources, e.g., from different shifts or locations.

- Some distributions might be "skewed," with the greatest concentration of data at one end of the distribution rather than in the center of the "bell." Therefore, the distribution may look more like a ski slope than a bell. A "positive skew" is when most of the data is concentrated on the left. (The concentration of data "tails off" on the right.) A "negative skew" is when most of the data is concentrated on the right. (The concentration of data "tails off" on the left.) These differences in skewness usually occur when the data have values greater than zero. A positive skew indicates the data values are decreasing and approaching zero and a negative skew indicates values that are increasing and moving away from zero.

Ask: *"Is the shape what we expect from the process?"*

If the answer is no, *"What can we find in the process that's causing the shape to be other than what we expect?"*

▶ **Normal Distribution**

The normal or Gaussian distribution is a bell-shaped curve that describes the distribution of many natural processes: heights of people, hardness, density, wait times, and so on.

The normal distribution is based on the assumption that most of the output of a process will be close to the mean value with fewer and fewer observations occurring as you move away from that mean. The *mean* identifies location of the center of the distribution and the sample *standard deviation*, *s*, describes the variation from that mean.

What are the three characteristics of a normal distribution?

- The mean = median = mode.

- The curve is symmetrical.

- The area under the curve is equal to 1 (or 100%).

▶ **Bell Curve Height:** The height of the curve at any point is related to the probability of occurrence for a particular value.

▶ **Bell Curve Width:** If the sample standard deviation is large, the bell curve will be wide. If the sample standard deviation is small (approaching zero), then the bell curve will be narrow. Regardless of whether the curve is narrow or wide, the relationship between the sample standard deviation and the total area under the curve remains the same.

▶ **Area Under Bell Curve:** The percentage of normally distributed data that fall under the curve can be predicted as follows:

$\pm 1s$	=	0.6826 or approximately	68% of the total area
$\pm 2s$	=	0.9544 or approximately	95% of the total area
$\pm 3s$	=	0.9974 or approximately	99.7% of the total area

See the illustration on the next page.

Bell Curve

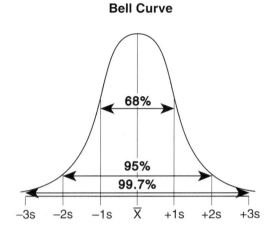

Many organizations use ±3*s*, however, some organizations, for example the automotive industry, have moved to ±4σ, and others beyond that.

EXAMPLE

This example is illustrated using the same steps that are shown in *The Memory Jogger*™ *II* on pages 66–74. The example shows you the preparation of a frequency table, the appropriate calculations to make, the Histogram in final form, and provides an interpretation of the chart.

▶ **Step 1 Process Measure**

For this example, the data could measure the time, in minutes, to do a chemical analysis, to process the results of a blood test or a roll of film, to train someone to make a pizza, to make a bank transaction with a branch in another country, to prepare a monthly report, or any variety of situations. If it makes it easier to follow the example, make up your own process measure.

▶ **Step 2 Gather Data**

The following table has 75 data points. This data will be used to prepare a frequency table, which is shown at the end of Step 3 in this section.

123	134	135	127	134	136	129	142	126	132
131	130	131	133	132	124	132	131	134	135
131	133	125	137	129	126	138	133	131	132
127	139	132	128	136	131	128	127	136	132
132	128	134	131	127	134	133	132	125	137
133	131	124	129	131	130	135	129	133	131
142	129	131	133	135	132	131	131	139	129
135	132	136	130	133	–	–	–	–	–

▶ **Step 3 Prepare a Frequency Table**

The appropriate calculations to prepare a frequency table are shown below. **Don't forget:** this example follows along with Step 3 shown on pages 67–69 in *The Memory Jogger*™ *II*.

a) **Number** of data points in sample is

n = 75

b) **Range** of data points for the sample is

$$\mathbf{R} = X_{max} - X_{min} = 142 - 123 = 19$$

c) Number of **class intervals** can be determined in two ways:

Method 1: Take the square root of the total number of data points and round to the nearest whole number.

$$k = \sqrt{75} = 8.660254 \quad \text{Round up to 9}$$

Method 2: Use the table on page 68 of *The Memory Jogger*™ *II* to determine the number of classes for the sample. Since n is >50 and <100, divide the sample into 6–10 classes.

Let's use Method 2. Let

$$k = 7$$

d) Determine **class width**, **H**

Use the formula:

$$H = \frac{R}{k} = \frac{19}{7} = 2.714 \quad \text{Round up to 3}$$

e) Determine **class boundaries**, or end points

The lowest number is 123, and the lower boundary for the first class interval.

Add the **class width**, H, to the lower boundary of the *first* class interval to get the lower boundary for the *second* class interval: 123 + 3 = 126.

Since each class interval must be mutually exclusive, that is, every data point will fit into *one, and only one* class interval, the first class interval begins with 123 and includes every data point up to, but not including 126.

The lower boundary for the third class interval is 126 + 3 = 129.

Consecutively add the **class width** to the lowest class boundary until the k class intervals and/or the range of all the numbers are obtained. (This level of detail isn't shown.)

f) Construct the frequency table based on the data.

Class #	Class Boundaries	Midpoint	Frequency	Total
1	123 – 125	124	‖‖‖	5
2	126 – 128	127	‖‖‖ ‖‖	9
3	129 – 131	130	‖‖‖ ‖‖‖ ‖‖‖ ‖‖‖ ‖	22
4	132 – 134	133	‖‖‖ ‖‖‖ ‖‖‖ ‖‖‖ ‖‖	23
5	135 – 137	136	‖‖‖ ‖‖‖ ‖	11
6	138 – 140	139	‖‖	3
7	141 – 143	142	‖	2

▶ Step 4 Draw a Histogram

Here's the result!

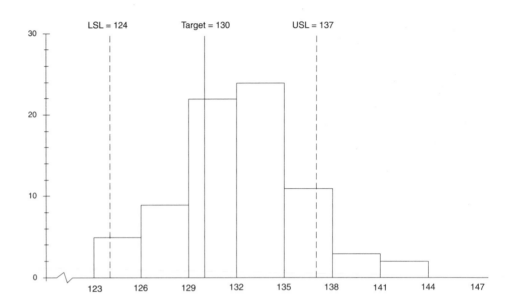

▶ Step 5 Interpret the Histogram

Don't forget: this example follows along with Step 5 shown on pages 71–73 in *The Memory Jogger™ II.*

a) Centering = Slightly/somewhat above target

The purpose of the Histogram is to provide a quick visual of the process' performance. A team can "eyeball" or determine "best guesstimates" of the process.

Mode: the most frequently occurring bar is Class #4 with 23. Therefore, use the class midpoint value of 133. (This information is taken from the frequency table in f), Step 3 above.)

Median: When sampled data are rank ordered, lowest to highest, the median is the middle number. This example has 75 data points. Find the middle number by dividing 75 by 2 = 37.5. The 37th and 38th values (132 and 132) fall in Class #4. Again, use the midpoint value of 133. (The midpoint value is taken from the frequency table in f), Step 3 above.)

Mean: There are three methods for figuring out the mean, $\overline{X}$, which is the sum of the values of the sample divided by the total number, n, of sampled data.

Method 1:
$$\frac{\Sigma X}{n} = \frac{(123 + 124 + 125 \ldots 139 + 142)}{75} = \frac{9879}{75} = 131.72$$

This method can be extremely tedious if n is large. Make sure you use a calculator and be careful in entering the numbers.

Method 2: Set up another frequency table, shown on the next page, and use the calculations to figure out the mean.

Histogram

Class #	Midpoint x	Frequency f	fx	fx2 (optional for calculating s)
1	124	5	620	76880
2	127	9	1143	145161
3	130	22	2860	371800
4	133	23	3059	406847
5	136	11	1496	203456
6	139	3	417	57963
7	142	2	284	40328

Σf or the sum of each frequency = 75
Σfx or the sum of each frequency x the midpoint = 9879
Σfx^2 or the sum of each frequency x the midpoint squared = 1302435

$$\text{Mean} = \frac{\Sigma fx}{\Sigma f} = \frac{9879}{75} = 131.72$$

Using the frequency table above provides a good approximation to the mean. Although the calculations can become tedious, they are preferable when n is large.

Method 3: Use a computer program to calculate and draw the Histogram. Be careful in entering each data value.

b) Variation = The process does not meet the specifications. 8 of the 75 numbers exceed the specification limits. $\frac{8}{75}$ = .107 x 100 = 10.7% defective material.

Range: $X_{max} - X_{min} = 142 - 123 = 19$

Standard Deviation: The frequency table in Method 2 above can also be used to calculate the sample standard deviation, s.

$$s = \sqrt{\frac{[\Sigma fx^2 - n(\overline{X})^2]}{n-1}}$$

$$= \sqrt{\frac{[1302435 - 75(131.72)^2]}{75-1}}$$

$$= \sqrt{\frac{[1302435 - 75(17350.1584)]}{74}}$$

$$= \sqrt{\frac{1302435 - 1301261.88}{74}}$$

$$= \sqrt{\frac{1173.12}{74}}$$

$$= \sqrt{15.85297297}$$

$$= 3.9815$$

c) Shape = approximately normal bell-curve distribution

Calculations for determining whether the shape is near normal are beyond the scope of this book. For a listing of some SPC book resources, see the appendix.

d) Process capability = Process cabability is about comparing the variation in a process, (represented here by the range), to the spread of the specifications, which is also referred to as "tolerance."

$$\text{Specifications} = 130 \pm 5\% = 130 \pm 6.5$$
$$130 - 6.5 = 123.5 = \text{LSL}$$
$$130 + 6.5 = 136.5 = \text{USL}$$
$$\text{Specifications width} = 136.5 - 123.5 = 13$$
$$\text{Process width} = \text{Range} = 19$$

From these numbers, it can be seen that the process, at this point in time, is producing more variation in the product than is allowed by the specifications. The process width, range = 19, exceeds specifications, 13, and therefore the process cannot meet the specifications no matter what.

Action: Reduce the amount of variation in the process. Since the process is centered slightly higher than the target of 130, work to move the process down (to the left).

Recommendation: The team needs to initiate a Control Chart to monitor the process over time. For information on this, see the Control Chart and Process Capability chapters.

▶ **Learning Activity**

Getting Started:

For the full bowl, the following values were found:

$$\textbf{Mean} = \text{median} = \text{mode} = 6$$
$$\textbf{Range} = 10 \ (11 - 1 = 10)$$
$$\textbf{Standard deviation} = 1.715$$

Follow Up:

n = 45

Range, $R = X_{max} - X_{min} = 73 - 64 = 9$

Class interval, k

Method 1: $k = \sqrt{45} = 6.7$ Round up to 7

Method 2: since n <50 use k = 5,6, or 7

Let's try k = 7

Class width, $H = \frac{R}{k} = \frac{9}{7} = 1.28$ Round down to 1.0

Class boundaries and frequency table:

Since the class width is 1.0, there are 10 class intervals.

Class	Frequency	Total
64	I	1
65	II	2
66	IIII	4
67	IIIII II	7
68	IIIII IIII	9
69	IIIII IIIII	10
70	IIIII I	6
71	IIII	4
72	I	1
73	I	1
	Total =	45

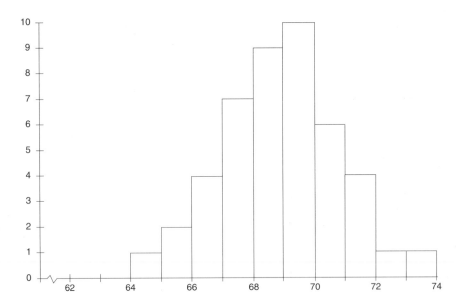

a) If the requirement is for the percent moisture to be between 62 and 72, then according to the sampled data, the supplier is not meeting specifications. That is, 1/45th or roughly 20% of these shipments (and possibly future shipments if no changes are made) will be too high.

The width of shipment is 9. This is within the requirement of 62–72 or width of 10. Therefore, the supplier is capable of meeting the specification width. The midpoint of the requirement is 67. By eye, looking at the Histogram below, the centering appears to be 68 or 69. Thus, the supplier is providing material that is centered higher than requested. This is also confimed by the defective materials on the high end of the desired range.

b) Inform the supplier that the process is capable of meeting the specifications, but currently is running high. Get the supplier to improve the process by slightly reducing the moisture content of the process.

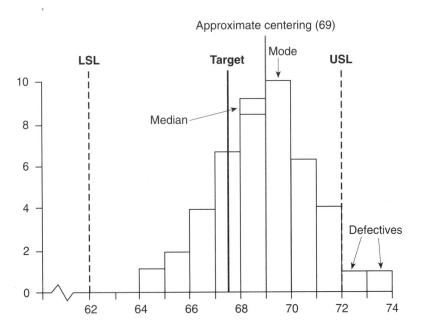

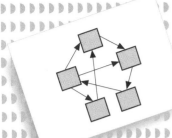

Interrelationship Digraph (ID)

Looking for drivers & outcomes

▶ Does your team have limited resources and need to focus its efforts on one or two priorities?

▶ Do you need a way to help your team use its collective experience and instinct, not just scientific data, to determine its best course of action?

▶ Does your team need to identify the cause and effect relationships among various issues?

▶ Is your team ready to identify not only the root issues, but also possible areas for measuring the success in treating those issues?

▶ Do you need a way of surfacing the values and priorities of team members?

STEPS AT A GLANCE

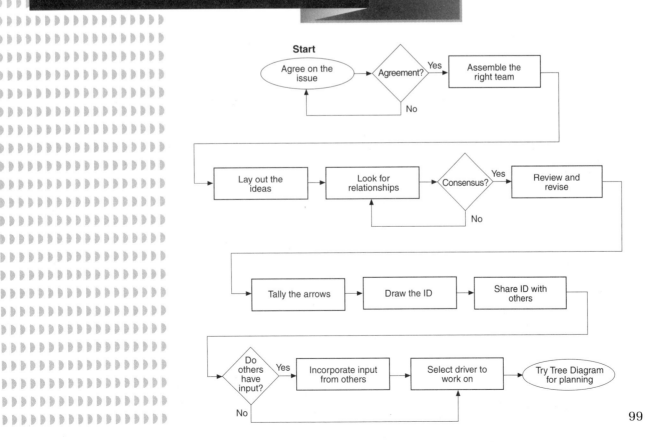

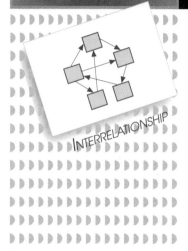

INTERRELATIONSHIP

Q. **How can this tool achieve credible results when it doesn't use any quantifiable data?**

A. Teams are foolhardy if they don't faithfully gather and use data to guide them. However, it's important to remember that the collective experience and intuition resident in most working teams can be as powerful and reliable as much of the data they generate. If you encounter skepticism, remember to involve key stakeholders in the generation of the tool and the discussion that follows. Helping key players understand the logic behind the tool might make them more comfortable accepting the results.

Q. **Why not just have everyone determine the relationships individually and then compile the results?**

A. The tool's explicit value is to help a team identify cause and effect relationships. A less obvious, but equally important benefit is the direct and often revealing discussion that occurs while constructing the ID. Besides forfeiting the chance to understand each other's logic and assumptions, you'd also lose an opportunity for the people to surface and address, in a healthy way, the conflict and disagreement that is part of team maturation.

Q. **What's so bad about drawing two-headed arrows?**

A. The purpose of the ID is to determine cause and effect or influencing relationships between items. If people use a two-way arrow, they are essentially negating the impact of the relationship between two variables. Using two-headed arrows can also inadvertently allow team members to take an "easy out" of a meaningful discussion of why team members' viewpoints may differ. Insisting on one-way arrows compels the team members to make their priorities and perceptions explicit.

Q. **Is the item with the highest number of "out" arrows always the one the team should work on?**

A. No. A team should apply common sense when reviewing its completed ID. Sometimes the team, for a variety of reasons, needs to have a quick and certain success. Team members might want to temporarily set aside an issue that surfaces as a driver if it is very complex or has a high degree of risk. Other reasons for not jumping into the issue with the most "out" arrows might include: the people needed to work on that issue are unavailable; the funding to address the issue properly is not available; team members have the energy and spirit to work on another issue that surfaced as a secondary driver, i.e., the item next closest in number of "out" arrows.

If: **The team gets bogged down in a circular discussion on one specific relationship . . .**

Then: Keep the statement of the problem the team is working on within sight at all times. Remind the team of its purpose, and try the "ID mantra": state each of the two issues under consideration and then ask the questions *"Is there a relationship?" "Which drives which?"* Continually repeat this verbal cycle. The constant sing-song pattern seems awkward at first, but once you and the team get accustomed to the rhythm, it can really improve the pace and quality of the team's work.

If: **The team cannot decide which way the arrow should go . . .**

Then: Remind the team that while it may seem appropriate for the arrow to go both ways, it should represent the relational direction that is strongest. The team can also use dotted lines, sparingly, to represent weak, but existing relationships. These will count for .5 when adding up the arrows. Consensus on the direction of the arrow is the objective. While "majority rules" decisions should be avoided, it can sometimes be helpful to ask all members to state their position. This also ensures that each team member has a chance to state his or her case. If after all this, the team is just "stuck," draw the line in a different color without an arrowhead. Return to this relationship later. In the end it may be critical to fight for consensus or the result might be inconsequential in light of the final chart.

If: **When the ID is complete, the team does not like or believe the result . . .**

Then: Teams are frequently surprised by the results of their IDs. It's that very revelation that sometimes leads the team to a breakthrough. Encourage people to apply logic to the result and to explore their discomfort: Does it make sense? Why does the result trouble team members?

LEARNING ACTIVITY

Often the most difficult part of getting accustomed to this tool is understanding the sequence and direction of placing the arrows. To help a timid group get more comfortable with this, try using a hands-on means to illustrate the process.

Put an almost complete ID on a flipchart, using Post-it™ Notes and visually appealing colors and icons. Have some of the arrows filled in, but leave five or six out. Fill in the missing arrows with the group. Spend a lot of time on each arrow, until you're sure that each member of the team is comfortable with the decision.

Interrelationship Digraph

101

> "The ID helped us to separate ourselves from the past and forced us to consider the merits of each issue."
>
> *Buzz Stapczynski*

Written by Buzz Stapczynski, Town of Andover, Massachusetts

What was the problem?

Andover, a town of nearly 30,000 people, located north of Boston, already enjoyed a reputation for its quality of life and excellent management. The challenge was to create a shared vision and practical plan for the future supported by citizens, elected officials, and employees.

Who was on the team?

Citizens provided input at a series of 6 public forums and there were separate IDs done by the Board of Selectmen (5 people), and the town department heads (12 people). The Town Manager participated in all meetings.

How long did the process take?

The citizen forums were done over a 4-month period. Each ID took about 1 hour and 30 minutes to complete.

What did we learn?

We learned that the keys to our future were extremely interdependent. Much of what our citizens told us we must be, depended on making progress on many fronts. Based on the issues with the greatest number of outgoing arrows, the ID showed us that there were a few key drivers that would create leverage if we made significant progress in those areas. We always have scarce resources and the ID showed us where we might get the greatest return on our investment. Likewise, the issues with the greatest concentration of incoming arrows showed us the key outcomes that would be the measure of success or progress for the entire process.

How was the team affected?

As with any team, both the Board of Selectmen and the municipal department heads have a history, some positive, some negative. The ID helped us to separate ourselves from the past and forced us to consider the merits of each issue. There was less "positioning" and more listening.

What else did we use?

The issues that we used in the IDs were actually header cards from separate Affinity Diagrams that each team had created. The input for the Affinities came from common issues that each team member took from the citizen forums.

TOWN SEAL

What was the conclusion?

The Board of Selectmen and the municipal department heads, at a joint meeting, brought together the results of the separate processes. We were all pleasantly surprised at the level of agreement among team members on the overall issues, as well as those issues that included key drivers and results. Next, the Selectmen created a town vision statement that emphasized the critical importance of "treating citizens as valued, active customers" and "preserving the legacy of Andover." Then the municipal department heads created mission statements for their departments that supported the vision statement.

What were the results?

With the creation of the vision complete, the real challenge is to likewise agree on reasonable budgets and plans that will move us closer to the vision each year.

A Vision of Andover
in the 21st Century

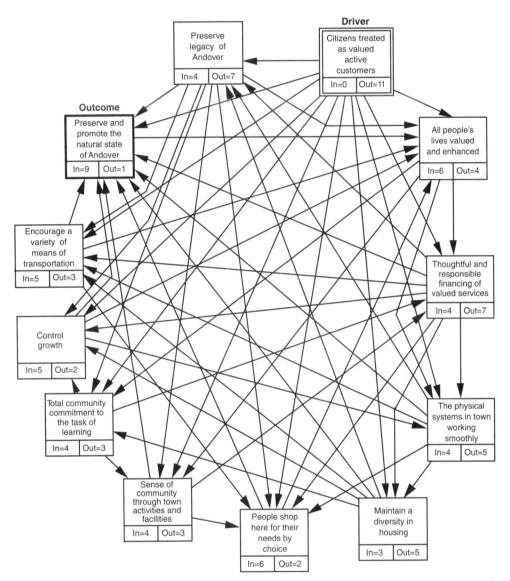

Information provided courtesy of Town of Andover, MA

Driver: If the focus on the citizen as a customer becomes the core of the town's vision then everything else will be advanced.

Outcome: It puts the preservation of nature in the town as a key indicator of the vision working.

> "The ID allowed senior leaders to vent their ideas, concerns and frustrations, and later on we were able to make decisions with the information."
>
> MSgt. Kemper Watkins

Written by MSgt. Kemper S. Watkins, ACC Quality Center, U.S. Air Force

What was the problem?

The ID was the next logical step after the Affinity. We chose the Affinity statement, "How do we effectively maintain quality initiatives in our organization?" to address critical issues many of the senior leaders are now facing. Many of the leaders in Air Combat Command (ACC) are now at the critical juncture where philosophy meets application.

Who was on the team?

The team was composed of ACC senior leaders. Senior leaders in this case were colonels and senior civilians from throughout the Command. Functional areas represented were Operations, Logistics, Civil Engineering, Inspector General, and Information Management.

How long did the process take?

The process took approximately 1 hour and 30 minutes. After completion, a discussion and refinement lasted about 30 minutes.

What did we learn?

Until we actually went through the process, we had originally concentrated on education and training as our cure-all for quality. As senior leaders, we felt that if everyone went through some sort of training, the implementation would sustain itself. Not so! By using the ID, we determined that leadership involvement and customer satisfaction were the main drivers. Only by agreeing to focus on these two key elements as key drivers to success, were we able to move forward effectively.

How was the team affected?

To realize the full impact of how the team was affected, it is helpful to know the attitude of the group before coming together. ACC has been formally working on quality for about 3 years. During that time, many senior leaders still harbored reservations about this "quality stuff." By using the Management and Planning tools, especially the ID, we were able to capture those reservations and do something with them. This is key, in that previous discussions about quality led nowhere. It didn't occur to us that a tool existed that could help us capture these thoughts and do something constructive with them.

What else did we use?

From the Affinity to the ID to the Tree, and finally to the T-Matrix.

What was the conclusion?

The ID helped us come to consensus that even if we trained 100% of the base population, leadership support and customer satisfaction were paramount to sustaining quality. Individually, we all knew this. Collectively, we were able to do something about it and stop placing the blame elsewhere.

Senior Leaders Team, ACC Quality Center, U.S. Air Force

What were the results?

Using the results of the ID and our Culture and Leadership survey, we are now tapping the unparalleled resource of senior leadership instruction. From the Commander of ACC on down, senior leaders are now teaching their peers. We have found this is monumental in sustaining our quality journey.

Interrelationship Digraph

104

Maintaining Quality Initiatives:
Exploring Leadership Involvement and Customer Satisfaction
ID–Matrix Format (Variation)

	Logistic Support	Customer Satisfaction	Education & Training	Personnel Incentives	Leadership	Cause/ Driver	Result/ Rider	Total
Logistic Support	■	⊙	○	△	○	3	1	16
Customer Satisfaction	⊙	■	○	⊙	○	0	4	24
Education & Training	○	○	■	○	⊙	2	2	18
Personnel Incentives	△	⊙	○	■	⊙	1	3	22
Leadership	○	○	⊙	⊙	■	4	0	24

Information provided courtesy of U.S. Air Force,
Air Combat Command

Relationship Strength

⊙ = 9 Significant
○ = 3 Medium
△ = 1 Weak or none

STEP 1 AGREEING ON THE ISSUE

MJII pp. 76–77

▶ **Keep the Issue Visible:** It's absolutely essential to keep the problem/issue statement visible throughout the entire ID exercise. If you can fit the statement in the space that the team is using to work on the tool, do.

▶ **Agree on the Issue:** Invest as much time as the team needs to get agreement on this statement. Keep a single focus. Statements that are multipart, complex, or ambiguous will cause the team to have problems later. To test the statement, ask, *"If we achieve this, what will things/our situation/the world look like?"* If the team members can paint a clear scenario, then they will be clear about what they're working toward.

STEP 2 ASSEMBLING THE RIGHT TEAM

MJII p. 77

▶ **Team Makeup:** It's been said before, but it warrants reinforcement. This tool requires a team with in-depth knowledge of the issue at hand. Large variations in knowledge and understanding within the team will result in frustration as those less informed struggle to keep up and those with more information reach for a higher level of discussion.

▶ **What to Do with Big Teams:** IDs with large groups (more than 10 people) can be very positive experiences. After all, more minds means more ideas and information. Potential challenges and suggested solutions include:

Challenge
   Some people simply won't have the courage to speak up in a crowd that size. The team could lose some valuable input.

Solution
   It's impractical to call on everyone, but keep your eye out for people who seem to have something to say, but never quite get it out. Look directly at them or just gesture with your hand. Usually everyone else will follow your gaze.

Challenge
   It's difficult to assess the consensus of the group, since there are almost always views representing different sides of an issue.

Solution
   This is one of the rare cases where hand voting might actually be okay. Don't count hands in detail, but asking for a show of hands should give you a general idea of where potential consensus might lie.

Challenge
   Not everyone can read the ID items from a distance.

Solution
   Forego the use of Post-its™ and write as large as is needed over multiple sheets of flipchart paper.

STEP 3 LAYING OUT THE IDEAS

MJII p. 77

▶ **This Tool is Messy**

If the team has more than eight items, consider using two sheets of flipchart paper side by side. Spread out the issues in a circle over the two pages. Leave a lot of space between each issue so that later the arrows don't become clumped together and illegible. Draw distinctive arrowheads to make counting easier. Colored-in triangles as arrowheads work well. Also, using different colored pens for arrows coming from each issue can help.

▶ **ID-Matrix Variation:** For some, drawing in the arrows seems too chaotic while in process. If the group is less "free-wheeling" and prefers more order, try using the matrix variation. See an example on page 105 of this book or page 81 of *The MJII.*

▶ **Maintain a Paper Trail**

If you take the ID issues from the team's Affinity headers, simply copy the headers onto new Post-its™, leaving the original Affinity intact. This will help the team maintain an accurate record of its thought process, and it can be a useful exercise for those who learn best by kinesthetic means. Physically moving the copied header cards from the Affinity to the ID also helps illustrate the practical connections between the tools.

STEP 4 LOOKING FOR RELATIONSHIPS

MJII pp. 78-79

▶ **Who's in Charge Around Here?**

With this tool, it's important for you not to participate in the content of the discussion if you are to be an effective facilitator. It's also best not to be overbearing in your guidance of the group. However, when it comes to the mechanics of the tool, you must project a sense of authority and confidence and help people trust the process. Here are some tips.

Do's

– Do step in when the discussion is only taking place between two people. This is not the appropriate environment for personal duels.

– Do point out patterns in the discussion and areas of commonality.

– Do encourage the team to help shape the process in terms of scheduling, people who should be on the team, and the issue to be worked on, but again, preserve the main essence of the tool process.

Don'ts

– Don't draw an arrow just because one person insists. Keep asking questions and make sure that when an arrow is drawn, it represents the whole team.

– Don't judge the comments of team members. Even a subtle gesture from you can sway the direction of the team.

– Don't give in on the essential elements of the tool process. It might be tense at times, but team members will thank you for it later.

▶ **Anchors Away**

Don't lose track of where the team is. It's easy in the midst of a heated discussion to forget which relationship is being discussed. Try drawing an anchor on a Post-it™ and placing it next to each issue as it's being addressed. Then move the anchor to the next issue as the team completes the one before. Also, put a check next to each issue as it is completed. It helps team members feel they're making progress and allows you to know when they've completed the full cycle.

▶ **Are We There Yet?**

IDs take time, especially if you want to foster good discussion throughout the process. Be sure to set aside sufficient time so that the team won't feel rushed or frustrated.

Also, if the tool goes on for more than an hour, take a break. This work can be fatiguing, and tired, cranky people are not very productive. An ID with 10 items might take between one and three hours.

STEP 5 REVIEWING AND REVISING

MJII p. 79

▶ **Sanity Check**

It's a good idea to invite people outside the team to provide feedback on the ID the team has generated. As the team's coach, you can serve as an impartial liaison for the flow of that feedback.

People who might be invited to review the ID include:

— Those who will be affected by work on the issue that surfaced as the driver and/or was selected for further attention.

— People who will be key to providing leadership and authority over the processes related to the issue selected.

— Members of other departments who the team members might want to solicit support from in the future as they work on the selected item.

▶ **Making Changes**

It's important to preserve the integrity of the team's original work. People frequently refer back to old versions of tools to remember their logic or to capture something that was lost in a later iteration.

The Memory Jogger Plus+® Software is useful in this instance. A person can draw the ID in the software, make an electronic copy of it, and incorporate changes onto the copy without disrupting the original.

STEP 6 TALLYING THE ARROWS

MJII pp. 79–80

▶ **Time Saver**

Have each team member count the arrows going in and out for an issue. This adds to the fun in the group and keeps everyone involved. It doesn't matter how the arrow information is recorded as long as it is consistent among the issues.

What are some variations in recording the direction of the arrows?

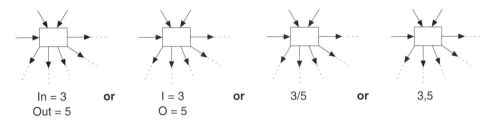

| In = 3 | **or** | I = 3 | **or** | 3/5 | **or** | 3,5 |
| Out = 5 | | O = 5 | | | | |

▶ **What Does It All Mean?**

The team is not done when the arrows are counted. Help them process the results of their effort by asking, *"Does this make sense?" "Are you surprised at the result?" "What now?"*

This is often the most rewarding discussion in the process. Congratulate the team and let them linger in the discussion. This will help reinforce the result and buoy them for the next steps.

STEP 7 DRAWING THE ID

MJII p. 80

▶ **Visual Guidance**

As mentioned in *The Memory Jogger™ II*, you can indicate the drivers and outcomes with a bold box and double box, respectively. Other options include using different colors or shapes to distinguish them from each other. Let the team decide and then have them stick to the same method in the future to avoid confusion.

▶ **It's Alive!**

It might look like something from the arthropod family, but the ID is the child of the team's work together. Don't be surprised if team members seem possessive and protective of their ID. You may hear them say things like, *"Yeah, it might look stupid, but it really does make sense," "I know it's confusing, but let me explain,"* or *"You really had to be there."*

When sharing the ID with others, suggest that the team leave out the lines and arrows. Just keep the number of ins and outs next to each item. This will present a more palatable image to the recipient. The team can share the glory of the lines and arrows later.

Another alternative, when the ID is being shared with others, is to use the ID-Matrix format to summarize the results.

Taking a Fun Camping Trip

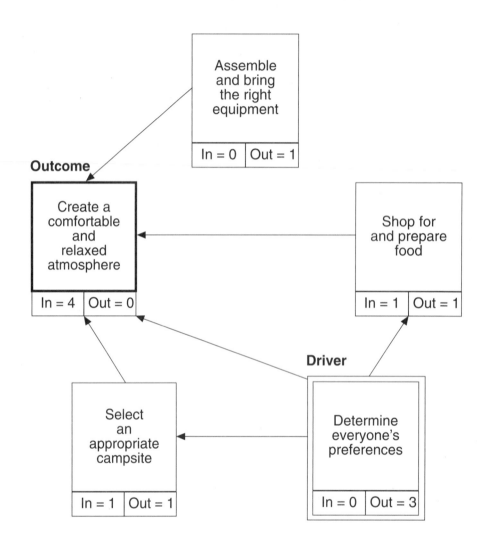

Matrix Diagram
Finding relationships

IS THIS THE RIGHT TOOL? ASK . . .

▶ Does your team need to take a hard look at two or more sets of data to establish priorities or to decide which issue to address?

▶ Would it help to list all the tasks involved in a project and to clearly define levels of responsibility for those tasks?

▶ Does your team need to see how or if different projects or activities will impact each other?

▶ Does your team need a systematic way to see the cumulative effect of many individual decisions?

STEPS AT A GLANCE

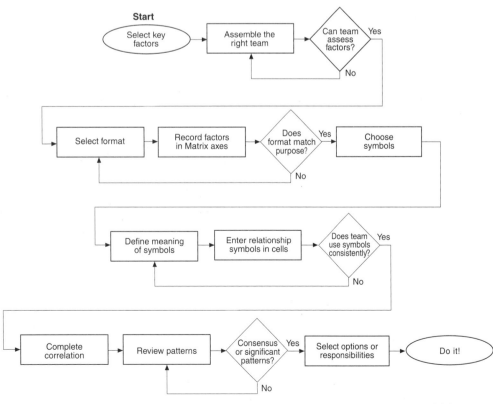

111

MATRIX DIAGRAM

Q. **How do we choose the right format for the matrix?**

A. If your team clarifies its purpose, decides how many data sets it needs to correlate, and understands the complexity of the issue, the format will almost choose itself. The L-shaped matrix, which shows two sets of factors at once, is the most popular. Check it out: draw the matrix and see if it works for you before introducing it to the team. The matrix is very versatile—be creative!

Q. **Does this tool sometimes overwhelm a team?**

A. There is no theoretical limit to the number of cells in a matrix, however, it's much more practical to help the team keep a smaller focus. It's possible to create a 100 x 100 cell matrix, but this size matrix would overwhelm most teams. Start as simply as possible. Teams build capability with practice. Refer to a familiar matrix like those in *Consumer Reports* or a baseball scorecard when you introduce this tool.

Q. **Can the team "break up" the matrix? Can individuals do pieces of it—a few weightings per team member?**

A. It's better not to do this. Team members learn more from the discussion than from the technical aspect of completing the matrix. Team members learn where they disagree and the reasons for their disagreements. Having the team reach consensus on the correlation ratings is important.

Q. **Does the "winner" always indicate the course of action?**

A. Not always. The team reviews the patterns and results in reaching an agreement. In many cases the matrix will indicate the action to take. Sometimes, though, if the team is not comfortable with the results of the matrix, they will look for more data or ask for input from others not on the team before a final decision is reached.

Q. **Why are the numbers "9," "3," and "1" the values assigned to the double circle, single circle, and triangle (respectively)?**

A. Many different rating systems have been tried over the last twenty years in Japan and western countries. The values "3," "2," "1" and "5," "3," "1" have been used. The values "9," "3," and "1" were settled on as common practice in order to create a meaningful gap between the very important and the important. Matrix users have found that these values establish an appropriate differentiation between each level.

Q. **Why are symbols often used, rather than numbers or words?**

A. The matrix is one of the most powerful tools to use to detect patterns among decisions or data. The ability to detect patterns requires that team members step back from the individual cells in the matrix to see the "forest AND the trees" across all rows and columns. Symbols or colors allow team members to detect patterns quickly, without focusing attention on each cell. A helpful reminder: each cell of a matrix is simply a box for useful information; look at each cell with this in mind and the overall matrix will be a valuable document.

If: **The team has difficulty differentiating correlations, and everything seems to be important . . .**

Then: ◗ Stop the process and review the purpose of the tool.

◗ Remind the team that resources are limited and that they need to focus on the truly most important issue.

◗ Remind the team that in a responsibility matrix, it's usually best to assign prime responsibility to only person per item.

◗ Show some examples from other teams in which it was helpful to differentiate correlations by either different strengths or an absence of a correlation.

If: **The team is uncertain or disagrees sharply about the relative strength of correlation values . . .**

Then: ◗ Have members discuss their understanding of the data. They may decide to gather more or different data or may choose to look at the data with different criteria.

◗ If the matrix is based on team experience, rather than quantitative data, discuss the reasons for differing views.

◗ Mark the cell or cells in question with color or a question mark and come back to it. Do this after a reasonable discussion period, for example, five minutes. Make progress and come back to the tough ones at the end.

LEARNING ACTIVITY

1. Form small groups of 3–4 people.

2. Prepare for each group a 4 x 5 cell matrix (empty) that fills a flipchart sheet. Each cell should be at least 3" wide by 3" tall.

3. Ask each group to list 4 customer demands for one of the following: a good family restaurant, a great vacation, or a great sports car. If a "good family restaurant" was chosen as the topic, the group could list: 1) clean, 2) quick service, 3) inexpensive, and 4) food selections that the kids like. Let each group decide which topic to choose.

4. Ask each group to list 5 specific examples of ways to meet any of the 4 customer demands they already listed. If a "good family restaurant" was chosen as the topic, the group might think of these 5 ways to meet customer demands: 1) customers clear their own tables, 2) customers pay before eating, 3) customers prepare their own meals, 4) customers are allowed to split orders, and 5) self-service dessert buffet is available. **An example of a completed matrix is shown in the Coach's Answer Key at the end of this chapter.**

5. Ask the groups to fill in the matrix. List customer demands down the left column, and the four specific examples across the top row.

6. Ask each person to facilitate the correlation of one row. Use Post-it™ notes with large symbols drawn to fill the Post-it™. Do it quickly, and encourage the group to make it fun.

7. Review the pattern. Discuss the results.

Matrix Diagram

> "*The matrix is a tool that can communicate a tremendous amount of information on one piece of paper.*"
>
> *Robert Brodeur*

Written by Robert Brodeur, Bell Canada

What was the problem?

The team had the responsibility to put together an implementation plan for Total Quality in the Logistics organization, which includes 3500 employees. The plan had to be clear, concise, and actionable (measures, goals, schedule, responsibility, etc.).

Who was on the team?

The team included one representative of each of these services: Administrative Services, Realty, Material Purchasing, Environmental Affairs, Internal Telecommunications, Material Distribution, and Motor Vehicles Maintenance.

How long did the process take?

It took 2 full-time days to assemble the strategies, tactics, and the measures.

What did we learn?

We learned that it is feasible to elaborate a plan that is contained on a few pages, easy to understand and to review.

How was the team affected?

The Matrix helped save the team from the headache of writing on hundreds of pieces of paper and creating documents to support the different types of information. We use the Matrix very often because it helps us to summarize a lot of information in one place.

What else did we use?

We were using various tools during this exercise. The Affinity Diagram, brainstorming sessions, and NGT were some of the most useful tools we used to build the plan. The result of this work has been displayed on Matrix and Tree Diagrams.

ROBERT BRODEUR,
TEAM MEMBER

What was the conclusion?

Preparing a plan that is precise and actionable is not an easy task. Finding the right measurement has been the most difficult part of the job. Some tactics had to be discarded because it was impossible to get a reliable metric.

What were the results?

This planning exercise has been very profitable to communicate to everybody the direction of the department; it has also allowed the management team to follow-up closely the evolution of each strategy.

Logistics Annual Plan

TQ Implementation (Tree)		LQC Objectives (Matrix)				Measures	Schedules (AND)								
							1994				1995				
		Reduce customer cost	Continue implementation of total quality	Continue upgrading tech., prof., & managerial skills of employees	Promote environmental responsibility in our operations		Quarter				Quarter				
							1	2	3	4	1	2	3	4	
Goal Continue to implement total quality	Survey customer satisfaction	△	⊙		◯	% satisfaction via survey			►					►	①
Delight our customers	Research customer needs via QFD	△	⊙	△	◯	List of customer needs by key processes				►					
	Capture customer comments	◯	⊙	△	△	# of comments or # of complaints				►					

⊙ = 9 Strong influence/relationship
◯ = 3 Some influence/relationship
△ = 1 Weak influence/relationship
Blank = No influence/relationship

Goals (AND)		Co-Responsibility (Matrix)					Cost/Benefit Analysis				Status*
1994	1995	LQC	Departments	Boards of management	Logiqual	Other stakeholders	Resources required ($)		Tangible benefits ($)		
							94	95	94	95	
① 75% customer satisfaction	80% customer satisfaction	⊙	◯	△	◯	△	25K	25K			
Field trial	100% customer needs gathered	△	⊙	◯	⊙	△	25K	25K			
1% transactions	1.9%	△	⊙			△					

*Status: ▉Caution ▉Stopped ☐On target

⊙ = 9 Prime responsibility
◯ = 3 Secondary responsibility
△ = 1 Kept informed

Information provided courtesy of Bell Canada

STEP 1 SELECTING THE KEY FACTORS

MJII p. 87

▶ **Examples of Key Factors**

Common sets of two factors that teams use are:

- Tasks and who is responsible
- Selection criteria and possible project team members
- Selection criteria and proposed solutions to problems
- Customer demands and product or service characteristics
- Organizational goals and department objectives or action plans

▶ **Start Small and Grow**

The basic matrix can "grow" to meet the team's needs. Start by working with two specific sets of data. Once the team has experienced "matrix thinking," and won't be intimidated by a larger matrix or different format, consider other data that would be helpful to correlate, and add on. In addition to finding relationships between groups of items, the matrix can be expanded to display a complete action plan with time lines, resources and costs. The team should discuss what information they want to include in an expanded matrix. For examples of what other matrix formats look like, refer to *The Memory Jogger™ II* and *The Memory Jogger Plus+®*.

▶ **Review Data Needs**

At this point the team will decide what data must be gathered. The team may need data to be able to effectively compare the matrix items and find relationships. Plan who will do this and how it will be completed.

STEP 2 ASSEMBLING THE RIGHT TEAM

MJII p. 87

▶ **The Right Team**

As with all the tools, the matrix analysis will be as good as the team brought together to do the job. The factors being correlated should determine the team. Include those responsible for implementing the tasks, for providing the resources, for contributing the appropriate technical expertise, or for gathering and analyzing the data. Include customers, suppliers, subcontractors, line workers, orderlies, students—whomever it takes to complete a quality analysis of the chosen factors.

▶ **"Assembling" in the '90s**

Virtual teams in remote locations can exist through conference calls, video conferencing, exchange of faxed information, or E-mail.

A team's initial work can be reviewed and confirmed by others who might be affected by the analysis. **Note:** If you use this option, prepare your team to accept changes. Teams have been known to develop a "don't touch our matrix" mentality.

STEP 3 SELECTING THE FORMAT

Which Format is Best?

The team's decision in Step 1 determines the format. Ask:

- How many key factors have we identified?
- Which format would best help us find the relationships?
- Do we want to display additional information beyond the identification of the relationships?

Consider this information:

- The L-shaped matrix does the job for any two sets of data compared to each other, or one set compared to itself.
- The T-shaped matrix is used for comparing two sets of data to a common third set.
- The T-shaped matrix is not complicated and can add depth to the team's analysis.

Shown below is an example of the data one team used in constructing their T-shaped matrix. (The matrix below is a portion of the full matrix in *The Memory Jogger Plus+®* page 149.) Other combinations of data elements could be: sales representatives, customers, and product lines; curriculum advisors, theory or skills, and courses.

Company-Wide
Continuous Improvement Training Program

	Courses	7 Basic QC Tools	7 Tools for Management & Planning	Problem Solving	Design of Experiments (DOE)	Total Productive Maintenance	Just in Time (JIT)	New Supervisor Training	Total Quality Control (TQC)	Facilitation Skills	Quality Function Deployment (QFD)
Who Trains	Human Resource Dept.										
	Managers										
	Consultants										
	SPC Coordinator										
	University										
	Technology Specialists										
	Engineers										
Who Attends	Executives										
	Marketing										
	Sales										
	Engineers										
	Clerical Workers										
	Quality Professionals										
	Employee Involvement Teams										
	Suppliers										

Key for "Who Trains"

◉ Development Responsibility

○ Individual Training Responsibility

△ Team Member

Key for "Who Attends"

X = Full

O = Overview

Teams can modify the basic formats to include all the information that is needed. An expanded matrix is a powerful way to display decision elements or implementation plans. Multi-page reports may just become a thing of the past!

For examples of what other matrix formats look like, refer to these sources: 1) *The Memory Jogger*™ *II* pages 85–86 (L- and T-shaped matrix), 89–90 (several tools combined), and 125 (matrix and Gantt combined), and 2) *The Memory Jogger Plus*+® pages 138–139 (generic examples of the L-shaped, T-shaped, Y-shaped, X-shaped, and C-shaped matrix), and numerous other examples sprinkled throughout the Matrix Diagram chapter, pages 135–170.

STEP 4 DEFINING THE SYMBOLS

MJII pp. 87–88

▶ Understanding Matrix Symbols

The most commonly used symbols are ◉, ○, △. Teams may also create their own. What is important is that their *meaning* be well defined, clearly understood, and consistently applied. Always display a legend to communicate the meaning of the symbols. The following examples show some common uses of the symbols:

Supportive/Negative Relationships Matrix

To help differentiate between supportive and negative correlations, either a "+" or "–" is used in addition to the matrix symbols.

◉ +/- Strongly positive/strongly negative

○ +/- Some positive/some negative

△ +/- Possible positive/possible negative

Responsibility Matrix

In a responsibility matrix, the matrix symbols take on these meanings:

◉ Primary responsibility
○ Secondary responsibility
△ Inform

Knowledge Or Skills Matrix

To indicate the level of knowledge or skill needed, the matrix symbols can be used to mean this:

◉ Master
○ Use
△ Understand

Numerical Values Commonly Used

The usual numerical values are:

◉ 9
○ 3
△ 1

▶ Simple Symbol Logic

Keep these notes in mind:

– It's perfectly okay for teams to make up additional symbols to meet their needs. It's possible that a team may want to weight four or five levels of relationships. Remember to use a legend!

– The team may want to expand on the purpose and metrics of the matrix. In an action plan matrix, headings can be added for data such as cost, cost and benefit, resources needed, % of goal reached, and time lines can be included. (MJII pages 89–90 for example.)

– Test the team's understanding of the symbols as they begin filling in the matrix. Clarify the definitions of the symbols if the team is not consistently applying them.

STEP 5 COMPLETING THE MATRIX

MJII p. 88

▶ Just Do It

Start at the top? Work down or across? Where do we begin?

Begin by correlating the first item listed in the first row with the first item in the first column and then work across the columns. Most facilitators take an item on the horizontal row and work across the columns and then do the same with the next row. However, it's really a matter of personal preference as to how the team chooses to move through the matrix. The important thing is to be consistent so that the team doesn't become confused about where they are.

Okay, we've agreed on a system; where to from here?

For each cell in the matrix, ask *"Is there a relationship?"* If there is relationship, ask *"What is the strength of the relationship?"* Some cells should be empty to indicate there is no relationship. Be sure the team carefully thinks through the weightings of the relationships of each cell. Clear thinking, not speed, determines the quality of results.

We disagree on the weightings: what now?

If the team expresses strong disagreement over the weightings, additional data may be needed. Note the points of conflict and discuss them. Mark the cells to indicate that the team agrees there is a relationship but hold the decisions on the weightings for items that team members disagree on until the matrix is completed. If an item is key to the final decision or plan, decide what additional data to gather and plan to complete the matrix at the next meeting.

Wrap it up

Review the results. Look for new insights. They often emerge without using the numerical values of the symbols. In other instances, the numerical values are computed and posted to determine the results.

▶ **The Next Step**

Now what? Should the team move forward with the project or conclude it? Decide on how to follow through on the proposed plan? Agree on what to do with the matrix information? The team should decide on the action they need to take, based on the completed matrix. Here are three possibilities:

— The matrix may *immediately* indicate a course of action.

— The results of the matrix may be combined with outcomes from other tools for decision making.

— An expanded matrix may become a "living tool" for further planning and documentation.

INCIDENTALLY

The matrix symbols ◉ Win, ◯ Place, and △ Show originated in the posting of Japanese racing results. Use of these symbols has spread rapidly in the United States through the use of the Seven Management and Planning Tools and Quality Function Deployment.

Summary of TQC Education and Training in Japan
Content Distribution by Levels/Functions

People / Topic	Top Management	Middle Mgmt./ Staff	Engineers	Supervisors	Function & Administration	General Workers
TQC Concepts	○	○	○	○	△ / ◎	○
QC Techniques	○	○	◎	◎		○
Statistical Methods	○	○	◎	○	○	○
Quality Assurance	△	○	◎	○	△	△
Product Development	△	△	◎		△ / ○	
Role in TQC	◎	◎	◎	◎	◎	◎
QC Circle	△	○	△	◎	△	○ / ◎
New Product Introduction	○	△	◎	○		
Hoshin Planning	◎	○	△		△	
Company Production System			○	◎		○

Educated to: △ = Understand   ○ = Use   ◎ = Master

Sources: JUSE, JSA, Deming Prize Companies

Printed in 1989 GOAL/QPC Research Committee Research Report, "Total Quality Control Education in Japan," page 9.

▶ **Learning Activity**

Finished Matrix Example

**Customer Demands
of a Good Family Restaurant**

	Customers clear their own tables	Customers pay before eating	Customers prepare their own meals	Customers allowed to split orders	Customers can choose self-serve dessert buffet
Clean	◉				
Quick Service	◯	◉	◉	△	◉
Inexpensive	◯	△	◉	◉	△
Good food selection for the kids			◉	◉	◉

◉ = Strong impact on meeting customer demand

◯ = Some impact

△ = Weak impact

Blank = No impact

The pattern that emerges is in the column "Customers prepare their own meals."

A. 2+2
B. 1+1
C. 3+4
D. 4+3

Nominal Group Technique (NGT)

Ranking for consensus

Is This the Right Tool? Ask . . .

▶ Do you need a way to "level the playing field" for a team—a way to give everyone the same opportunity to contribute?

▶ Does the team need a fairly quick process to get a general consensus on the priorities among 5 or more alternatives?

▶ Does the team need a way to prioritize its options by using each person's opinion?

▶ Does the team need a break from intense, conflict-oriented discussion?

Steps at a Glance

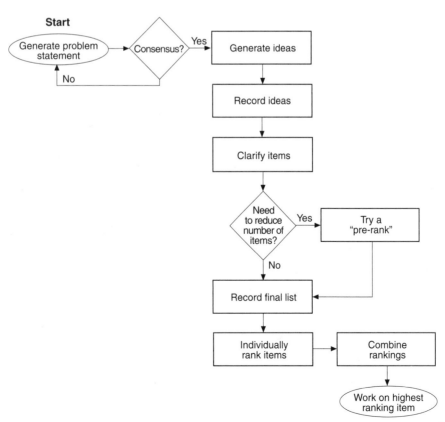

A. 2+2
B. 1+1
C. 3+4
D. 4+3

NOMINAL GROUP TECHNIQUE

Q. **Why is it called Nominal Group Technique (NGT)?**

A. Because it engages the group in minimal or "nominal" interaction relative to the usual amount of exchange that takes place in a group session. NGT can depersonalize the process of working through an issue and provide team members with breathing room when they are dealing with controversial or difficult issues.

Another rationale for the name is that the groups who use this tool are often new or unformed and are a group by name only—a nominal group.

Q. **When is NGT not the right tool to use?**

A. If a team is trying to decide among issues based on data that can be compared, it is better to use the Pareto Chart or another data-gathering tool. Likewise, if a team has brainstormed different ideas for how to improve something, NGT might be a way to reduce the list, but then a criteria matrix should be applied to make a final selection.

Q. **So what *is* the best situation to use NGT in?**

A. To truly maximize the value of this tool, use it when you need to find out the range of the team's opinions. Reserve NGT for when *opinions* are important and when the discussion of the opinions is not a vital part of the process. (If it is, use a criteria matrix.) But when *data* are important, don't substitute this opinion tool for an appropriate data tool.

FACILITATION ESSENTIALS

If: **You don't have the time for a full cycle of NGT . . .**

Then: ▶ You can apply the tool verbally to get a quick sense of the team's opinions. This variation is described further in the Step 5 section of this chapter.

Beware: this is not a good option if the team is new or the subject matter is complex or controversial.

If: **The team is not satisfied with the result of applying the NGT . . .**

Then: ▶ First explore the reason(s) for the team's dissatisfaction. Is it related to the process of using the tool or the final result? With a strong facilitator at hand, this might be a good time to more openly discuss the conflict areas.

▶ Remember that the NGT is best used to gauge and make visible *opinions*. It is frequently appropriate to follow NGT with the use of a more data-driven tool. The team may then have more confidence in the validity of their NGT outcome.

▶ For an example, refer to pages 92–93 in *The Memory Jogger™ II*. NGT revealed the team members' combined opinion that "No documented process" was the strongest reason why the department had inconsistent output. If team members are not satisfied with this result, they might start a Check Sheet to record each time the department's output was unacceptable and why. Then they can put this data into a Pareto Chart to display the occurrences of poor output categorized by the reasons for the poor output. They can prove or disprove their assumption that "no documented process" is the most frequently occurring reason for inconsistent output.

LEARNING ACTIVITY

The following are sample questions for practicing NGT:

◗ Where should we go for lunch?

◗ What are the best movies out this year?

◗ What are the best vacation places?

If you choose to use this tool because there is conflict in the team or the issue is controversial, keep the topic of the warm-up activity neutral.

Nominal Group Technique

STEP 1   GENERATING IDEAS

MJII p. 91

▶ **Individual Brainstorming**

Nominal Group Technique is applied most often to a group-generated list of ideas. (Then each person ranks the ideas.) However, NGT can also be applied to ideas generated by individual brainstorming.

By removing the pressure of public presentation of ideas, individual brainstorming can harness the input of people who might otherwise be too intimidated or frustrated to contribute. This is especially true when the issue being addressed has high stakes attached to it.

▶ **Connections**

NGT is a very versatile tool. It can be used as a follow-up to any brainstorming tool, as a way to prioritize items on a Tree Diagram, as a supplement to an Interrelationship Digraph to "test" the team's comfort level with the driver, as a simpler alternative to a decision matrix, and it can be used in conjunction with any number of other tools, as well.

Once people have learned NGT, it can be conjured up "just-in-time" in meetings as a means for assessing a team's position and priorities on just about anything.

STEP 2   RECORDING IDEAS

MJII p. 91

Each person should record his or her own ideas on a sheet of paper, but someone should also be committing all the ideas to a common, visible area as the ideas are suggested. As with other tools that call on people to give their views, each person's ideas should be recorded verbatim to avoid misinterpretation.

It may be helpful to shorten ideas into manageable form, but the originator of the idea should be checked with before making changes.

STEP 3   CLARIFYING ITEMS

MJII p. 92

▶ **Idea Overload**

If the team generates a large number of ideas, it may be necessary to do a "pre-rank." Ask each team member to pick the most important two or three items from the ones generated. To keep the number of items reasonable, use this general principle: the larger the team, the fewer number of items you should have each member pick. Then use only those selected items for the final ranking process. A similar process, the "One Half Plus One" method, is described in *The Memory Jogger*™ *II* on page 93.

STEP 4 RECORDING THE FINAL LIST

MJII p. 92

Once the items have been clarified and the number of items reduced if necessary, record them on a large, vertical, and visible surface. Identify each item with a letter or symbol. Avoid using numbers for these identifiers, since that may confuse team members later as they use numbers to rank order the items.

STEP 5 RANKING ITEMS INDIVIDUALLY

MJII pp. 92–93

▶ Making Choices

Each person writes the letter or symbol identifiers on a sheet of paper and writes a rank next to each one. The higher the rank, the higher the importance the person is placing on the item. Team members should rank all the items this way. For example, if there are 10 items, the most important is marked with "10" and the least important is marked with "1." (See the "literacy" example in this chapter.)

▶ Singing from the Same Song Sheet

Before each person on the team begins to rank the items individually, it's useful to have the team agree on a small number of criteria against which they will each evaluate the items. One or two "must haves" agreed on by everyone can help each person's reasoning during the ranking. Examples of such criteria include:

— Must cost under $1000.

— Must be able to be completed within six months.

— Must be conducive to strengthening the team spirit.

▶ Ranking Variations

Verbal Ranking: In a team where the members are comfortable with each other and individually confident of their contributions, a verbal version of the Nominal Group Technique can be used. A recorder/facilitator stands at a flipchart, pen in hand, and asks each person to rank the same item. This round robin approach is repeated for each item on the list.

Active Ranking (Multivoting): One way to keep the energy level high is to get moving. Once the final list is posted, you can give team members different colored markers and ask them to place marks next to the items they think are most important. A person can give more than one vote to an item.

Another alternative is to hand out 3–5 stickers to each person and ask them to place the stickers next to the items they rank highest. Then count the stickers. Items with the highest number of stickers are the highest priority for the team.

Nominal Group Technique

▶ **Organizing**

Once each person has ranked each item, construct a simple matrix to combine all the rankings.

Item	Member A	Member B	Member C	Total
A	rank	rank	rank	
B	rank	rank	rank	
C	rank	rank	rank	
D	rank	rank	rank	

Total the rankings across for each item. The item with the highest number suggests the highest overall priority for the team.

EXAMPLE

A team of trainers and managers for a large manufacturer convened and asked, "What are ways to increase literacy among all employees in the organization?"

After brainstorming and reducing their list of ideas, the team agreed on the following two criteria as a guide for ranking the items on the final list.

– Must have a high potential for success.

– Must be sensitive to the unique needs of adult students.

Item	Maya	José	Sidney	Rebecca	Pete	Total
Provide confidential on-site literacy training	3	3	1	2	3	12
Start a confidential network to connect students with tutors	4	1	3	4	4	**16**
Offer the resources for potential students to organize monthly reading parties	1	2	2	1	1	7
Give a small bonus for reading milestones achieved	2	4	4	3	2	**15**

In this case, setting up the network was the highest ranking item, with bonuses close behind. These two items were the first ones the team investigated and tried.

Nominal Group Technique

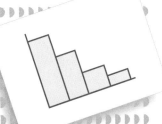

Pareto Chart

Focus on key problems

IS THIS THE RIGHT TOOL? ASK . . .

▶ Would it help to tackle problems in a systematic way, starting with the most important cause?

▶ Do you want to find the 20% of sources that cause 80% of the problems?

▶ Would comparing problems using different measurement scales (such as frequency and cost) help you decide where to start?

▶ Do you want to get closer to the root cause by breaking a problem into smaller problems and identifying their causes?

▶ Do you need a clear, easy-to-understand visual to track your progress?

STEPS AT A GLANCE

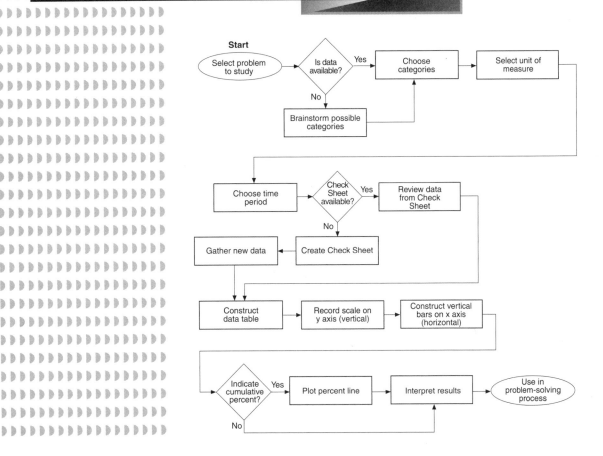

129

PARETO

Q. **How does the Pareto differ from a bar chart?**

A. The Pareto *is* a bar chart, distinguished by the fact that categories are displayed in descending order of impact, from the left to the right on the chart.

Q. **Isn't this a pretty simple tool?**

A. Yes, but don't let that fool your team. The Pareto can be extremely helpful. In *Guide to Quality Control*, page 44, Dr. Kaoru Ishikawa says "A Pareto Diagram can be the first step in making improvements." It helps a team select a goal, has a strong visual impact, creates enthusiasm for starting the team's work, and ultimately serves as a consistent measure of progress.

Q. **How does the Pareto Chart fit in a problem-solving process?**

A. A team can use the Pareto to select a problem to work on, or to look at probable causes from different angles, such as cost, frequency, and customer demand. Following up a Cause and Effect Diagram with a Pareto analysis of selected causes will focus the team. The Pareto Chart also plays a role in monitoring processes.

Q. **Should the team always work on the "tallest bar?"**

A. No, it depends on what the Pareto is measuring and whether that measurement is critical to the team. For example, on page 104 of *The Memory Jogger*™ *II*, a team was looking at the relative importance of various field service problems. On the basis of *relative frequency*, "Shipping" would be the highest priority since it represents 42% of all complaints. However, when the same data is composed using the *relative cost* to rectify complaints, "Installation" emerges as the tallest bar. Using the cost standard, "Shipping" represents only 13% of the total cost. If cost is the most important dimension, preventing installation problems has a much larger impact than similar improvement in the shipping area would have.

If: **There is confusion about which set of data to use on the x and y axes of the chart . . .**

Then: Remind the team of a simple rule: The items/categories/types are always on the x axis (horizontal line), and the units of measurement are always on the y axis (vertical line).

If: **The team wants to jump to a quick decision . . .**

Then: Suggest that they look at several measurement scales to get a complete picture. For example: In a hospital, the greatest number of medication errors could be due to "wrong time of medication." A shorter bar showing "wrong medication given" would represent fewer errors, but more serious outcomes and greater potential costs.

If: **The team thinks the data is incomplete or insufficient . . .**

Then: ▶ Review the length of time data was collected, the Check Sheets used, the consistency of the collection process in different locations, or other factors the team suggests.

  ▶ Create a legend to indicate where (location), when (time period), and by what group the data was collected to facilitate data review.

  ▶ Confirm that the data was collected over a period of time that represents the "typical" performance of the organization.

If: **There is a flat distribution: the Pareto principle "didn't work" . . .**

Then: Try taking a different look at the data. If the team used a frequency measure, try cost, location, time, or another measure important to the customer. In the end, a flat distribution may also indicate that the process is in a state of chaos, in which any problem has an equal chance of occurring.

LEARNING ACTIVITY

1. Prepare a Check Sheet ahead of time, or quickly do one with the team on typical problems that cause them to be late for work. First brainstorm and post a list of the top ten problems on a flipchart. Ask team members for "guesstimates" on the number of times each problem occurs every week.

2. Record on the flipchart each person's "guesstimate" for each problem, and tally the number for each problem.

3. Provide graph paper or paper prepared with an x- and y-axis format.

4. Have each person construct a Pareto Chart based on the Check Sheet.

5. Review any construction questions and check team members' reactions to this tool.

Suggested Issues for Pareto Charts:

1. Frequency of defects, errors

2. Causes of lost, late, or incorrect shipments or billing

3. Reasons for feeling stress on the job

4. Level of business activity at various time intervals

Pareto Chart

A TEAM'S EXPERIENCE . . .

Written by Gary Starcher, Goodyear Tire & Rubber Company

> "The Pareto Chart enabled us to analyze and identify the major areas so that we could address each toward a viable solution."
>
> *Gary Starcher*

Pareto Chart

What was the problem?

The team was formed to address outstanding freight invoices and specifically to eliminate past due billings.

Who was on the team?

This was a cross-functional team including Goodyear team members from Traffic, Accounts Payable, Data Processing, and Consolidated Freightways members form Collections, Rate Audit, Edi Systems, and support from each organization's quality management group.

How long did the process take?

The team decided on a 6-month time frame to reach our goal of eliminating past due billings.

What did we learn?

The team used various tools to learn each company's systems in order to better understand the processes involved in freight invoice payment. Through these tools, the team was able to analyze and identify the major areas of payment delays and address these to reach a viable solution.

How was the team affected?

The process of working together created an atmosphere of cooperation and understanding among the team members. We found that by meeting face to face and working together, we were able to create opportunities for improvements that we were unable to accomplish in the past.

What else did we use?

We analyzed all past due invoices for a given time period and then used several Pareto Charts to identify the causes and chart our progress over the time frame chosen by the team.

What was the conclusion?

We were able to isolate and identify all of the causes for payment delays. With this information it was obvious what the major problems were and the areas we needed to concentrate on in order for us to reach our goal. We implemented changes such as electronic data interchange enhancements and contract changes that were necessary to eliminate past due billings.

What were the results?

After six months, the past due invoices dropped from a high of 329 bills to 56 bills. Through the efforts of our cross-functional team, we found that the procedures and processes we used and implemented were applicable with other companies as well. We learned that open lines of communication and understanding are extremely important and that partnering does work.

Major Cause Breakdowns

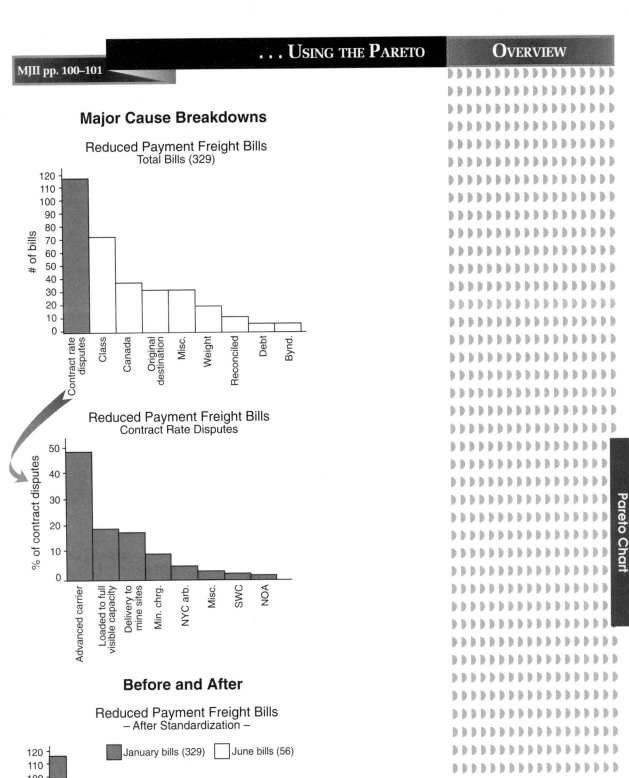

Reduced Payment Freight Bills
Total Bills (329)

Reduced Payment Freight Bills
Contract Rate Disputes

Before and After

Reduced Payment Freight Bills
– After Standardization –

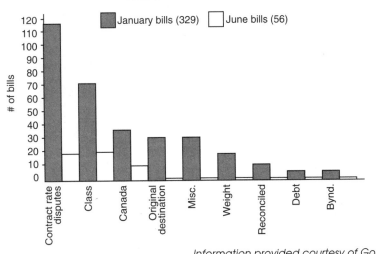

January bills (329)   June bills (56)

Information provided courtesy of Goodyear

Pareto Chart

A TEAM'S EXPERIENCE . . .

> "As a team we learned that the best way to find out what your customers want and need is to ask them!"
>
> Robert McMahon

Written by Robert McMahon, U.S. Navy, Naval Dental Center

What was the problem?

The appointment system was not conducive to the needs of the patients who could not receive instant attention.

Who was on the team?

The team was comprised of members who worked in every facet of the patient appointing process.

How long did the process take?

We developed a customer survey to find out the reasons why patients were not showing up for their dental appointments. We collected data for 5 weeks from both the shore and fleet population. It took about 3 hours to diversify reasons for failed appointments and put it into a Pareto Chart.

What did we learn?

As a team we learned that the best way to find out what your customers want and need is to ask them! By using a Pareto Chart we then prioritized those needs on the basis of highest to lowest. By doing that, we decided which need would affect the majority of the population first. We then improved the process that caused that need to be in such high demand. After the need was worked on, we then started working on the next highest need, and so on and so forth. What we had to remember is that the Pareto Chart will always change as the paradigm shifts. In turn, we learned customer surveys are essential for continuous process improvement.

How was the team affected?

The team was effected drastically in realizing how important customer input actually was, and how useful a Pareto Chart can be in organization of customer needs.

What else did we use?

We used an Affinity to organize the comments of the customers so that we could better understand the results.

What was the conclusion?

The Pareto Chart showed us that the major reason shore and fleet patients failed their appointments was because they forgot about the appointment being scheduled. So we knew that if we could both take care of the forgetfulness and share the responsibility of showing up for the appointment with the patient that we could improve our patient appointing procedures.

Front row (L to R): Roger Hunter, Kelly Miller, Dr. David Katzer. Back row (L to R): Ervin Borja, Tony Prestridge, Robert McMahon (facilitator), Dr. Mark Waterman. Not present: Dawn Pradia

What were the results?

We as group set forth our recommendations for process improvement through what we gained from the customer survey and the use of the Pareto Chart. These recommendations are now in the testing stage. We are continuously collecting data to monitor those recommendations. From this evolution we learned that if the recommendations did not work, we know how to step out of our paradigm and find another intuitive alternative to our problem.

Pareto Chart

Change the Source of Data

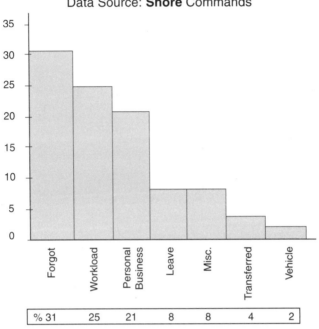

Reasons for Failed Appointments
Data Source: **Shore** Commands

%	31	25	21	8	8	4	2

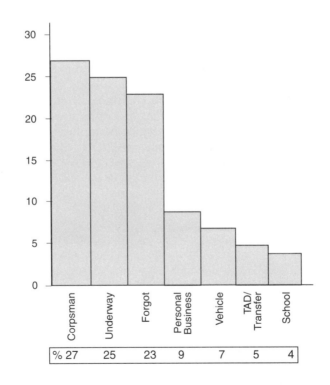

Data Source: **Fleet** Commands

%	27	25	23	9	7	5	4

*Information provided courtesy of
U.S. Navy, Naval Dental Center, San Diego*

Pareto Chart

STEP 1   CHOOSING A PROBLEM TO STUDY
MJII p. 95

Begin with an issue of importance to your customers. Problems that are causing a ripple effect of additional problems, or issues that are generating a lot of blame but no agreed upon solution are good starting points.

STEP 2   CHOOSING CATEGORIES
MJII pp. 95–96

Existing Check Sheets or data reports can provide the categories of causes or problems. Using previously collected data is a good way to get started. Or, the team can brainstorm categories. Data must be collected and classified by the categories selected. The team will need to modify existing Check Sheets or construct new data collection forms to correspond to the categories they want to study.

STEP 3   SELECTING A UNIT OF MEASURE
MJII p. 96

One set of data can be viewed through a variety of measures. Determine which measure would be most helpful for your analysis, but plan to take a second or third look from a different point of view. Frequency and cost to the customer and/or to the company are most commonly used.

STEP 4   CHOOSING A TIME PERIOD
MJII p. 96

There is no set rule for choosing the time period. It varies by the situation. The period should be based primarily on the "pace" of the process. For example, if the team is measuring the frequency of defects in a three-shift, high-speed process, a 5–6 *day* data collection period may be adequate. However, if a Pareto is based on reasons for accidents, a 5–6 *month* data collection period may be necessary. In any case, the time period should be convenient: use periods like weeks, months, or quarters. Many teams have found that two weeks is a minimum but sufficient time to begin the study. **Note:** Remember to keep data collection periods consistent if the team is building related Pareto Charts. This will allow the team to make meaningful comparisons.

STEP 5   GATHERING DATA
MJII pp. 96–97

▶ **Use Check Sheets:** Create a Check Sheet for data gathering or review existing Check Sheets. Remember to post a legend showing the data source, the time period in which data was collected, the team or unit, and the location. Make sure that data is collected consistently, and don't forget to keep the Check Sheet visible.

▶ **Purpose of Study:** Explain the purpose of your study to the data collectors. Share the completed Pareto Charts with them. People are motivated to participate if they understand the purpose of the project and their efforts are recognized.

STEP 6   COMPARING DATA

Construct a table with columns for the category, measurement data, and the percent each category is of the whole. Keep this data with the finished Pareto Chart for documentation.

STEP 7   CONSTRUCTING THE CHART

▶ **Do It: Construct the Chart**

The time has arrived to construct the chart. Draw the x and y axes. Graph paper helps here.

▶ **Record the Scale on the Y Axis (Vertical Line):** There are two methods to determine the scale and the upper limit on the y axis.

1) Cover the highest value. Use the highest value in the measurement data set to determine the scale. Divide the scale proportionately, using even multiples. Commonly used units are 0, 5, 10 . . . or 0, 10, 20 . . . for frequency or percent. Units for cost are determined by the highest cost. This method is the simplest and most often used. Examples of this approach are on pages 100–104 of *The Memory Jogger*™ *II*.

2) Cover the range of data. In this method, the scale is based on the number of total occurrences or events represented in the Pareto. In the example on page 98 of *The Memory Jogger*™ *II*, there was a total of 206 problem calls to the help line. The y axis of the Pareto Chart therefore included at least this total. Since the y axis was based on a unit measure of 20, the y axis continued from 200 to the next highest break of 220. This method makes it possible to draw a cumulative percentage line, which shows the cumulative percent that each bar and all the bars to the left of it represent of 100 percent. See Step 8 in this chapter for more explanation of the cumulative percentage line.

▶ **Construct the Vertical Bars in Descending Order on the X Axis (Horizontal Line):** Label each bar. The height of each bar corresponds to the measurement values on the y axis (vertical line). Keep the bar width constant and create a staircase look by placing the bars side by side so that they are touching each other.

▶ **Combine Smallest Bars:** The smallest bars can be combined into one bar, placed as the last bar to the right, and labeled "Other." The "Other" category is generally larger than the bars just before it. (MJII page 98.)

▶ **Make It Clear:** Include a legend that shows the source of the data, the location, and the time period covered. Color code the bars if you are creating more than one chart for the same categories, breaking out subsets of a key cause or category, or doing a before and after study.

STEP 8 SHOWING CUMULATIVE PERCENTS

MJII pp. 97–98

▶ **Optional Step**

Some people feel that it is critical to plot a line to show the cumulative percent reached as each bar is added to the x axis (horizontal line). This line indicates what percent of the data collected is represented as each bar is added until 100% is reached. A unit scale is always on the left, the y axis (vertical line), and the percent scale is added on the right. A simpler option is to place the percentage that each bar represents either above or inside each bar. This approach doesn't show the cumulative percent total, but it can be easily calculated at any time. Generally, when the cumulative percent line is shown, the individual percentages are not shown, and vice versa. However, there is no rule that says both can't be shown (MJII page 98).

STEP 9 INTERPRETING THE RESULTS

MJII p. 99

The team now uses the results in their problem-solving or process-improvement activities. The most important thing to focus on is the relative impact on the goals of the business and the customer. This focus generally translates into the tallest bar on the Pareto, but the team should choose this bar only after a thorough review of the impact of the other problems. The team should also monitor the performance of the shorter bars over time, to be sure that other bars are not "popping up" while the largest bar is pushed down. For example, in the Stop 'N Go Pizza example (MJII pages 115–131), the team improved delivery time by improving training, reducing turnover, *and* simplifying the menu. If you compare the Pareto Chart on page 127 of *The Memory Jogger™ II* with the chart on page 128, you will see that the chart on page 128 shows dramatic improvement in "Late deliveries," but customers began to complain about the menu selections available, which did not even appear as a category in the chart on page 127. The "Selection" category may not be a serious problem but it is one that deserves close monitoring over time.

▶ **For Further Study of the Pareto Chart**

These two books are good references:

– *Understanding Statistical Process Control* by Donald Wheeler and David Chambers interprets Pareto Charts for out-of-control processes. Published by Statistical Process Controls, Inc., Second Edition, 1992.

– *Guide to Quality Control* by Dr. Kaoru Ishikawa includes practice problems. Published by Asian Productivity Organization, Second Revised Edition, 1986.

Pareto Chart

The Pareto Chart is named after Vilfredo Pareto, an Italian economist in the 19th century who studied the distribution of wealth in Italy. He found that 20% of the people controlled 80% of the wealth. Hence, the Pareto principle that 20% of the categories represent 80% of the trouble. If we work on the correct 20%, we will use our time and resources to their maximum benefit.

EXAMPLE

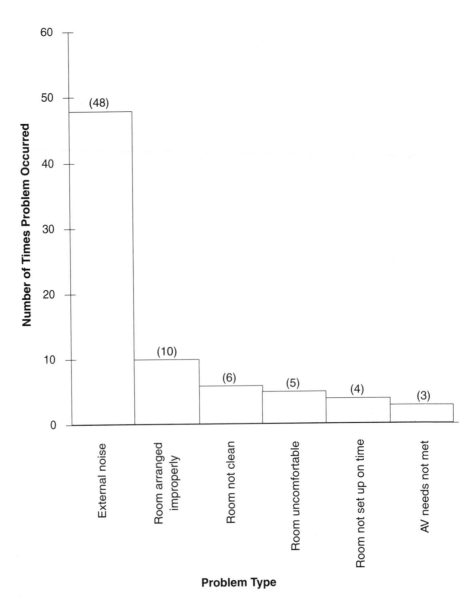

**Problem Areas in
Setting Up Meeting Rooms**

Information provided courtesy of Sewickley Valley Hospital, PA

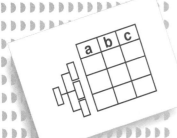

Prioritization Matrices
Weighing your options

IS THIS THE RIGHT TOOL? ASK . . .

▶ Are team members having difficulty getting past "hidden agendas" when they are narrowing down options?

▶ Are there at least three criteria that the team needs to consider in making an important decision?

▶ Will the success of the team's decision have a major impact on the business?

▶ Is the team willing to spend at least two hours to compare alternatives?

▶ Does the success of a decision depend on each member being committed to the outcome?

▶ Do the team's options represent competing "pet projects"?

STEPS AT A GLANCE

Start

Agree to use FACM* or CCM** → Agree on the goal → Do criteria exist? —Yes→ Choose a workable number

Do criteria exist? —No→ Generate list → Choose a workable number

Are criteria defined? —No→ Define each criterion → Create weighting scale → Compare and calculate weight for criteria

Are criteria defined? —Yes→ Create weighting scale

Create an option matrix for each criterion → Rate options by criteria → Calculate and transfer score per option

More criteria to rate? —Yes→ Rate options by criteria

More criteria to rate? —No→ Build summary matrix → Choose best option

Calculate and transfer score per option → Transfer criteria weight scores

* FACM = Full Analytical Criteria Method
** CCM = Consensus Criteria Method

141

Q. **How can we justify spending from two hours to two days going through this form of tool torture?**

A. Hey, if the the boss insists, we can justify *anything!* Joking aside, consider the example from Novacor that's featured in the mini case study and on pages 112–114 of *The Memory Jogger™ II*. Novacor needed to choose which word processing, spreadsheet, and presentation graphics software would be used throughout the entire organization. It was an important decision to make because everyone in the company would be affected. Instead of spending 3–6 months to make the decision, Novacor dedicated a 16-person team, made up of mainly system users and some information systems staff, to a five-day process. During that time the team members agreed upon selection criteria, heard vendor presentations, compared options and made a choice. The result was a decision made in five working days that was sound, supported by everyone on the team, and successful.

Q. **Why use the 1, 5, 10, 1/5, 1/10 rating scale? Why not 1, 2, 3, or any other scale?**

A. The Prioritization Matrices tool was developed by GOAL/QPC using the work of Thomas Saaty as a starting point. In his book *Decision Making for Leaders*, Saaty uses a more continuous scale from 1 to 9. The 1, 5, 10, 1/5, 1/10 scale was chosen by GOAL/QPC because the computation is easy. This simplicity was important since the Prioritization Matrices tool was designed to be used by "mainstream" managers without the use of a computer. The GOAL/QPC rating scale is not as sensitive to small distinctions between ratings as some of the other rating scales that are used are, however, the GOAL/QPC scale has proven to lead to the same result.

Q. **How long does it take to complete a typical series of matrices?**

A. The Prioritization Matrices tool has been used in such a wide variety of applications that it's difficult to define "typical." Say that a team has 3–5 established criteria, which will be applied to 6–8 options. The team should plan on approximately 3 hours to complete the matrices. This time estimate assumes that the criteria and the options are "average" in both their level of complexity and controversy to the team. There have been instances in which very "small" matrices have taken a great deal of time because the criteria and/ or options were so charged with emotion and history. The strength of this tool/method is that fundamental differences of opinion and/or approach are forced to the surface for consideration, and with some effort, are reconciled. In situations in which consensus is vital to the success of the effort, this is time well spent.

If: **The team or a key member sees no benefit to using a structured decision-making process and insists on a traditional open discussion . . .**

Then: Ask the team to answer three questions: 1) What are the risks if we choose the wrong options? 2) How important is consistent, honest team support for the final decision in determining whether it succeeds or fails? 3) Is there an example of a recent major decision that everyone agrees fell short of expectations, (read "failed" depending on the team environment), and would have been improved by a more disciplined review of options?

If: **An influential team member insists on "selling a solution" right from the start and won't agree to work out a decision using the tool . . .**

Then: Ask the influential team member: *"On what basis will we decide that this option has succeeded or failed?"* Try to briefly capture both the direct and indirect factors that the team member is using. For example, he/she may say *"It's the cheapest thing we can do!"* Record that on a flipchart as "cost to implement." *"The customer would see a big impact right away!"* may be rewritten as "visibility to the customer." Once you have captured three to four criteria, ask the team, *"Are these the key criteria that we need to apply at this time?"* The purpose of this questioning is two-folded: 1) to confirm that the influential team member is actually using criteria but that the criteria are hidden in the solution, and 2) to get the team to confirm (or counter) that these are indeed the criteria that it wants to apply to all of the options. The benefit is that the influential team member's idea is not rejected, (it might be a great idea), and that the discussion shifts to the criteria that *the team* wants to apply.

LEARNING ACTIVITY

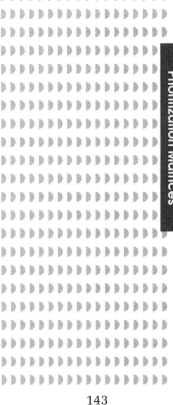

The following activity will help coaches reinforce the importance of creating sound criteria and using a structured process for comparing options.

1. Select four brands of any common snack food product. For this example, let's choose chocolate chip cookies.

2. Ask each person to divide a letter-size sheet of paper into four quadrants, marking them one through four.

3. Give everyone a cookie, identifying the brand only with a number. Be sure that you have recorded each brand and its corresponding number for your own use; don't share this information with the group. Distribute the other cookies, one brand one at a time, and call out their numbers. Ask everyone *not to eat* the cookies yet. This is the tough part!

4. Brainstorm and record criteria for selecting the "best" cookie. Select a maximum of four criteria. Also record a definition of each criterion. Any list is okay, but encourage everyone to include at least one criterion that is fact-based and commonly listed on the package, i.e., nutritious, low in fat, (use nutritional information), inexpensive or expensive (use purchase price).

5. Use the Full Analytical Method, (illustrated in Steps 4 and 5 of this chapter and the MJII pages 107–111) to: a) weight the criteria using a criteria matrix, b) do an options matrix comparing all cookies relative to each criterion (four criteria = four matrices), c) transfer the criteria weightings and option ratings from each matrix to a summary matrix, and d) announce the brand of the winning cookie!

Prioritization Matrices

> "The prioritization process separated the big decision into many small decisions, which helped diffuse the bias that team members had for a favorite software program."
>
> *Jack Waddell*

Written by Jack Waddell, Novacor Chemicals (Canada) Ltd.

What was the problem?

The corporation, with sites across North America, was using many different PC software packages for doing basic word processing, spreadsheets, and graphics presentations. There were three or four spreadsheet programs being used within individual sites. A team was formed with a mandate to set software standards for the corporation.

Who was on the team?

The team of 16 was selected with a majority of its members representing the user community and a minority from information systems to support a user-focus process.

How long did the process take?

Group members, who came from across the United States and Canada, were given 5 days to reach consensus on a recommendation.

What did we learn?

The team took a complex, emotional issue, with a lot of individual bias and worked through a process that left the participants feeling they had all contributed, and had produced a sound recommendation backed up by numerical data.

How was the team affected?

We took a monumental amount of information and processed it to meet the needs of individual team members, the whole team, and the corporation. The team grew as a group to understand and be empathetic to the issues and needs of every team member. The process helped a group of strangers pull together to resolve a difficult problem.

What else did we use?

We took 14 headers from the Affinity we created and used these as our criteria. The criteria were ranked using the Full Analytical Criteria Method. The criteria were also sent to the software companies and they were each given 2 hours to present their product, demonstrating how it met our criteria. This information was used in ranking each software company against the criteria.

What was the conclusion?

The prioritization of the software companies against the criteria helped diffuse the emotion and bias of the decision making. The ranking of the criteria let us see what was most important in the choice of the product. The ranking against the criteria gave a distinct advantage to the spreadsheet package company. Two products in the other two categories were very close so the team decided to use the three products from one company.

What were the results?

The team reached consensus on the selection of the products we recommended to the team sponsor. This happened despite the lack of any previous use of the products by the majority of the team members. The recommendation was accepted by the corporation and implemented. The employees accepted and are happy with the decision.

Prioritization Matrices

Choosing a Standard
Corporate Spreadsheet Program

① Weighting criteria (described in Step 3)
This is a portion of a full matrix with 14 criteria in total.

Criteria	Best use of hardware	Ease of use	Maximum functionality	Best performance	Total (14 criteria)	Relative Decimal Value
Best use of hardware		.20	.10	.20	3.7	.01
Ease of use	5.0		.20	.20	35.4	.08
Maximum functionality	10.0	5.0		5.0	69.0	.17
Best performance	5.0	5.0	.20		45.2	.11
			Grand Total (14 criteria)		418.1	

② Comparing options (described in Step 4)
These are just 2 of 14 matrices.

Best integration –internal	Program A	Program B	Program C	Total	Relative Decimal Value
Program A		1.00	1.00	2.00	.33
Program B	1.00		1.00	2.00	.33
Program C	1.00	1.00		2.00	.33
			Grand Total	6.00	

Lowest ongoing cost	Program A	Program B	Program C	Total	Relative Decimal Value
Program A		.10	.20	.30	.02
Program B	10.00		5.00	15.00	.73
Program C	5.00	.20		5.20	.25
			Grand Total	20.50	

③ Summarize Option Ratings Across All Criteria
(described in Step 5)
This is a portion of a full matrix with 14 criteria in total.

Criteria / Options	Easy to use (.08)	Best integration int. (.09)	Lowest ongoing cost (.08)	Total (across 14 criteria)	Relative Decimal Value
Program A	.03 (.01)	.33 (.03)	.02 (0)	.16	.18
Program B	.48 (.04)	.33 (.03)	.73 (.06)	.30	.33
Program C	.48 (.04)	.33 (.03)	.25 (.02)	.44	.49
			Grand Total	.90	

Information provided courtesy of Novacor Chemicals

Note: This constructed example represents only a portion of the prioritization process and only a portion of Novacor's spreadsheet evaluation process. Novacor Chemicals assembled a 16-person team, comprised mainly of system users and some information systems staff. The team developed and weighted 14 standard criteria and then applied them to choices in word processing, spreadsheet, and presentation graphics programs.

Result: Program C was chosen. Even though 14 out of the 16 team members were not currently using this program, the prioritization process changed their minds, and prevented them from biasing the final decision.

Prioritization Matrices

145

STEP 1 AGREEING ON THE GOAL

MJII p. 107

▶ **Every Word Is Important**

Don't dismiss the importance of getting consensus on the wording of the team's goal statement—recall that the criteria for decision making flow directly from the goal. In the vacation example in *The Memory Jogger™ II*, consider how the decision-making process would have been different if the goal statement was: "Choose the best vacation." It may seem obvious but the addition of the words "enjoyable" and "whole family" takes the discussion in entirely new and more focused directions. If the goal statement is clear up front, the team will have to consider far fewer possible criteria.

STEP 2 AGREEING ON THE CRITERIA

MJII p. 107

It's satisfying for a team to come to an agreement on a final list of criteria to be applied since it's often not an easy process. So expect some resistance when you ask the team to create an "operational definition" for each criterion. Consider the criteria used for the vacation example in *The Memory Jogger™ II* on page 107:

No Operational Definition	With Operational Definition
Cost	Price of food, lodging, and transportation
Educational value	Everyone can learn something interesting first-hand
Diverse activity	Every day the family can change direction and preferences
Escape reality	The family can leave their everyday problems behind

▶ **How Many Criteria Are Too Many?**

There is no absolute rule. If the team is moving through the process for the first time, it's wise to choose three to four criteria. Any fewer than this, and the team may feel that the matrices were too simple to warrant the time spent. Any more criteria than this would probably tax the patience of a team that is likely to be skeptical anyway. *Keep in mind that for every criterion, the team needs to create a matrix to compare all the options.* That's right, if the team comes up with 17 criteria, they need to create 17 matrices! This is just what one team did when selecting a new dean for their college. These 17 criteria were important enough that they applied them to the six finalists for the position. The process took them three months, but the old process generally took over one year and left everyone with a very unsatisfied feeling. The team agreed that this process was far superior. It really does depend on the importance of the decision and the acceptance of the outcome.

STEP 3 WEIGHTING CRITERIA

MJII pp. 107–108

▶ **Which Method Is the Best to Construct this Tool?**

The Full Analytical Criteria Method or the Consensus Method? The example described on pages 107–110 in *The Memory Jogger™ II* illustrates the Full Analytical Criteria Method. The Consensus Criteria Method is also widely used. Please refer to page 106 of *The Memory Jogger™ II* for an outline of the typical situations for using each method. Described below is an overview of the strengths and weaknesses of both the Full Analytical Criteria and Consensus Methods.

Prioritization Matrices

Full Analytical Criteria Method

Strengths

- This method forces a team to compare *each criterion* and option to *every other* criterion and option. This method is superior to a general discussion because it allows the team to make detailed comparisons and conclusions, whereas a general discussion will tend to ramble, lose direction, or go in circles.

- Breaks down a large number of factors and choices into individual decisions. These decisions can be made thoroughly by using the matrix to focus on just one "cell" at a time.

- Uncovers very basic assumptions and biases of team members when directly comparing and weighting criteria.

- Reduces the chance that any one individual will "push through" a pet project or specific criteria.

Weaknesses

- Can be very time consuming, especially when the criteria and/or options are controversial or when the team members have a high personal stake in the outcome.

- The process can create intense conflict, which may be a new experience for many teams.

- Requires more skilled facilitation than most of the other tools because of the need to deal positively with conflict and to maintain a high quality discussion throughout the process.

Consensus Criteria Method

Strengths

- Provides a quick way for a team to build on the consensus around the criteria, which is a major step forward for many teams.

- It is a comfortable decision-making method because it is based on techniques that are already widely used in teams such as the Nominal Group Technique and many forms of weighted voting.

- The procedures of ranking and weighting are simple to carry out and easy to communicate.

Weaknesses

- Because all the team members rank or weight their choices individually, the result is simply an addition process. Therefore, it only represents a type of "mathematical" consensus, not one based on full discussion and compromise.

- Because of the lack of discussion and full exploration of each team member's position, everyone "votes" as they currently stand. The team members really don't learn from each other and everyone's present "paradigm" (world view) stays untouched and intact.

▶ Criteria Matrix Examples

For examples of a criteria matrix created with both the *Full Analytical Criteria Method* and the *Consensus Criteria Method*, see the "Example" section, Step 3, at the back of this chapter. (Also *The Memory Jogger™ II* pages 107–108, Step 3, for the Full Analytical Criteria Method.)

STEP 4 RATING OPTIONS BY CRITERIA

MJII pp. 108–109

▸ **Customizing the Rating Scale**

Full Analytical Criteria Method

Unlike the rating scale for the *criteria matrix* (MJII page 108), which always stays the same, (e.g., 1 = equally important, 5 = more important, 10 = most important), the rating scale for each *options matrix* (MJII page 109) is customized, based on the specific criterion the team is rating. For example, there are four unique legends for the criteria "cost, educational value, diverse activity, and escape reality." For examples of each legend, see the "Full Analytical Criteria Method" matrices in the "Example" section, Step 4, at the back of this chapter.

Notice that the "5" and the "10" ratings are always used for the positive or desirable ratings. In the case of the criterion "cost," it is desirable if an option is "less expensive" (unless you work for a monopoly or if you're trying to price products so as to get the maximum profit margin). Therefore, "less expensive" would get a rating of "5." On the other hand, in the case of the criterion, "diverse activity," it is better to have "more diverse activity" (unless you're a couch potato). Therefore, "more diverse activity" would also get a "5" rating.

Consensus Criteria Method

When using this method, each team member *ranks* all of the options for each criterion. The similarity between this method and the Full Analytical Criteria Method is that the team will need to create a matrix for every criterion. *The difference, however, is that each team member ranks rather than compares all options*, and so team members need to agree on the definition and value of both the top and bottom of the rating scale. For example: if there are six options that the team is considering on the basis of "cost," team members may agree to list on the matrix: "6" as the "Least expensive," and "1" as the "Most expensive." Team members could also agree to "6" as the "Most expensive," and "1" as the "Least expensive," and the process would still work; what's important is that team members discuss and agree on the rating scale.

▸ **Options Matrix Examples**

For examples of options matrices using weighted criteria created with both the *Full Analytical Criteria Method* and the *Consensus Criteria Method*, see the "Example" section, Step 4, at the back of this chapter. (Also *The Memory Jogger™ II* pages 108–109, Step 4, for the Full Analytical Criteria Method.)

STEP 5 BUILDING A SUMMARY MATRIX

MJII p. 110

In both the Full Analytical Criteria Method and Consensus Criteria Method, creating the summary matrix is simply a mechanical step to transfer the relative decimal values from the criteria matrix and each of the criterion versus options matrices. The summary matrix should contain as many rows (horizontal) as there are options and as many columns (vertical) as there are criteria. It should also include two additional columns for the row total and relative decimal value, as well as a box for the "Grand Total" at the bottom of both of these columns. An additional row at the bottom of the matrix, which shows the totals of each column, is optional. This extra row can be helpful as a check on the math.

▶ **Summary Matrix Examples**

For examples of a summary matrix created with both the *Full Analytical Criteria Method* and the *Consensus Criteria Method*, see the "Example" section, Step 5. (Also *The Memory Jogger*™ *II* page 110, Step 5, for the Full Analytical Criteria Method.)

STEP 6 CHOOSING THE BEST OPTIONS

MJII p. 111

▶ **Decisions Based on Data or Opinions?**

In the vacation example, the decisions each family member made on the criterion "cost" were based on real numbers, real data. Mom or Dad simply needed to calculate a daily cost for each destination, then ask everyone to compare or rank order the options based on these costs. All of the other decisions the family made on the other criteria (educational value, diverse activity, and escape reality) were based on less factual information; each person's decision was "subjective." The prioritization process didn't eliminate subjectivity but it did tap the knowledge and judgment of each person to *systematically* come to an agreement that the whole family could support.

Data should always be the first choice as the basis for making a decision. But in the many situations when data is only one of the inputs or when data is not available, these matrices can help tap the knowledge and wisdom of the *entire* team rather than that of any one individual.

EXAMPLE

This example, which starts on the next page, is illustrated using the same steps that are shown in *The Memory Jogger*™ *II* on pages 107–110. The example shows you how the criteria for the goal "Choose the most enjoyable vacation for the whole family," are weighted and the vacation options are narrowed down systematically by using the Full Analytical Criteria Method (FACM) and the Consensus Criteria Method (CCM).

Prioritization Matrices

149

FULL ANALYTICAL CRITERIA METHOD

▶ **Step 1 Agreeing on the Goal**

The matrices shown in this "Example" section are based on the goal statement, "Choose the most enjoyable vacation for the whole family."

▶ **Step 2 Agreeing on the Criteria**

The list of criteria is taken from page 107 of *The Memory Jogger*™ *II*. The criteria are:

▶ Cost

▶ Educational value

▶ Diverse activity

▶ Escape reality

▶ **Step 3 Weighting Criteria**

Full Analytical Criteria Method

Criterion vs. Criterion

Criteria \ Criteria	Cost	Educ. value	Diverse activity	Escape reality	Row Total	Relative Decimal Value (RT ÷ GT)
Cost	■	$\frac{1}{5}$	$\frac{1}{10}$	5	5.3	.15
Educ. value	5	■	$\frac{1}{5}$	5	10.2	.28
Diverse activity	10	5	■	5	20	.55
Escape reality	$\frac{1}{5}$	$\frac{1}{5}$	$\frac{1}{5}$	■	.60	.02
				Grand Total	36.1	

1 = Equally important	**Row Total**
5 = More important	Rating scores added
10 = Much more important	**Grand Total**
$^1/_5$ = Less Important	Row totals added
$^1/_{10}$ = Much less important	**Relative Decimal Value**
	Each row total ÷ by the grand total

▶ **Step 4 Rating Options by Criteria**

In *The Memory Jogger*™ *II*, Step 4, "Compare all options relative to each weighted criterion," only the options matrix using the cost criterion was shown completed. The other criteria—educational value, diverse activity, and escape reality— were not illustrated as completed matrices. The four completed matrices, which follow, pick up where *The Memory Jogger*™ *II* (page 109) could not venture because of space limitations.

Full Analytical Criteria Method

Options vs. Each Criterion (Cost Criterion)

Cost	Disney World	Gettys- burg	New York City	Uncle Henry's	Row Total	Relative Decimal Value (RT ÷ GT)
Disney World		$\frac{1}{5}$	5	$\frac{1}{10}$	5.3	.12
Gettys- burg	5		10	$\frac{1}{5}$	15.2	.33
New York City	$\frac{1}{5}$	$\frac{1}{10}$		$\frac{1}{10}$	.40	.01
Uncle Henry's	10	5	10		25	.54
				Grand Total	45.9	1.00

1 = Equal cost
5 = Less expensive
10 = Much less expensive
$^1/5$ = More expensive
$^1/10$ = Much more expensive

Full Analytical Criteria Method

Options vs. Each Criterion (Educational Value)

Educa- tional value	Disney World	Gettys- burg	New York City	Uncle Henry's	Row Total	Relative Decimal Value (RT ÷ GT)
Disney World		$\frac{1}{5}$	$\frac{1}{5}$	10	10.4	.24
Gettys- burg	5		1	10	16	.375
New York City	5	1		10	16	.375
Uncle Henry's	$\frac{1}{10}$	$\frac{1}{10}$	$\frac{1}{10}$		.30	.01
				Grand Total	42.7	1.00

1 = Equal educational value
5 = More educational value
10 = Much more educational value
1/5 = Less educational value
1/10 = Much less educational value

Full Analytical Criteria Method

Options vs. Each Criterion (Diverse Activity)

Diverse activity	Disney World	Gettys-burg	New York City	Uncle Henry's	Row Total	Relative Decimal Value (RT ÷ GT)
Disney World	■	10	$\frac{1}{5}$	10	20.2	.40
Gettys-burg	$\frac{1}{10}$	■	$\frac{1}{10}$	5	5.2	.10
New York City	5	10	■	10	25	.49
Uncle Henry's	$\frac{1}{10}$	$\frac{1}{5}$	$\frac{1}{10}$	■	.40	.01
				Grand Total	50.8	1.00

1 = Equally diverse activity
5 = More diverse activity
10 = Much more diverse activity
1/5 = Less diverse activity
1/10 = Much less diverse activity

Full Analytical Criteria Method

Options vs. Each Criterion (Escape Reality)

Escape reality	Disney World	Gettys-burg	New York City	Uncle Henry's	Row Total	Relative Decimal Value (RT ÷ GT)
Disney World	■	10	10	10	30	.65
Gettys-burg	$\frac{1}{10}$	■	5	5	10.1	.22
New York City	$\frac{1}{10}$	$\frac{1}{5}$	■	5	5.3	.12
Uncle Henry's	$\frac{1}{10}$	$\frac{1}{5}$	$\frac{1}{5}$	■	.50	.01
				Grand Total	45.9	1.00

1 = Equal escape from reality
5 = Greater escape from reality
10 = Much greater escape from reality
1/5 = Less of an escape from reality
1/10 = Much less of an escape from reality

▶ **Step 5 Building a Summary Matrix**

Full Analytical Criteria Method

Summary Matrix
Options vs. All Criteria

Criteria ⟍ Optns.	Cost (.15)	Educational value (.28)	Diverse activity (.55)	Escape reality (.02)	Row Total	Relative Decimal Value (RT ÷ GT)
Disney World	.12 x .15 (.02)	.24 x .28 (.07)	.40 x .55 (.22)	.65 x .02 (.01)	.32	.32
Gettysburg	.33 x .15 (.05)	.37 x .28 (.10)	.10 x .55 (.06)	.22 x .02 (0)	.22	.22
New York City	.01 x .15 (0)	.37 x .28 (.10)	.49 x .55 (.27)	.12 x .02 (0)	.37	.38
Uncle Henry's	.54 x .15 (.08)	.01 x .28 (0)	.01 x .55 (.01)	.01 x .02 (0)	.09	.09
				Grand Total	1.00	

.54   **x**   **.15**
(from Step 4 matrix)   (from Step 3 matrix)
(.08)
Option score

▶ **Step 6 Choosing the Best Options**

Analysis

The results in this "Example" section happen to be the same using either the Full Analytical Criteria or Consensus Criteria Method. In either method, the family is still going to New York City. It's very likely, however, that the two experiences are quite different: The Full Analytical Method forces a discussion of assumptions right from the beginning of the comparison of criteria. Each step of the process gives team members the choice to understand why people may agree or disagree. It is difficult to simply gloss over fundamental disagreements that could later return to block the implementation of the team's decision. In the end, the Full Analytical is one of the best methods for encouraging and harvesting the fruits of honest discussion and true consensus. No small accomplishment!

153

CONSENSUS CRITERIA METHOD

▶ **Step 1 Agreeing on the Goal**

The matrices shown in this "Example" section are based on the goal statement, "Choose the most enjoyable vacation for the whole family."

▶ **Step 2 Agreeing on the Criteria**

The list of criteria is taken from page 107 of *The Memory Jogger™ II*. The criteria are:

▶ Cost

▶ Educational value

▶ Diverse activity

▶ Escape reality

▶ **Step 3 Weighting Criteria**

Consensus Criteria Method
Criteria Matrix

Members \ Criteria	Mom	Dad	Rick	Karen	Row Total Weight
Cost	.25	.10	.10	.30	.75
Educational value	.15	.45	.25	.20	1.05
Diverse activity	.50	.20	.45	.40	1.55
Escape reality	.10	.25	.20	.10	.65
Total	1.00	1.00	1.00	1.00	4.0

Each column represents a value of 1.00 distributed across the criteria.

Analysis

Overall, there is fair amount of consistency across the ratings of the different family members. Where do you think there might be some conflict in evaluating the vacation options? Notice that Dad values the educational aspects of a vacation far more than anyone else. The other family members seem to be much more interested in finding a destination with diverse activities (not necessarily educational activities.)

Talking Through the Weightings: Another area worth watching is the contrast between Mom and Dad's attitudes toward the role that cost plays in the final selection. Such diverse views are to be expected within any team, but this process, (unlike the Full Analytical Criteria Method), throws them together into a mathematical weighting. Without discussion up front, options aren't explored and it's easy for everyone to be isolated from one other by "tunnel vision." One possibility is to review each matrix to note deep splits within the group, discuss the nature of the disagreement, and then repeat the weighting. However, in the interest of speed, this step is often skipped and there remains only the appearance of consensus.

▶ **Step 4 Rating Options by Criteria**

The four matrices that follow are based on the same vacation options and the same weighted criteria shown in the "Full Analytical Criteria Method" matrices in this "Example" section.

Consensus Criteria Method

Options vs. Each Criterion (Cost)

Members / Options	Mom	Dad	Rick	Karen	Total	Rank
Disney World	2	2	2	2	8	2
Gettys-burg	3	3	3	2	11	3
New York City	1	1	1	1	4	1
Uncle Henry's	4*	4	4	4	16	4

*Doesn't account for the cost of marriage counseling after the week at Uncle Henry's.

1 = Most expensive

4 = Least expensive

Consensus Criteria Method

Options vs. Each Criterion (Educational Value)

Members \ Options	Mom	Dad	Rick	Karen	Total	Rank
Disney World	2	2	3	3	10	2
Gettys-burg	3	4	2	2	11	3
New York City	4	3	4	4	15	4
Uncle Henry's	1	1	1	1	4	1

1 = Least educational value

4 = Most educational value

Consensus Criteria Method

Options vs. Each Criterion (Diverse Activity)

Members \ Options	Mom	Dad	Rick	Karen	Total	Rank
Disney World	3	4	3	3	13	3
Gettys-burg	2	2	2	2	8	2
New York City	4	3	4	4	15	4
Uncle Henry's	1	1	1	1	4	1

1 = Least diverse activity

4 = Most diverse activity

Consensus Criteria Method

Options vs. Each Criterion (Escape Reality)

Members / Options	Mom	Dad	Rick	Karen	Total	Rank
Disney World	4	3	4	3	14	4
Gettys-burg	3	4	2	2	11	3
New York City	2	1	3	4	10	2
Uncle Henry's*	1	2	1	1	5	1

*Uncle Henry hasn't touched reality in years.

1 = Least escape reality

4 = Most escape reality

▶ **Step 5 Building a Summary Matrix**

Consensus Criteria Method

Summary Matrix
Options vs. All Criteria

Criteria / Options	Cost (.75)	Educa-tional value (1.05)	Diverse activity (1.55)	Escape reality (.65)	Row Total	Rank
Disney World	2 x .75 (1.50)	2 x 1.05 (2.10)	3 x 1.55 (4.65)	4 x .65 (2.60)	10.85	3
Gettys-burg	3 x .75 (2.25)	3 x 1.05 (3.15)	2 x 1.55 (3.10)	3 x .65 (1.95)	10.45	2
New York City	1 x .75 (.75)	4 x 1.05 (4.20)	4 x 1.55 (6.20)	2 x .65 (1.30)	12.45	4
Uncle Henry's	4 x .75 (3.00)	1 x 1.05 (1.05)	1 x 1.55 (1.55)	1 x .65 (.65)	6.25	1

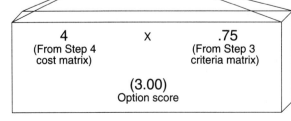

4
(From Step 4 cost matrix)

x

.75
(From Step 3 criteria matrix)

(3.00)
Option score

1 = Lowest rated option

4 = Highest rated option

▶ **Step 6 Choosing the Best Options**

Analysis

From this process it's clear that the only thing that everyone agrees on is that there is very little to support going to Uncle Henry's for vacation, other than it would be dirt cheap. Mom and the kids seem to see the options in much the same way. Then there's Dad . . . It's clear from both the criteria and option matrices that he would be happiest taking an educational stroll through Civil War history at Gettysburg. We can assume that he will take the high road and not pout as they cruise the shops and museums of New York. However, this does point out a basic weakness of this method in that there is no discussion through which people can share their thoughts and perhaps even change their minds! The primary advantage of this method is speed, but it may be at the expense of a true consensus.

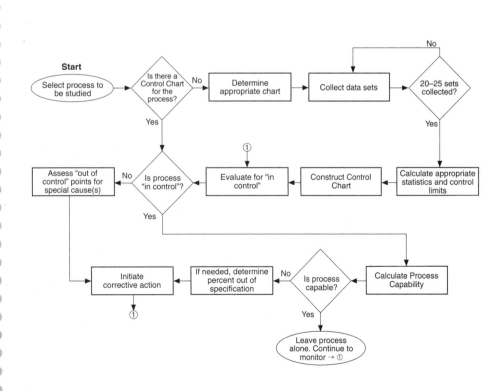

Process Capability

Measuring conformance to customer requirements

◗ Does the team want to link together the Control Chart with customer requirements?

◗ Does the team need to determine whether the process is capable of meeting the customers' requirements?

◗ Does the team want to determine if there has been a change in the process?

◗ Does the team need to estimate the percentage of product or service that exceeds the customer requirements?

STEPS AT A GLANCE

Q. **What is Process Capability?**

A. Process Capability means that a process is able to consistently produce products or services within the requirements set by the customer. A process operating within its control limits is said to be operating in statistical control, i.e., consistent and predictable, but not necessarily capable. Once statistical control is achieved, only then can the capability of the process to meet customer requirements (specifications) be evaluated.

Q. **What is a Process Capability study?**

A. A Process Capability study will help a team find out whether a process can meet specifications and, if not, to estimate the fraction (or percentage) that does not meet specifications.

Q. **Where do customer requirements, or specifications, come from?**

A. Customer requirements are the defined numeric descriptions of product or service quality. They can be tolerances from drawings for a component, e.g., the diameter of a hole that best matches the diameter of a plug to go into that hole, or the earliest and latest times for students to be dropped off at school. Customer requirements can also be delivery specifications: time to complete a banking transaction, turnaround time of blood analyses, or the percent of on-time arrivals of planes at the airport.

Q. **What is six sigma (or 6σ)?**

A. Six sigma is a code name made popular by the quality improvement work at Motorola. Six sigma is a measure of the amount of variation resulting from the inherent factors affecting an undisturbed process in statistical control. It is the process standard deviation. It is what the process *can do*. This is different from what you *would like it to do*—meet customer requirements. Some organizations today are moving beyond six sigma, to 8σ.

Q. **Is there a difference between Control Charts and Process Capability?**

A. Yes. Control Charts are based on charting the means and ranges of subgroupings, and assessing variation between and within subgroupings. Process Capability is based on the variation exhibited by all the individual data points. Control Charts determine whether a process is *in control* whereas Process Capability determines whether a process *is capable*.

Q. **What is a capability index?**

A. A capability index measures the ratio of process requirements (specifications or tolerances) to process capability. C_p and C_r are simple ratios that compare natural process spread and specification width. However, C_p and C_r do not look at how well the process is centered to the desired target (average). C_{pl} and C_{pu} (for single-sided specification limits) and C_{pk} (for double sided limits) measure the process spread to specification width as well as process average to nearest specification. C_{pk} is considered a measure of the process capability.

If: **The team wants to determine whether the process is capable of meeting the customer requirements and whether it is making defective product or service, but they don't know where to start . . .**

Then:

▶ Help the team define the process and the customer requirements for the process. Talk to the customer. Clearly define the process you are studying.

▶ Review the Control Chart for the process. Make sure the team is working with a process that is in control. Set up a charting system if one doesn't exist. (You may also want to review the Control Chart chapter.)

▶ Make sure the process has a normal distribution. Have the team construct a Histogram on the individual data points, or plot the data on normal probability paper. (This method of determining normality extends beyond the scope of this book. Three good resources to consult are *SPC Simplified: Practical Tools for Continuous Quality Improvement*, *Total Quality Transformation*, and *Fundamental Statistical Process Control Reference Manual*, which are listed in the appendix.)

▶ Once the team is sure the process is in control and normally distributed, the team can proceed with Step 1 of Process Capability.

If: **The team is struggling between understanding the difference between Process Capability and Control Charts . . .**

Then: Explain that they are two completely different techniques:

▶ Process Capability requires more data. It uses individual data points, which are usually consecutively drawn, to see whether a process is capable of meeting customer requirements (specifications). It is a snapshot of the untouched process.

▶ Control Charts determine the type and amount of variation acting on a process, and are used to to determine stability. Control Charts use small sample sizes drawn over time, because it is less time consuming and less costly than measuring every data point. Control limits are natural limits of variation of the *averages*. These limits are not to be confused with specification limits which are for *individuals*. The Control Chart is used to improve and control a process over time; it determines the type of variation and process direction, such as a trend. Information from the Control Chart, however, can be used to estimate the process variation ($\overline{R}$ or $\overline{s}$) needed to calculate process capability.

Situation:

A manufacturer of light bulbs is interested in determining the performance of two machines and whether each machine is capable of meeting the customer requirement of 100 LPW (lumens per watt) ± 5%. A team, named *Bright Ideas* obtained 10 measurements from each machine.

Machine A	98	95	96	95	93	95	99	93	95	96
Machine B	98	99	101	98	100	101	99	100	99	99

Conditions:

Normally, before a team can determine the capability of a process, the team must be sure the process is stable. By using a Control Chart, the team can determine whether or not the process is stable. However, *for this exercise **only**, keep in mind the following conditions:*

1. *Assume* the individual data points for Machines A and B come from stable processes.

2. The number of data points (10) for both machines is purposely small for ease of calculation. Under normal circumstances, 10 data points are not enough to determine process capability. Use industry standards for the minimum number of data points you will need.

3. The calculated standard deviation, s, for the individual data points, can be substituted for $\hat{\sigma}$.

Learning Activity Questions:

1. Are both Machines A and B capable of meeting the customer requirement?

2. How does the performance of Machine A and Machine B compare to one another?

3. What action needs to be taken?

Hint

Since this is all the data available, and the number of data points from each machine is small, start by calculating the mean, $\overline{X}$, and sample standard deviation, s, for each data set. Then replace $\hat{\sigma}$ with s to calculate process capability. (The formula for calculating process capability is shown on page 163.)

Bright Ideas Team Investigation:

Under normal circumstances, before the *Bright Ideas* team can evaluate the capability of the process, they need to know that the process is stable and distributed normally. They would know the process is stable by looking at the process spread (variation) on the average and range Control Chart, and they would know the distribution of the data is normal by looking at the shape of the distribution on a Histogram or a probability plot. (The probability plot method is not discussed in this book. A good explanation of this method is described in *SPC Simplified: Practical Steps to Quality*, pages 123–131.) Normally, the team would next calculate the estimated process variation using this formula:

$$\hat{\sigma} = \frac{\bar{R}}{d_2}$$

They would find the value for the average range on the Control Chart and the value for d_2 in the Table of Constants, which is shown on page 165.

However, *for this exercise **only***, the team will use the above three conditions and will substitute s, the sample variation for individual data points, for the estimated process variation, $\hat{\sigma}$. (See the formula below for calculating process capability.)

Evaluating Simple Process Capability

Use the index C_p to determine the capability of the process. C_p is the ratio of specification width (tolerance) to process variation. The formula for C_p is:

$$C_p = \frac{USL - LSL}{6\hat{\sigma}}$$

Remember: While the index C_p relates the spread of the process relative to the specification width, the capability index does not tell you how well the process average is centered to the target value.

The answers for this activity are printed in the "Coach's Answer Key" at the end of this chapter.

▶ **Determining Process Grand Average and Average Range**

Important Note

This entire section, Steps 1 through 4, focuses on determining process capability for the $\overline{X}$ and R chart **ONLY**. For the other variables control charts, ($\overline{X}$ and s, $\tilde{X}$ and R, and X and R_m charts), determining process capability is identical to that of the $\overline{X}$ and R chart. Just substitute the appropriate constant, using the Table of Constants shown in *The Memory Jogger™ II* page 42.

Process capability for attributes control charts is represented simply by the process averages, $\overline{p}$, $n\overline{p}$, $\overline{c}$, $\overline{u}$.

▶ **Limitations of Process Capability**

Proceeding to determine process capability is meaningless if the process is not stable. Therefore, stay true to these three questions:

Is it a new process?

If the team is studying a new process, set up an $\overline{X}$ and R chart using the steps in the Control Chart section, otherwise refer to the team's current Control Chart.

From the Control Chart, select the process grand average, $\overline{\overline{X}}$, or determine it by taking the average of the averages for each subgrouping. Select the process average range, $\overline{R}$, or determine it by taking the average of the ranges for each subgrouping.

Is the process in control?

Evaluate the process for being in control. To determine if the process is "out of control," refer to pages 45 and 46 of *The Memory Jogger™ II*. Remove all assignable, or special causes, and collect more data if it's necessary. (Remember that you need 20–25 subgroups.)

Does the process show a normal curve?

Determine normality. A simple process to determine normality is to draw a Histogram of the individual data points and assure, by eye, that the process follows a bell-shaped curve. Unilateral, or one-sided tolerances, have a nonnormal distribution by design and require special statistics. Unilateral tolerances are common. A more exact method for determining normality is to use probability paper, which is a method that extends beyond the scope of this book. Three good resources to consult are *SPC Simplified: Practical Tools for Continuous Quality Improvement*, *Total Quality Transformation*, and *Fundamental Statistical Process Control Reference Manual*, which are listed in the appendix.

▶ **Specification Limits**

Specification limits are based on what the customer requires, which can be defined by specification, customer, or management requirements. Talk to the customers of the process to clearly understand their needs.

Upper Specification Limit

The Upper Specification Limit (USL) is the highest allowable measurement that will satisfy the requirement.

Lower Specification Limit

The Lower Specification Limit (LSL) is the lowest allowable measurement that will satisfy the requirement.

STEP 3   CALCULATING STANDARD DEVIATION

MJII pp. 132–133

▶ **Estimating Process Standard Deviation**

If we could measure every *individual* product or service we produce, the process variation would be represented by σ, the *population* standard deviation. A team can calculate an estimated process standard deviation, $\hat{\sigma}$, using the value for the average range, $\bar{R}$, from a Control Chart of the process.

$$\hat{\sigma} = \frac{\bar{R}}{d_2}$$

▶ **Sample Size and Constants**

The constant d_2 is a weighting factor that is based on the sample size n. Use the table shown below to determine d_2 for an $\bar{X}$ and R Chart.

Sample size n	A_2	D_3	D_4	d_2
2	1.880	0	3.267	1.128
3	1.023	0	2.574	1.693
4	0.729	0	2.282	2.059
5	0.577	0	2.114	2.326
6	0.483	0	2.004	2.534
7	0.419	0.076	1.924	2.704
8	0.373	0.136	1.864	2.847
9	0.337	0.184	1.816	2.970
10	0.308	0.223	1.777	3.078

This is a portion of the table shown on page 42 of *The Memory Jogger™ II*.

▶ **Determining Process Capability For An Average and Range Chart**

Simple Process Capability Indices, C_p and C_r

Determining C_p or C_r will answer the question of whether the variation within the process is acceptable, as specified by the requirement. These indices do not answer to whether the process variation is targeted appropriately.

C_p Index

C_p is the ratio of specification width (tolerance) to process capability:

$$C_p = \frac{USL - LSL}{6\hat{\sigma}}$$

When $C_p < 1$ Process variation exceeds specification limits. 99.73% of the data will not fit within these limits.

When $C_p = 1$ Process variation just meets specification limits. 99.73% of the data fits just within these limits.

When $C_p > 1$ Process variation is less than specification limits. 99.73% of the data will easily fit within these limits.

See page 134 in *The Memory Jogger™ II* for illustrations of $C_p < 1$, $C_p = 1$, and $C_p > 1$.

C_r Index

C_r is the ratio of process capability to customer requirements. C_r is the inverse of C_p:

$$C_r = \frac{6\hat{\sigma}}{USL - LSL}$$

When $C_r > 1$ Process variation exceeds specification limits. 99.73% of the data will not fit within these limits.

When $C_r = 1$ Process variation just meets specification limits. 99.73% of the data fits just within these limits.

When $C_r < 1$ Process variation is less than specification limits. 99.73% of the data will easily fit within these limits.

Remember the limitation of C_p or C_r: They compare only variation against requirements, they do not look at how the process is centered relative to customer requirements.

C_{pl}, C_{pu}, C_{pk} Indices

These indices compare the process variation to the centering or target value, and answer the question *"Will this process produce bad quality product or service?"* These indices do not answer the question of how much bad product or service will be produced if the process is left unchanged.

C_{pl} and C_{pu} Indices

C_{pl} and C_{pk} are used for one-sided requirements.

C_{pk} Index

C_{pk} is used for two-sided requirements. It is the lesser value of C_{pl} and C_{pu}.

When $C_{pk} < 1$ Process variation exceeds specification limits. 99.73% of the data will not fit within these limits.

When $C_{pk} = 1$ Process variation just meets specification limits. 99.73% of the data fits just within these limits.

When $C_{pk} > 1$ Process variation is less than specification limits. 99.73% of the data will easily fit within these limits.

C_{pk} can be used to estimate the proportion of the process output that falls outside the specification limits. The formulas used to develop C_{pk} result in a Z score that can be converted into the percentage area under the curve, using the Standard Normal Table. These calculations are beyond the scope of this book and can be found in statistical books, such as *Fundamental Statistical Process Control Reference Manual*, which is listed in the appendix.

EXAMPLE

The W"req" ing Crew

A team within the purchasing department was chartered to study the capability of the "requisitioning" process to meet a management objective of 6 ± 3 processing days.

Each day for four weeks the team randomly chose five "processed" requisitions, determining the number of days to process it. The team knew that n was equal to 5 samples, and k was equal to 20 subgroups. (On each work day, from August 1 through August 26, five sample measurements were taken for a total of 20 days.) The W"req" ing crew used the value for k to calculate the total average, and the average range, of all the sample measurements. Next, they calculated the upper and lower control limits for the averages chart and the ranges chart. Using n = 5 as the sample size, the team found the values for A_2, D_3, and D_4, (0.577, 0, and 2.114 respectively), in the table shown in Step 3 under "Sample Size and Constants." The team's calculations are shown on the next page.

**Average
of Averages**

$$\bar{\bar{X}} = \frac{\sum \bar{X}}{k}$$

$$= \frac{(5.2 + 5.2 + 5.6 \ldots 5.4 + 4.0 + 5.8)}{20}$$

$$= \frac{118.8}{20}$$

$$= \mathbf{5.94}$$

**Average
Range**

$$\bar{R} = \frac{\sum \bar{R}}{k}$$

$$= \frac{75}{20}$$

$$= \frac{(6 + 7 + 5 \ldots 5 + 2 + 4)}{20}$$

$$= \mathbf{3.75}$$

**Averages
Control
Limit
(Upper)**

$$UCL_{\bar{x}} = \bar{\bar{X}} + A_2\bar{R}$$

$$= 5.94 + (0.577)(3.75)$$

$$= \mathbf{8.10}$$

**Averages
Control
Limit
(Lower)**

$$LCL_{\bar{x}} = \bar{\bar{X}} - A_2\bar{R}$$

$$= 5.94 - (0.577)(3.75)$$

$$= \mathbf{3.78}$$

**Ranges
Control
Limit
(Upper)**

$$UCL_R = D_4\bar{R}$$

$$= (2.114)(3.75)$$

$$= \mathbf{7.93}$$

**Ranges
Control
Limit
(Lower)**

$$LCL_R = D_3\bar{R}$$

$$= (0)(3.75)$$

$$= \mathbf{0}$$

Process Capability

This is what the W"req" ing crew's Control Chart looked like after the data was plotted.

Process: Time in Days to Process A Requisition

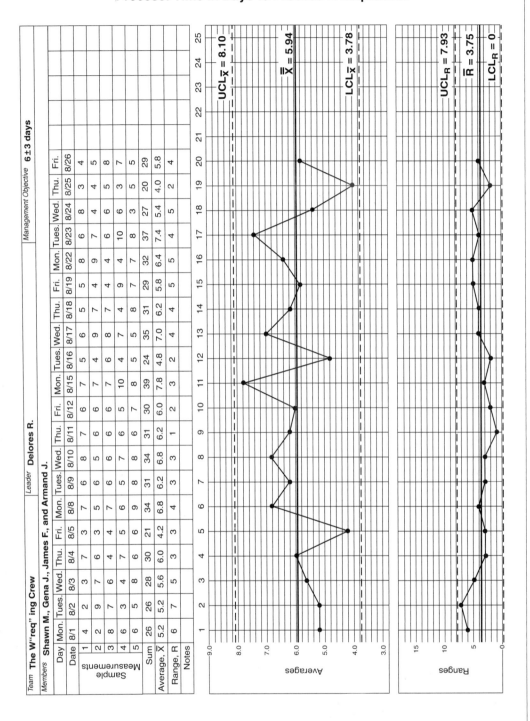

▶ **Simple Process Capability**

Process Standard Deviation

$$\hat{\sigma} = \frac{\bar{R}}{d_2}$$

$$= \frac{3.75}{2.326}$$

$$= \textbf{1.61}$$

The team again consulted the table shown in Step 3 to find the value for d_2, based on a sample size of n = 5.

C_p

Spec = 6 ±3

LSL = 6 − 3 = 3

USL = 6 + 3 = 9

$$C_p = \frac{USL - LSL}{6\hat{\sigma}}$$

$$= \frac{9 - 3}{6\,(1.61)}$$

$$= \frac{6}{9.66}$$

$$= \textbf{0.621}$$

Since C_p is < 1.0, the team determined that they were processing requisitions outside the desired management objective. The process currently was not capable.

Since the team knew C_p compared only the process spread, they decided to also look at C_{pk}, which would take into account the centering of the process.

$$C_{pl} = \frac{\bar{\bar{X}} - LSL}{3\hat{\sigma}}$$

$$= \frac{5.94 - 3}{3\,(1.61)}$$

$$= \frac{2.94}{4.83}$$

$$= \textbf{0.609}$$

$$C_{pu} = \frac{USL - \bar{\bar{X}}}{3\hat{\sigma}}$$

$$= \frac{9 - 5.94}{3\,(1.61)}$$

$$= \frac{3.06}{4.83}$$

$$= \textbf{0.634}$$

Since C_{pl} and C_{pu} are almost equal, the process is almost centered. However, if:

$$C_{pk} = min (C_{pl}, C_{pu})$$
$$= min (0.609, 0.634)$$
$$= \mathbf{0.609}$$
$$C_{pk} < 1.0$$

Then: requisitions are being processed outside of the management objective.

The team decided to construct a Histogram to get a picture and calculate the percentage of requisitions not meeting the requirement.

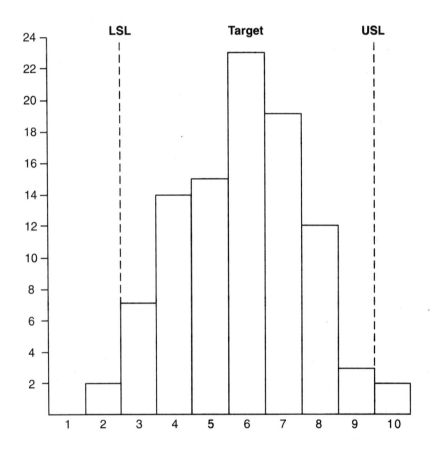

Percent outside of requirement was 4 / 100 = 4%

The team decided to focus on how they could reduce the variation in the amount of processing time. However, since they could process some requisitions in under the management objective, they thought they would also see if they could shift the process downward and subsequently change the management objective to be that requisitions were processed faster.

▶ **Learning Activity**

Conditions:

Normally, before a team can determine the capability of a process, the team must be sure the process is stable. By using a Control Chart, the team can determine whether or not the process is stable. However, *for this exercise* **only**, keep in mind the following conditions:

1. *Assume* the individual data points for Machines A and B come from stable processes.

2. The number of data points (10) for both machines is purposely small for ease of calculation. Under normal circumstances, 10 data points are not enough to determine process capability. Use industry standards for the minimum number of data points you will need.

3. The calculated standard deviation, *s*, for the individual data points, can be substituted for $\hat{\sigma}$.

Learning Activity Questions:

1. Are both Machines A and B capable of meeting the customer requirement?

2. How does the performance of Machine A and Machine B compare to one another?

3. What action needs to be taken?

Bright Ideas Team Investigation:

Under the three conditions listed above, the *Bright Ideas* team needed to calculate the mean and standard deviation for each machine, since these statistics are necessary to calculate process capability. The *Bright Ideas* team used these formulas:

$$\overline{X} = \frac{\Sigma\,(X_i)}{n} \qquad s = \sqrt{\frac{\Sigma\,(X_i - \overline{X})^2}{n-1}} \qquad C_p = \frac{USL - LSL}{6\hat{\sigma}}$$

where Σ is the Greek symbol for summation, X_i represents the individual data points, n is equal to the sample size, and $\hat{\sigma}$, estimated process standard deviation, is substituted with *s*, sample standard deviation.

Machine A

$$\overline{X}_A = \frac{98 + 95 + 96 + 95 + 93 + 95 + 99 + 93 + 95 + 96}{10}$$

$$= \frac{955}{10}$$

$$= 95.5$$

$$s_A = \sqrt{\frac{\begin{array}{c}(98-95.5)^2 + (95-95.5)^2 + (96-95.5)^2 + (95-95.5)^2 + (93-95.5)^2 \\ + (95-95.5)^2 + (99-95.5)^2 + (93-95.5)^2 + (95-95.5)^2 + (96-95.5)^2\end{array}}{10-1}}$$

$$= \sqrt{\frac{(2.5)^2 + (-0.5)^2 + (0.5)^2 + (-0.5)^2 + (-2.5)^2 + (-0.5)^2 + (3.5)^2 + (-2.5)^2 + (-0.5)^2 + (.05)^2}{9}}$$

$$= \sqrt{\frac{6.25 + 0.25 + 0.25 + 0.25 + 6.25 + 0.25 + 12.25 + 6.25 + 0.25 + 0.25}{9}}$$

$$= \sqrt{\frac{32.50}{9}}$$

$$= \sqrt{3.6111}$$

$$= 1.90$$

$$C_{pA} = \frac{105 - 95}{6\,(1.90)}$$

$$= \frac{10}{11.4}$$

$$= 0.877$$

Since $C_{pA} = 0.877$, which is less than 1.0, Machine A *is not* capable of meeting the customer requirement. The variation exceeds that allowed under the requirement. Further, since the process is centered near the lower specification, the process is making defective product. **(Answer to question 1.)**

Machine B

$$\overline{X}_B = \frac{98 + 99 + 101 + 98 + 100 + 101 + 99 + 100 + 99 + 99}{10}$$

$$= \frac{994}{10}$$

$$= 99.4$$

$$s_B = \sqrt{\frac{\begin{array}{c}(98-99.4)^2 + (99-99.4)^2 + (101-99.4)^2 + (98-99.4)^2 + (100-99.4)^2 \\ + (101-99.4)^2 + (99-99.4)^2 + (100-99.4)^2 + (99-99.4)^2 + (99-99.4)^2\end{array}}{10-1}}$$

$$= \sqrt{\frac{(-1.4)^2 + (-0.4)^2 + (1.6)^2 + (-1.4)^2 + (0.6)^2 + (1.6)^2 + (-0.4)^2 + (0.6)^2 + (-0.4)^2 + (-0.4)^2}{9}}$$

$$= \sqrt{\frac{1.96 + 0.16 + 2.56 + 1.96 + 0.36 + 2.56 + 0.16 + 0.36 + 0.16 + 0.16}{9}}$$

$$= \sqrt{\frac{10.4}{9}}$$

$$= \sqrt{1.1556}$$

$$= 1.07$$

$$C_{pB} = \frac{105 - 95}{6\,(1.07)}$$

$$= \frac{10}{6.42}$$

$$= \mathbf{1.56}$$

Since $C_{pB} = 1.56$, which is greater than 1.0, Machine B *is* capable of meeting the customer requirement for allowable variation. Since the process is nearly centered within the customer requirement, no defective material is being made. **(Answer to question 1.)**

These two outcomes can be visualized with the following frequency distribution:

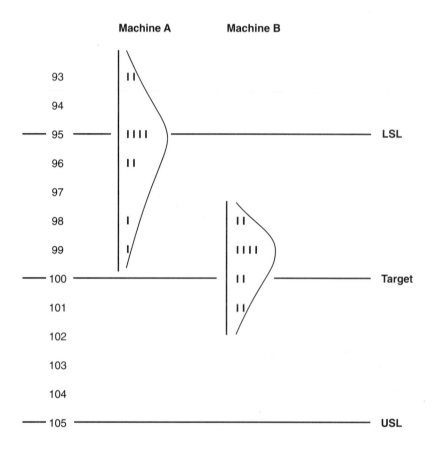

The *Bright Ideas* team determined that light bulbs from Machine B were on target and not producing defectives. Machine B was meeting the customer requirement and should be left alone. Machine A, however, was targeted low and making defective product. **(Answer to question 2.)**

Action:

Even if the *Bright Ideas* team is able to center the process for Machine A, the variation is still too excessive. The team needs to study how to change the current process for Machine A to reduce the variation as well as re-target it. They need to use Machine B as a model to understand differences and similarities between the two machines, and work to bring the level of performance of Machine A up to the level of Machine B. Thereby, this will get both machines performing at the customer requirement. **(Answer to question 3.)**

OVERVIEW

Radar Chart

Rating organization performance

IS THIS THE RIGHT TOOL? ASK . . .

▶ Would a user-friendly graphic help the team assess the strengths and weaknesses of the organization, department, or a process?

▶ Do you need team consensus on where the organization currently is (a baseline) versus performance goals?

▶ Would a visual representation of current organizational status help the team communicate with customers and other teams?

▶ Does your team or your department need a simple, visual tool to track annual progress toward achieving goals?

STEPS AT A GLANCE

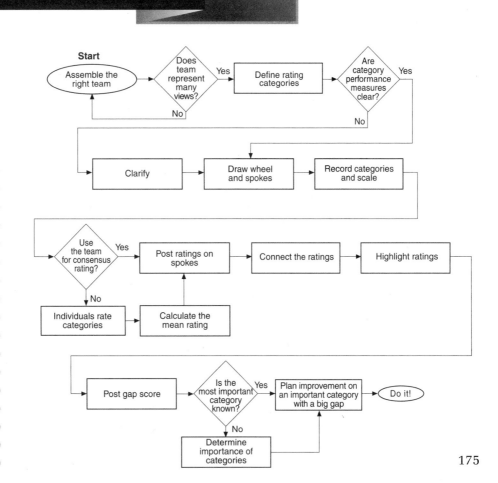

175

Radar Chart

RADAR CHART

Q. **Must data be collected for each category in order for a Radar Chart to represent a valid assessment?**

A. The Radar Chart can be completed subjectively or objectively. Sometimes, especially in strategic or hoshin planning, a team progresses from an Affinity to a Radar Chart. The Radar Chart then represents the collective knowledge and experience of the team, resulting in a subjective yet valid assessment, and should be presented to others in this manner. A Radar Chart gives the team a consensus graphic of their understanding of where they are. If there is a wide variation in scoring, more information is needed.

Q. **How many categories can be represented?**

A. There is no minimum or maximum number of categories. The chart should be based on the number of performance dimensions that must be rated. The team should be able to read the chart and be able to evaluate the categories chosen. Five to 10 categories is most common.

FACILITATION ESSENTIALS

If: **A team has difficulty reaching consensus on a rating . . .**

Then: ▶ Have each person rate the category and show the range and average of the ratings. Determine causes of wide variations.

▶ Gather more data and complete work at the next meeting.

If: **There is a reluctance to honestly rate categories; everything appears to be rosy . . .**

Then: ▶ Reiterate the purpose of the Radar Chart.

▶ Portray gaps as improvement opportunities.

▶ Declare the Radar Chart a "Draft." Ask the team members to distribute copies of the draft chart to coworkers, who work in the same department or unit respective to the team member, so the coworkers can anonymously rate each category on the chart. Team members should review the draft charts returned by coworkers, make modifications to one draft, and bring it to the next team meeting.

If: **Team members disagree over the meaning of performance within certain categories . . .**

Then: ▶ Review the definitions of the problematic categories. Ask team members to privately review and think about how they would respond to the following statements for each category in question:

1) We would fail in (category name) if _____.

2) We would succeed in (category name) if _____.

Now ask team members to write on a flipchart their responses to both statements. If the team can agree on a statement that expresses either minimum or maximum performance, then the "middle ground" of performance will become much easier to assess.

▶ If the categories were generated from an Affinity diagram, display the full Affinity nearby and refer to the items that "created" the header category.

176

The Radar Chart is generally easy to introduce and teams warm up to it quickly. To give team members an idea of what Radar Charts are like, try the following exercise:

1. Work in pairs.

2. Ask each person to share his or her New Year's resolutions or personal goals such as those related to exercise, personal learning, time management, and so on.

3. Have each person draw a circle, with one spoke representing each goal. Then ask each person to rate his or her current performance based on a scale of 1–10, with "1" as the low score and "10" as the high score.

4. Ask people in each pair to share their personal Radar Charts with each other. Give each person the option to share his/her chart with the entire team.

Suggested issues for Radar Charts:
1. TQM implementation progress
2. Self-assessment using Malcolm Baldrige Criteria
3. Progress on team, department, or unit annual goals
4. Baseline for elements of vision or mission statements

INCIDENTALLY

The Radar Chart is also called the Spider Diagram because the completed chart often looks like a spider web. One company took that name a step further and called it the "arachnid chart"! The term "Radar Chart" comes from the chart's resemblance to patterns on a radar screen.

STEP 1 ASSEMBLING THE RIGHT TEAM

MJII p. 137

▶ **Team Composition**

The performance to be measured determines the composition of the team. For example:

– If the Radar Chart will be used to measure current performance against elements of the vision or strategic plan, the team should consist of *executives*.

– If the Radar Chart will be used to baseline current performance on annual goals or for a Malcolm Baldrige self-assessment, the team should consist of *people from within the department* that is being assessed.

– If the Radar Chart will be used to baseline current processes or measure improvement, the team should be made up of *people who are most knowledgeable about, and responsible for the process*. These are people who work within the process.

▶ **Check the Member Mix**

Every team measuring performances must have members representing key functions and/or major steps in a process. This will ensure a variety of perspectives and thorough knowledge of the performance. A quick consensus on all ratings may indicate that the team does not have a thorough mix from all areas of the performance being measured.

STEP 2 DEFINING RATING CATEGORIES

MJII p. 137

▶ **Categories that Work**

For organizational assessments try:

– Malcolm Baldrige Criteria

– Dr. Deming's 14 Points

– Dr. Juran's or Phil Crosby's Steps for Improvement

– Supplier certification criteria

– State or local quality award criteria (often based on Baldrige)

For strategic planning try:

– Vision and mission elements

– Customer wants and needs

– Last year's goals

For process improvement try:

– Customer wants and needs

– Organizational quality indicators

– Benchmarked criteria, best in class for the process

▶ **Defining Performance Within the Categories**

Do's

- When using established assessment criteria such as supplier certification or Malcolm Baldrige Criteria, be prepared to clarify the meaning of the subcategories for the team.

- Have members of the team imagine what the organization would look like if the category were completely satisfied, with the organization achieving a "10." Get consensus.

- Have members of the team describe complete non-performance or performance. Get consensus.

- Clarify whether data will be used for rating and what data will be used.

Don'ts

- Don't let yourself, or someone else as the leader, establish the performance definitions of the categories for the team.

- Don't let the categories "take on a life of their own" and develop new meanings as the team fills in the chart.

MJII p. 138 **STEP 3 CONSTRUCTING THE CHART**

▶ **Plan Ahead**

It is helpful to prepare the wheel in advance. An even number of categories is easier to draw than an odd number.

▶ **Colors**

For the midpoints of each spoke: Using a color marker, put a small mark at the midpoint of each spoke to keep ratings in proportion to each other. This is a good idea because no matter how beautifully the wheel is drawn on a flipchart, without a compass, computer output of a perfectly drawn wheel, or other tool that allows you to draw a perfect circle, your Radar Chart will not be in proportion!

For the ratings: Use a different color marker or adhesive label to indicate the rating of each category.

▶ **Naming Categories**

Assigning a key word or phrase to each category helps the team stay focused and is usually easier than using a letter or number code.

▶ **Rating Scale**

Remember that the scale starts at zero at the center of the chart and increases to 10, (or whatever the highest number of the rating scale is), to indicate full performance, which is 100%, at the outer ring of the wheel.

STEP 4 RATING PERFORMANCE

MJII pp. 138–139

▶ **Choosing a Rating Method**

You can choose to have each person individually rate each category or have everyone work together to discuss and come to consensus on the ratings for each category. If you choose the first method, you can get a team rating by averaging together the individual scores.

Use a scale of 0–10 for consistency. 10 = excellent, 5 = satisfactory, 0 = non-functioning.

▶ **Team Consensus:** If the team is performing well, using a team consensus method will work. As the coach, you should review each category and ask for a rating of "where we are." The team should discuss the category until they agree on a rating.

▶ **Individual Rating:** A different method may be used to involve team members on an individual basis. Have each person rate the items and post the individual ratings on a large wheel. Use different colored adhesive labels, pens, or symbols to mark the individual ratings on the spokes of the wheel. Take an average of the individual ratings for each category and prominently mark the ratings on each spoke.

STEP 5 CONNECTING THE RATINGS

MJII p. 139

▶ **Go for It!**

Connect the dots (or tick marks) and you have a visual representation of current performance and the gaps between current performance and full performance. The current performance is represented by the team rating dot or symbol, and the gap is the area between the team rating point and the outside of the circle.

▶ **Calculate the Performance Gap**

Generally, the "gap score" is used to compare performance. To calculate the gap score for each category, subtract the average of the individual scores or the team consensus score (for that category) from the full performance number, which is often "10."

▶ **Complete the Picture**

Fill in the area inside the lines connecting the dots (or tick marks) to make the visual effect complete. Write the gap score near each spoke if this helps communicate the results.

STEP 6   INTERPRETING THE RESULTS

▶ **Addressing the Right Issue**

Should teams always address the biggest gap? Not necessarily. Use the Radar Chart in conjunction with other tools, such as the Interrelationship Digraph or Prioritization Matrix, to determine where to focus the team's energy. For example, when the Radar Chart is used with an ID, each gap score is generally multiplied by the number of outgoing arrows from that category item. This focuses the attention on making progress in the area that has the poorest performance, and that will have the greatest impact if addressed. Likewise, if the Radar Chart is used in combination with the Prioritization Matrices tool, the gap score for each category can be multiplied by the decimal value for that category in the summary matrix. As in the combined use of the Radar Chart and the ID (very common), this combination with the Prioritization Matrices (not very common), focuses attention on central issues that have the most significant performance gap to fill.

▶ **Tracking Annual Progress**

The Radar Chart can also be used to indicate annual goals. Add a circle on the spoke to show where you want to be in one year. Review at the end of the year and mark your progress. The Radar Chart then becomes a dynamic performance record.

EXAMPLE

First-Year Progress on Five-Year Plans

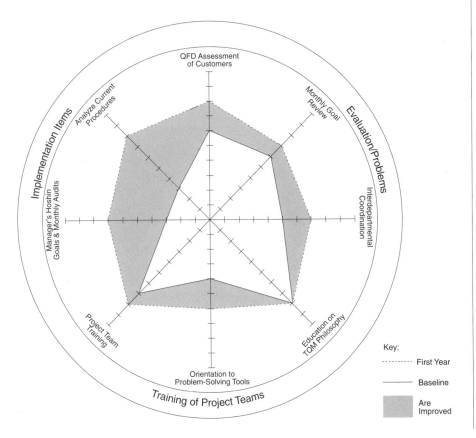

181

Vision Elements in the Development of a Strategic Plan

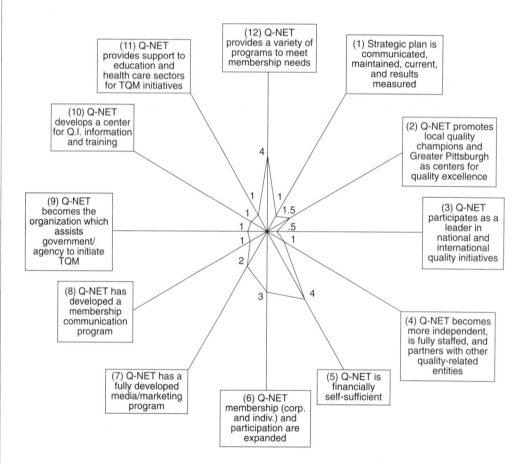

(12) Q-NET provides a variety of programs to meet membership needs

(11) Q-NET provides support to education and health care sectors for TQM initiatives

(1) Strategic plan is communicated, maintained, current, and results measured

(10) Q-NET develops a center for Q.I. information and training

(2) Q-NET promotes local quality champions and Greater Pittsburgh as centers for quality excellence

(9) Q-NET becomes the organization which assists government/ agency to initiate TQM

(3) Q-NET participates as a leader in national and international quality initiatives

(8) Q-NET has developed a membership communication program

(4) Q-NET becomes more independent, is fully staffed, and partners with other quality-related entities

(7) Q-NET has a fully developed media/marketing program

(5) Q-NET is financially self-sufficient

(6) Q-NET membership (corp. and indiv.) and participation are expanded

*Information provided courtesy of
The Greater Pittsburgh Quest for Quality Network*

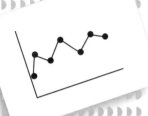

Run Chart
Tracking trends

IS THIS THE RIGHT TOOL? ASK . . .

▶ Do you need to show changes in data over time?

▶ Are you unsure of how to use the Control Chart, but need to collect some initial data?

▶ Do you want to measure one variable over time?

▶ Is the data that you are collecting sequential?

▶ Is the measured activity believed to have regular cycles?

STEPS AT A GLANCE

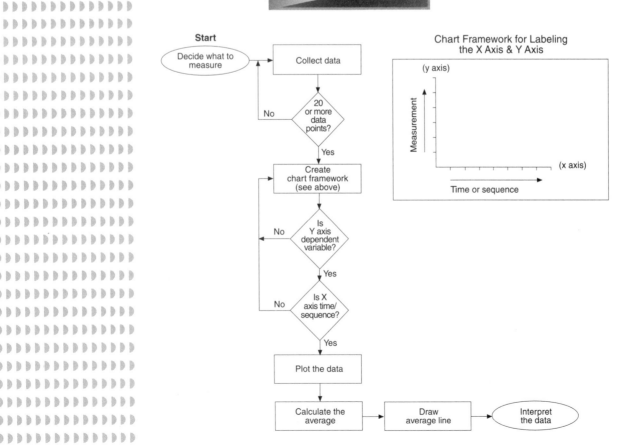

183

RUN CHART

Q. Why not just use a Control Chart?

A. It's really a judgment call. It depends on how critical it is to react quickly to unusual changes in the data. Run Charts are effective when it's important to detect and respond to gradual changes in trend data. However, if it is essential to react quickly to statistically significant variation in the data, then a Control Chart is appropriate.

A Run Chart can also be used as a simple first alternative to understanding statistically significant trends. For example, the various tests for trends, (see the Scatter Diagram chapter), allow a team to make a statistically safe bet that a run of data points is not happening by pure chance. Like a Control Chart, the Run Chart helps a team avoid reacting, (and possibly overreacting), to chance data. It may be appropriate to do a Run Chart for a process that is creating problems to look for significant trends first. If none are detected, then more detailed analysis using a Control Chart can be done. This is likely to pick up more subtle variation in the data.

Q. Can more than one variable be measured and represented on a single Run Chart?

A. Yes, but the *unit* of measure must be consistent. For example, a Run Chart may simultaneously show sales over the last 12 months of Products A, B, and C or sales by month over the last three years of Product A. However, a single Run Chart can't show both sales and unit values. Choose either dollars or units.

Sales Analysis of Three Types of Bicycles

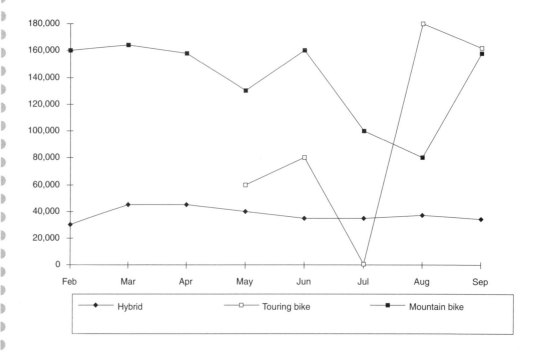

184

If: **The team wants to redraw the average line because they have fresh data . . .**

Then: Ask the team if anything has changed in the process. Are there any special conditions that didn't exist at the time of construction of the first Run Chart that exist now? If the answer to both of these questions is "no," then there is no need to recalculate the line.

If: **The team is frustrated that "nothing" is being revealed in their Run Chart . . .**

Then: Ask the team what the data points really reflect. Are they the average of several data points taken for that day? Are they taken from several subgroups that should be broken out and stratified? Is the measure of time appropriate? Should it be hourly instead of daily? Or vice-versa? Are any groupings of time significant to the process? Are there any breaks for shifts? Is end-of-the-month activity significantly different? Keep questions on consistency and accuracy of data collection for last so that the team can explore the data and sequencing of the data completely.

LEARNING ACTIVITY

To get the team to see a different perspective:

1. Work in groups of 4-6 people.

2. Have a pile of clippings of Run Charts taken from *USA Today*, *The Wall Street Journal*, a local paper, and any other publications from which you can harvest a well constructed Run Chart.

3. Have someone from each team select two unrelated Run Charts from the pile.

4. Ask the members on each team to see what information they can obtain from the first Run Chart. What was being measured? What was the sequence or time interval? Other observations?

5. Now have the teams repeat Step 4 for the second Run Chart.

6. Compare the learnings from the two Run Charts. Were there any significant differences in construction? What were the similarities? How did these observations help "make things visible"?

A TEAM'S EXPERIENCE . . .

> "The tool helped the team to see how it was doing on a monthly basis in reducing the time to make a decision about eligibility."
>
> Paula McIntosh

Written by Paula McIntosh, Georgia State Department of Human Resources, Division of Rehabilitation Services

What was the problem?

A group of employees, who were responsible for the process of determining which applicants were eligible for government-sponsored rehabilitation services, was formed into a team to analyze the process. The process required excessive documentation of decision making; on average it took 292 days in one of eight districts. Recent legislative action mandated it take no more than 60 days.

Who was on the team?

The team was comprised of rehabilitation counselors and a unit supervisor, all of whom were process workers under the sponsorship of a district director, the process owner.

How long did the process take?

Using historical data, it took the team several hours to create the first Run Chart, which we began to use as a tool for tracking the performance of the process. After the initial chart was created, the team updated it monthly. This took the team about 1 hour to update the data for each of the eight districts.

What did we learn?

With caseloads of 100+ people, process workers had no idea from day to day or month to month how they were doing in meeting the new timeliness measurement. The tool helped the team to see how it was doing on a monthly basis in reducing the time to make a decision about eligibility.

How was the team affected?

The team was very interested in the monthly updates to the Run Chart and began to ask how they could track the process daily by process workers, so as to give timely attention during the process to individual cases. Team members had to learn about variation in order to interpret the data and avoid overreaction to variation and understand when genuine progress was being made. Watching the trend line continue a downward course was encouraging to the team.

PAULA MCINTOSH,
QUALITY ADVISOR

What else did we use?

The team used a Flowchart to map and understand the process so that they could decide where time could best be saved. As the team discussed ways for individual process workers to track their own data, they used an Affinity Diagram to consider the issues for individuals who were tracking their own timeliness standard.

What was the conclusion?

With the Flowchart, we pinpointed the number of "wait" times and "decision points" in the process, any of which could add time to the final eligibility decision.

What were the results?

The timeliness of the eligibility decision was improved by 70 percent. Further improvement requires a process improvement team to drive cycle time down further. A team was formed to redesign the process to better meet customer expectations. The work is in progress.

Average Number of Days
for Determining Eligibility for Services

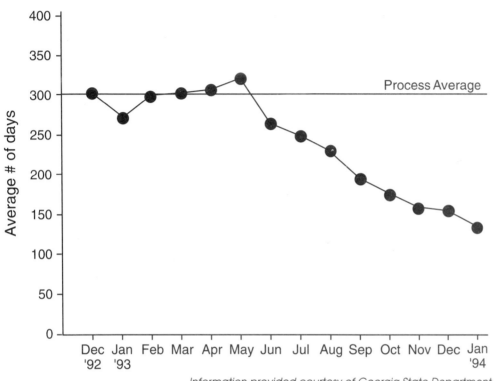

*Information provided courtesy of Georgia State Department
of Human Resources, Division of Rehabilitation Services*

Note: Eligibility requirements changed in May, making it much simpler for the department staff to make determinations. The trend is statistically significant because there are six or or more consecutive points declining.

Run Chart

STEP 1 DECIDING WHAT TO MEASURE

MJII p. 141

The team should ask two questions:

- What are we measuring?
- What unit of measure are we utilizing?

Consensus of the team must be reached on both of these questions.

STEP 2 GATHERING THE DATA

MJII p. 141

The data points collected must be in accordance with the two questions asked in Step 1. Although a trend can be seen with as few as six data points, either falling or rising consecutively, it would be highly unusual to see this immediately. Generally, having fewer than 20 data points makes trends difficult to see. A good rule of thumb for a Run Chart is 20–25 data points.

STEP 3 CREATING THE GRAPH

MJII pp. 141–142

▶ **Drawing the Vertical Line (Y Axis)**

The y axis will show the scale of the dependent variable that the team is measuring. The team will have to ask three questions in drawing the scale:

- What is the unit of measure for this variable?
- What is the range of the data?
- What increments should be used for the scale?

The team should keep these things in mind:

- The y axis should be drawn to cover approximately 1.5 times the range of the data.
- Remember to label the unit of measure. (Is it dollars or thousands of dollars?)
- Are the increments clear and consistent? (Is it obvious that each increment reflects 10%? 1000 dollars? 5 miles?)

▶ **Drawing the Horizontal Line (X Axis)**

The x axis will show the scale of the independent variable, which is time or sequence. The team has two questions for drawing the scale:

- What is the unit of time or sequencing used?
- What increments should be used for the scale? (Even though the team may have determined that months is the unit of time, the increment on the x axis may be in half months.)

The team should keep these things in mind:

- It is not necessary to draw beyond the time or sequence range.
- Label the unit of measure for time or sequencing. (Not every unit of measure needs to be recorded. For example, every other month can be written, and hash or tick marks can be used to indicate the months in between.
- Make sure the increments are clear and consistent.

STEP 4 PLOTTING THE DATA

Transfer the data to the Run Chart. If this is the first time the team is collecting this data, versus updating an existing data set, calculate the average or mean from the data points collected. Then draw the average line. The average line is helpful as a reference point for interpreting data.

STEP 5 INTERPRETING THE CHART

▶ **Look for Points and Patterns:** Remember these rules of thumb when the team is interpreting the Run Chart. Variation is significant when you see:

- – Nine consecutive points on one side of the average

- – Six consecutive points, increasing or decreasing

- – Fourteen consecutive points that alternate up and down

- – Repeated patterns based on a predictable cycle, i.e., seasons, peak business periods

▶ **Look at the Average:** As the team begins to "read the tea leaves," look at the average line. If the value of the average is a performance level that ordinarily would be desirable in your organization, but the data points bounce to very high and very low extremes, the actual performance is not reflected in the average line.

▶ **Look at the Time Unit:** Check to see if a pattern is revealed through the units of time on the horizontal line (x axis). If the team has drawn the scale for the days in a month, perhaps a pattern might become clearer if the days of the week were specified (for example, Friday night at the Emergency Room). It might also be helpful to show the duration of shifts. Is limiting the scale to single-day units obscuring a trend or pattern that might be discovered through increments of hours of the work day?

Finally, remember to look for subgroups. Are there two or more subgroups reflected in the data points that need to be broken out or stratified?

▶ **Holding the Gains**

A Run Chart is helpful not only in the initial analysis of a team's project, but also in standardizing and holding the gains of any improvement efforts. It becomes a strong tool in the Check and Act phases of the PDCA Cycle.

EXAMPLE

Miles Run Per Week
of Training for Boston Marathon

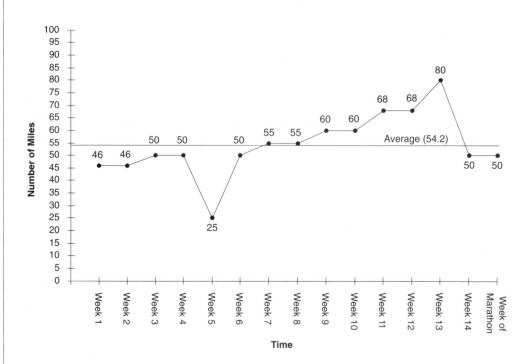

Analysis: (1) Dip in Week 5 is a result of getting the flu.

(2) Increased 10–15% every 2 weeks as part of training plan.

(3) Took one 22 mile run 2 weeks before marathon, which raised total to 80.

(4) Tapered off in last 2 weeks to rest before marathon.

Scatter Diagram

*Measuring relationships
between variables*

IS THIS THE RIGHT TOOL? ASK . . .

▶ Does your team need to statistically test a hunch about a possible cause and effect connection between two factors?

▶ Has a root cause been agreed upon that now needs to be tested with data to confirm that it actually causes or influences the original problem?

▶ Can pairs of data be gathered that simultaneously show the level of both variables at a specific point in time?

▶ Is there a pair of factors that seem to rise together, fall together, or move together in opposite directions that need to be confirmed with data?

▶ Are there at least 50 pairs of data to plot?

STEPS AT A GLANCE

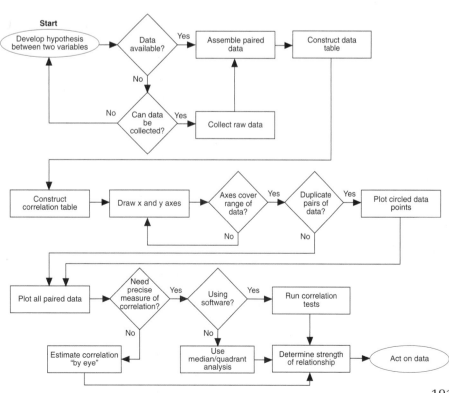

Q. **If two factors or variables show a positive correlation, (one factor increases as another factor increases), or a negative correlation, (one factor decreases as another factor increases), does one cause the other?**

A. No. The Scatter Diagram can only show the strength of a relationship, *not* its causality. The Scatter shows the strength of a relationship between two variables by graphically showing how tightly the pairs of data approximate a straight line. A straight line represents the strongest possible relationship between two factors since this would mean that one factor would increase one unit, (e.g., temperature), as the other factor increased by one unit, (e.g., BTU, or British Thermal Unit). The increase does not need to be one for one, but must be proportionate. Therefore, as the data looks more like a straight line, the *more likely* it is that one affects the other. Remember, statistics deals with probability, not certainty.

Q. **Is a positive correlation more important or desirable than a negative correlation?**

A. No, both are equally noteworthy! *Positive* or *negative* only refers to the direction of the relationship, not its desirability. For example: a study of the causes of driving fatalities could find a **positive correlation** between average speed (x axis) and the number of fatalities per 1000 miles driven (y axis). This *positive correlation* would mean that the average number of fatalities is likely to *increase* as the average driving speed *increases*. The data would be clustered, beginning from the lower left portion of the diagram, up to the upper right portion of the diagram. The same study could show a **negative correlation** between the average percentage of drivers using seat belts (x axis) and the average number of fatalities per 1000 miles driven (y axis). This *negative correlation* would mean that the average number of fatalities is likely to *decrease* as the percentage of seat belt usage *increases*. The data would be clustered, beginning from the upper left portion of the diagram, down to the lower right portion of the diagram. Remember to avoid the traditional connotations to either "positive," or "negative."

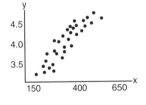

Positive Correlation
An increase in *y* may depend on an increase in *x*.

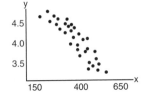

Negative Correlation
A decrease in *y* may depend on an increase in *x*.

Q. **If no correlation will ever look like a "perfect" straight line, how can anyone tell how strong a relationship is?**

A. There is a whole range of tests to show the strength of a correlation. For many purposes the "eyeball test" will suffice to distinguish between those factors that have a minimal relationship (loose patterned clustering) and those that appear to be have a strong relationship (tight patterned clustering). However, when conducting formal experiments it is usually necessary to perform standard correlation tests. The most common ones are described in this chapter.

If: **The team wants to use a Scatter Diagram with too few data points (i.e., less than 40–50 pairs) . . .**

Then: Plot the data to see if there is any clustering at all. If the data points are spread randomly, then agree to collect more pairs of data in sets of 10 to see if the lack of clustering continues. Review the Scatter Diagram after plotting each new data set to know when you can stop collecting data. It will become more clear with each review whether or not a tighter-formed pattern or cluster is emerging. The same process of collecting new data and reviewing the diagram also applies if the initial data show very tight clustering. In this case, observe whether the tight clustering continues or if the data points begin to spread more widely around the center line.

If: **"Experts" of the area being investigated reject the results of the Scatter Diagram because it flies in the face of their opinions (and possibly their experience) . . .**

Then: Examine as a team the *definition*, *collection*, and *analysis* of the paired data, by asking:

"What were the operational definitions that we used for both variables?"

"Were they clear and accurate?"

"Were the data on each variable collected consistently and validly?"

"What tests for correlation did we use?" "Were they interpreted correctly?"

Confirm the accuracy and integrity of these phases. As the team (including the "experts") signs off on each of these phases, list it on a flipchart as "approved." Resolve any challenges or questions when they are raised. Be prepared to collect the data again if the objections are legitimate. Remember, the experts' experience may be correct. Don't assume that objections are obstructionist and that the absolute truth always and only lies in the data.

If everyone agrees to the validity of each phase of *defining*, *collecting*, and *analyzing* the data, but one, some, or all reject the conclusion, ask those who reject the conclusion to suggest two alternative explanations for the results of the Scatter Diagram. For each alternative explanation, agree on at least one way of *objectively* testing it. Assign one or more team members to conduct the test and give a report at the next meeting. Be sure to choose data that can be easily and quickly collected.

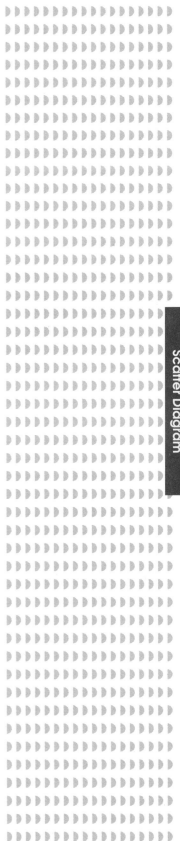

Scatter Diagram

Scatter Diagram

This activity is based on the detailed example shown at the end of this chapter. You will be walking the group through the example, step by step, to construct, then interpret a Scatter Diagram. To prepare for this activity, it will be helpful for you to copy the supporting data and diagram illustrations to distribute to each "member pair" in the group.

1. Ask team members to form pairs. Ask each pair to draw a horizontal line (x axis) and a vertical line (y axis) on a sheet of flipchart paper. Label the x axis "Height (Inches)," and the y axis "Weight (Pounds)."

2. Provide each team member with a copy of the data set shown below. (The same data set is also shown in the Height and Weight Table under Step 1 of the "Example" section at the end of this chapter.

Number	Height (inches)	Weight (pounds)	Number	Height (inches)	Weight (pounds)
1	83	350	26	79	240
2	73	220	27	81	230
3	73	200	28	68	170
4	71	180	29	74	210
5	75	210	30	80	270
6	71	180	31	82	280
7	69	190	32	68	160
8	83	250	33	83	220
9	73	200	34	82	350
10	67	180	35	79	230
11	68	190	36	81	250
12	84	290	37	76	210
13	79	250	38	81	230
14	80	230	39	83	280
15	80	220	40	71	170
16	85	240	41	79	240
17	81	240	42	81	240
18	79	270	43	72	180
19	81	230	44	77	200
20	77	200	45	69	170
21	71	180	46	80	220
22	85	290	47	73	200
23	71	180	48	83	300
24	73	200	49	74	190
25	81	240	50	71	180

3. Ask each pair of team members to create a Scatter Diagram, using the scales shown on the illustration below.

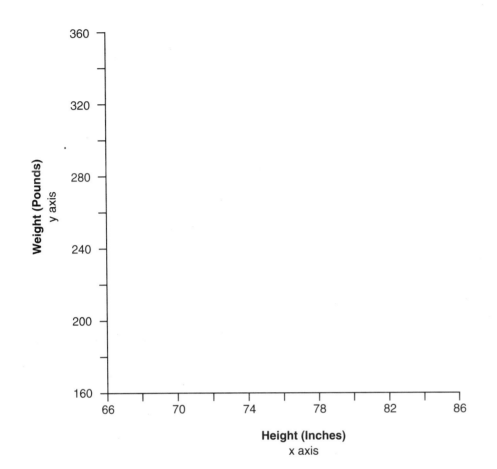

4. Ask each pair to interpret the Scatter Diagram by answering the four questions listed below. (You may want to write these questions on a flipchart.) When the pairs are finished discussing the questions, bring the whole group together and review the answers.

Question 1: Is there a relationship between "Height" and "Weight" in this data set?

Question 2: How strong or weak is the relationship?

Question 3: Does increased height *cause* increased weight? Why or why not?

Question 4: From what population(s) of people was this sample drawn? (Ask them to guess.)

The answers are on the last page of this chapter in the "Coach's Answer Key."

> "The Scatter Diagram helps teams to separate facts from feelings. It helps to uncover the important factors that drive processes toward consistently good performance."
>
> Tony Borgen

Written by Tony Borgen, Hamilton Standard

What was the problem?

The continuous improvement training team noticed that the approval rating of the weekly total quality training sessions had slipped significantly on several occasions. Various team members "knew" the factors that could change the rating, but had no quantitative evidence.

Who was on the team?

The team was made up of four trainers who were experienced in presenting the total quality sessions.

How long did the process take?

The brainstorming session where we arrived at the factor (average experience of the training team) that we thought was important lasted about 1 hour. Developing the spreadsheet and inputing the data was an individual task that took about 8 hours.

What did we learn?

The Scatter Diagram took the factor that the team members "knew" or at least suspected was important and showed graphically that it was. This put the discussion on the level of fact instead of feelings.

How was the team affected?

After using the Scatter Diagram, the team became more aware that many factors may have an effect on the outcome of a training session, and that the Scatter could be very useful in investigating these possible effects. Also, the fact that a Control Chart led to the use of the Scatter Diagram gave the team an appreciation for how powerful the tools are when they are used together.

What else did we use?

We went from a Control Chart (see the Hamilton Standard Case Study in the Control Chart chapter or page 51 of *The Memory Jogger™ II*) to brainstorming, to a spreadsheet for data reduction, and then a Scatter Diagram.

TONY BORGEN,
TEAM MEMBER

What was the conclusion?

The Scatter Diagram at first glance showed that there was no correlation between trainer experience and rating. Upon further study of the diagram, however, it was noted that the variability in ratings greatly decreased once the average experience of the training team exceeded 350 days.

What were the results?

We decided that the training sessions would have more consistent ratings if the average experience of the training team presenting the session was above 350 days. The recommendation was made to bring new trainers on board more slowly instead of the previous practice of starting a large group of new trainers every six months. This practice would keep the average experience at a more steady number above 350 days.

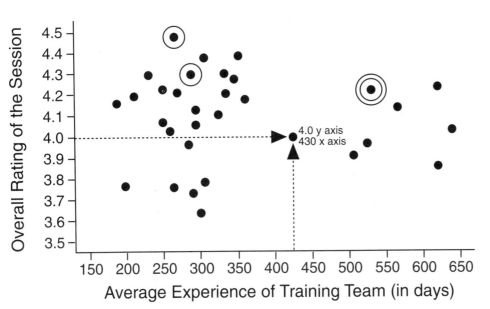

**Training Experience
and Course Session Ratings**

Information provided courtesy of Hamilton Standard

Scatter Diagram

Scatter Diagram

▶ **Confirming Root Causes: Three Popular Methods**

The Scatter Diagram is typically used after a team consensus has developed around the most likely root causes of a problem.

Described below are three methods for getting team consensus on the most likely root causes of a problem. The first two methods are *subjective* because they are based on getting team members' opinions. The third method (Scatter Diagram) is based on the comparison of two sets of variables. This method is *objective* because it is based on getting measurable confirmation of the root causes.

▶ **Confirming Root Causes with the Cause & Effect Diagram (Method 1):** For an example, look at the generic problem-solving/process-improvement model featured in *The Memory Jogger™ II*, pages 115–131. The Stop 'N Go Pizza team members discussed in Step 3 (MJII page 119) their theories for what the root causes were for late pizza deliveries. After this "theorizing," the team chose to use the Cause & Effect Diagram (MJII page 120) to see if any pattern of causes would emerge. (Then the team would be able to confirm or rule out some of the possible root causes.) The Stop 'N Go Pizza team's action to use the Cause & Effect Diagram is a typical action for many real teams as well. Usually when a team is using a Cause & Effect Diagram, members can come to agreement on the root cause of a problem through discussion, which draws upon the experiences and insights of the team members.

▶ **Confirming Root Causes by Ranking or Voting (Method 2):** Teams can also confirm possible root causes by using a voting or ranking process to pinpoint the consensus root cause. (MJII pages 91–94 for a description of NGT/Multivoting.) This may be appropriate when consensus is difficult to attain or when there are no repeated patterns of causes in the Cause & Effect Diagram.

▶ **Confirming Root Causes with the Scatter Diagram (Method 3):** The combination of the two methods described above are usually adequate to confirm root causes. However, *the Scatter Diagram is most helpful, and even essential, in situations in which it is possible to get measurable confirmation of the root causes of the problem.*

Beyond the fact that it may be possible and desirable to collect confirming data, the Scatter Diagram is frequently used because *someone just doesn't buy into the root cause.* Someone on the team may challenge the rest of the team's agreement on the root cause. This person may disagree with the other team members on the grounds that the team's agreement reflects some very traditional assumptions.

For example: Several teachers have been discussing the reasons for the unusually poor grades given for a particular exam. Many of the teachers could initially "conclude" that the students just didn't put in enough study time. But what will the conclusion look like with some data? If the teachers gather data that will identify how much time each student spent studying for the exam, and combine each data point with the exam score of the student, they can use the Scatter Diagram to look more closely at whether their initial conclusion was valid or whether they were simply making a traditional assumption. The teachers could see from the diagram if there were an actual correlation between the two variables. If the student who studied for several hours was just as likely to fail as the student who summarized a few pages in the book, then it's likely that the explanation for the poor grades lies elsewhere.

The team could dig further by using a Pareto Chart to see whether there were certain exam questions answered incorrectly by a disproportionately large number of students.

STEP 2 DRAWING THE AXES

MJII p. 146

▶ When to Use a Correlation Table Instead of a Scatter Diagram

In general, use a correlation table when the team collects data that include a large number of *identical paired values*. In the Scatter Diagram such repeated values are simply circled as many times as they repeat in the data set. For example, if the same paired data appears five times it would be circled four times since the data point itself represents the first time that the data is recorded. This is fine when a particular reading is repeated 2–3 times, but it may be unwieldly if it's repeated 4–5 times. If this occurs in your data set, an option is to use a correlation table. This is a frequency table using the same vertical and horizontal axes as would be used in the Scatter Diagram. The graphic shown below is a correlation table. This table shows the same height and weight data that is used in the "Example" section of this chapter.

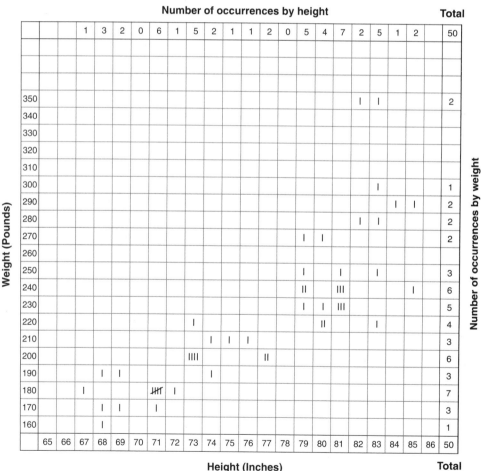

Number of occurrences by height — **Total**

Weight (Pounds) / Number of occurrences by weight / Height (Inches) / Total

Scatter Diagram

The Scatter Diagram below shows the result of plotting the data for the variable "Height" and the data for the variable "Weight." (The data was taken from the Height and Weight Table in Step 1 of the "Example.")

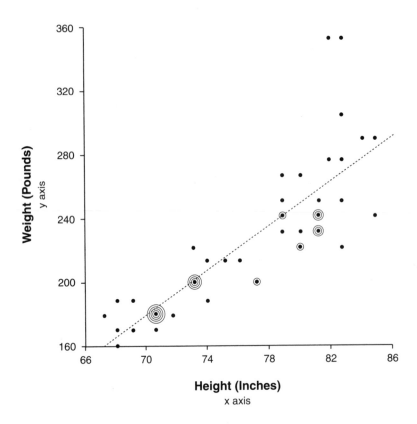

Why use a data table?

In every case a data table is constructed. A data table consists of columns in which paired data values are recorded. The variable names are listed at the top. The paired data points are transferred either directly to a finished Scatter Diagram or to a correlation table. (See an example of a correlation table in Step 2.)

Why use a correlation table?

It is not unusual to use a correlation table before constructing a finished Scatter Diagram. A correlation table is not only a convenient way to convert the data table to a finished Scatter Diagram, but it also provides an easy way to check all of the tabulations. Depending on the team's needs at the time, the table may be adequate to see the correlation pattern.

▶ **Determining the Strength of a Relationship**

This is where software can be of enormous help. *The Memory Jogger*™ Software automatically determines the strength of the relationship between two variables, as well as the confidence limits for "predicting" cause and effect. If the software is not available to you, there is a fairly simple analytical process that will help you determine the significance of the clustering. This process is described in Kaoru Ishikawa's book *Guide to Quality Control*, pages 92–93.

The following steps are based on the description in *Guide to Quality Control* for determining the strength of a relationship. The steps illustrate how to determine the strength of a relationship, in this case, between height and weight. The relationship between these two variables, height and weight, is used as the basis for the Learning Activity in this chapter, and also as an example to show the steps that lead up to and include the final diagram.

1. Calculate the median for the data plotted on the x axis (horizontal) and on the y axis (vertical). To calculate the median, use the method discussed in the Data Points chapter under the "Example" or on page 54 in *The Memory Jogger*™ *II*.

   In the height and weight example used in this chapter, the x axis median value, represented by x̃, is 79 inches. The y axis median value, represented by ỹ is 220 pounds.

2. Draw both the x axis and y axis median lines on the Scatter Diagram. The median lines for the Height and Weight example are shown in the diagram below.

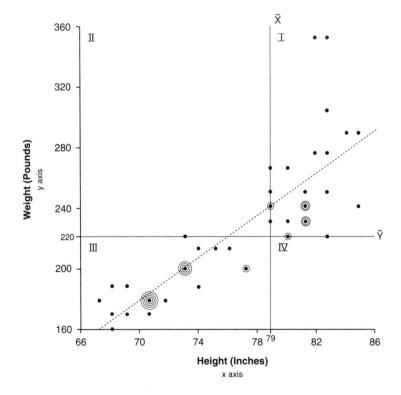

3. The median lines will form four quadrants on the Scatter Diagram. Label each quadrant I, II, III, and IV. Starting in the upper right portion of the diagram with I, move counterclockwise to end in the lower right portion with IV. These four quadrants are indicated in the Height vs. Weight Scatter Diagram shown above.

4. Create a simple table to record the number of points that fall within each quadrant. Be sure to have a category for those points that fall "on the line."

5. Count the number of data points that fall within each quadrant. Be sure to count those data points that appear repeatedly and are indicated with multiple circles. The table created for the Height vs. Weight Scatter Diagram is shown below.

Area	Data Points
I	18
II	0
III	23
IV	0
On the Line	9

6. Add the number of points that fall within Quadrant II to the number of points that fall within Quadrant IV. For the Height and Weight example: Quadrant II (0) + Quadrant IV (0) = 0.

7. Determine n by subtracting 2 from the total number of paired data points. For the Height and Weight example: n = 50 – 2 = 48.

8. Compare the total number of data points in Quadrants II and IV with the value in the column marked "Limit of Number of Points for I + III, II + IV" in the Sign Test Table shown below. Use n = 48 to find the correct value. If the total of Quadrants II and IV is less than the value in the "limit" column, then a correlation is statistically proven to exist.

n	Limit of Number of Points for I + III, II + IV	n	Limit of Number of Points for I + III, II + IV
20	5	42	14
21	5	44	15
22	5	46	15
23	6	48	16
24	6	50	17
25	7	52	18
26	7	54	19
27	7	56	20
28	8	58	21
29	8	60	21
30	9	62	22
32	9	64	23
34	10	66	24
36	11	68	25
38	12	70	26
40	13		

Note: This table is limited to n = 20 – 70 at a 5% level of significance.

The source of this table is *Guide to Quality Control*, page 93.

For the Height and Weight example, it isn't too surprising that there is *very* strong evidence of a positive correlation between height and weight. (As height increases, weight is also likely to increase.) Since the total of Quadrants II and IV is zero, and the limit number from the sign test table is 16, we know that 0 is <16, therefore a positive correlation exists. Don't expect all relationships to be as strong as this example.

▶ **Other Correlation Tests**

The procedure used to test the strength of the relationship in the Height and Weight example is a very simple linear model. More complex non-linear tests can be applied using software packages that feature the Scatter Diagram. *The Memory Jogger*™ Software is capable of producing the Scatter Diagram graphics shown in this chapter, and does a excellent job of both drawing the final product and providing all of the pertinent analytical statistics helpful to even the most sophisticated Scatter Diagram user.

EXAMPLE

This example is illustrated using the same steps that are shown in *The Memory Jogger*™ *II* on pages 145–147. The example shows you how the data for two variables, height and weight, are plotted on a Scatter Diagram, and how the resulting pattern should be interpreted.

▶ **Step 1 Collecting Paired Data**

The table below shows 50 paired samples of data.

Coach's note: Use the data set in the table below to begin the Learning Activity. Provide each pair in the group with a copy of this table.

Number	Height (inches)	Weight (pounds)	Number	Height (inches)	Weight (pounds)
1	83	350	26	79	240
2	73	220	27	81	230
3	73	200	28	68	170
4	71	180	29	74	210
5	75	210	30	80	270
6	71	180	31	82	280
7	69	190	32	68	160
8	83	250	33	83	220
9	73	200	34	82	350
10	67	180	35	79	230
11	68	190	36	81	250
12	84	290	37	76	210
13	79	250	38	81	230
14	80	230	39	83	280
15	80	220	40	71	170
16	85	240	41	79	240
17	81	240	42	81	240
18	79	270	43	72	180
19	81	230	44	77	200
20	77	200	45	69	170
21	71	180	46	80	220
22	85	290	47	73	200
23	71	180	48	83	300
24	73	200	49	74	190
25	81	240	50	71	180

▶ **Step 2 Drawing the Axes**

The diagram below shows the x axis scale for height and the y axis scale for weight.

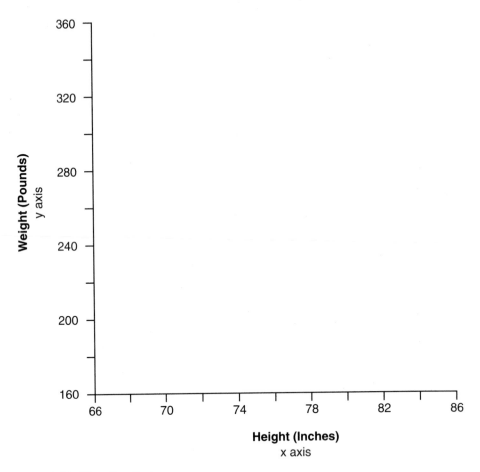

▶ **Step 3 Plotting the Data**

The Scatter Diagram below shows the result of plotting the data for the variable "Height" and the data for the variable "Weight."

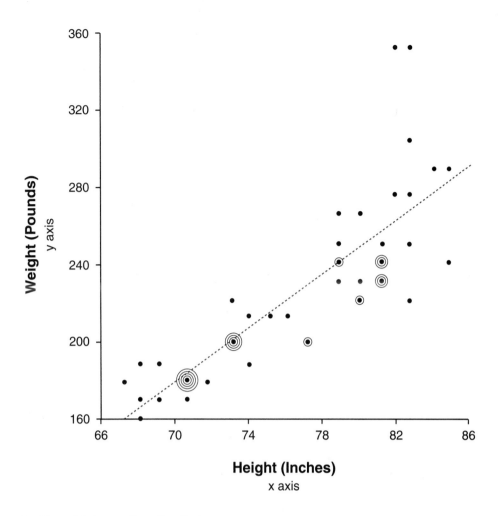

▶ **Step 4 Interpreting the Data**

There is *very* strong evidence of a positive correlation between height and weight. (As height increases, weight is also likely to increase.) To understand the full analysis that supports this interpretation, refer to "Determining the Strength of a Relationship" under Step 4 on page 201.

Scatter Diagram

COACH'S ANSWER KEY

▶ **Learning Activity**

Interpreting the Scatter Diagram

Question 1: Is there a relationship between "Height" and "Weight" in this data set?

Answer: Yes.

Question 2: How strong or weak is the relationship?

Answer: Very strong. In fact, considerably stronger than the typical Scatter Diagram.

Question 3: Does increased height *cause* increased weight? Why or why not?

Answer: You can't say that one *causes* the other, but only that the two characteristics *move* together. The tighter this connection is, the more confidence you can have in your ability to predict the future levels of both variables.

Question 4: From what population(s) of people was this sample drawn? (Ask them to guess.)

Answer: NBA basketball players.

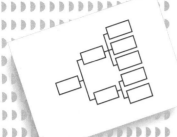

Tree Diagram
Mapping the tasks for Implementation

IS THIS THE RIGHT TOOL? ASK . . .

▶ Does the team need a "visual map" for implementation?

▶ Is the team underestimating the actual complexity that will be involved in achieving the goal?

▶ Is the team talking "solutions" with no idea of how to get there?

▶ Do team members need a "walk-away" piece of the project to work on?

STEPS AT A GLANCE

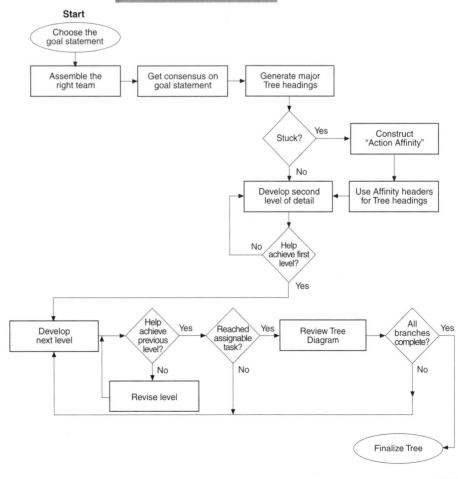

TREE DIAGRAM

Q. **Does each branch of the Tree have to be broken down into the same number of levels?**

A. No. Each major Tree heading carries its own scope of complexity. For example, in expanding one major Tree heading down to an assignable task, the team may only have to go to the third level of detail. In another Tree heading of the same Tree, it may be necessary to explore down to a fifth level of detail.

Q. **Why use Post-its™?**

A. It is recommended that the team doesn't draw lines on the Tree Diagram until it is complete. Use Post-its™ to create the branching, or "break down," in detail. This helps to keep the process flexible as the logic of the tasks emerge. By keeping the ideas "portable," the Tree can change as the team's thinking changes.

Q. **If the team's goal statement is from an Affinity Diagram, can they just move all the detailed Post-its™ from the Affinity to the Tree Diagram?**

A. No. Remember, the purpose of the detailed Post-its™ from the team's Affinity Diagram was to allow the major themes to emerge. These Post-its™ may not necessarily be the appropriate means for achieving the team's purpose. Frequently, the Affinity details are catalysts for further thinking rather than descriptions of the tasks themselves.

Q. **How can the team know when to stop "branching out" on the Tree?**

A. When the team has reached an assignable task level or the team's expertise has reached its boundaries, this is a good time to stop. Think of the goal as the trunk of the tree, leading to a branch, then to a twig, connecting to a leaf, then to a caterpillar on the leaf, then to the fuzz on the caterpillar. If the team starts discussing "caterpillar fuzz," perhaps they have expanded the Tree past a meaningful level of detail.

Q. **What should the team do when a series of tasks show up in two or more different branches?**

A. Sometimes, the means for carrying out a task may be the same for another subgoal. Simply repeat the means as they are generated. In fact, the repetition of a particular means may indicate that a "root task" has been found. For example, if the task "Ask supervisors for staffing requirements" is repeated in many branches, it may be an opportunity to have a meeting or conduct a survey to involve supervisors in all the aspects of staffing.

If: **The team is beginning to sequence items by time periods and is using the Tree Diagram almost like a Gantt Chart ...**

Then: Guide the team "back up" one or two levels of the Tree. Ask "What types of things must be done?" and "What kinds of action must be taken?" The branching out activity is intended to be a logical, not chronological, breakdown of the tasks at hand.

If: **The team positions itself in a "semantic spitting contest," such as: That's a goal! No, it's a means. Is that like a target? No, it's an objective!**

Then: Have the team look at only one pair of branches at a time, the current branch and the preceding branch. The questions they should focus on are:

"Does the current branch function as the means to accomplish the preceding branch?"

"Does the current branch answer the question, **'How?'** for the preceding branch?"

"Does the preceding branch answer the question, **'Why?'** for the current branch?"

The most important pairs of words to remember in this "sanity check" are goal/means and how/why. When you're moving from broad to more detailed tasks on the Tree, ask *how* you can accomplish the goal. What specific *means* will you use? When reviewing from the detailed to the broader tasks, ask *why* you're doing the tasks and what the *goals* are for completing the tasks. (See the MJII, page 159 for an illustration of this questioning/reviewing process.)

If: **The team gets "stuck in a branch". . .**

Then: Have the team brainstorm on Post-its™ the answer to the question *"How can we accomplish our purpose?"* If the team is "stuck" trying to come up with the major headings, sort the Post-its™ into a "mini" Affinity to get 3-5 major headings. The headings may serve as main Tree branches. If the team is further along in the Tree, simple brainstorming, without the structuring of an Affinity Diagram, may be enough. Use the best, or all of the Post-its™ generated.

LEARNING ACTIVITY

1. To get the team to think in progressive levels of detail, list these three categories on a flipchart: "the parts of General Motors," "the components of a symphony orchestra," "the elements of a great party or movie."

2. Ask each group to select one. No duplicate selections are allowed. Using Post-its™, have the group show the "breakout" in a Tree Diagram format of the products or parts for the category chosen. This is *not* an organizational chart. For example, the first level for General Motors might be Cadillac, then Buick, next Oldsmobile, Pontiac, and Chevrolet.

3. Ask the groups to break out the Tree to at least three levels of detail. Have the groups share and debrief with each other. Ask about the relationships between the branches of the Tree.

STEP 1 CHOOSING THE GOAL

MJII pp. 156–157

▶ **Where Goal Statements Come From**

Goal statements for the Tree Diagram can come from three general sources:

- The driver (primary outcome) identified in a previously constructed Inter-relationship Digraph (ID)

- The header cards from an Affinity Diagram

- An assignment from a team or an individual

▶ **Using the Driver from the ID:** Using the driver from an ID will help focus action planning on an issue or issues that will have the greatest leverage on the success of the project. Stated a little differently: when a team uses the driver from an ID, it will have a "ripple" effect and generally represents the most efficient path toward the goal.

▶ **Using the Affinity Diagram and the Header Cards:** Usually, the most difficult part in constructing a Tree Diagram is generating that first level of detail. By using the headers from an Affinity Diagram, the team has both its goal statement and its first level of detail.

A word of caution: By going directly into a Tree Diagram construction without first doing an ID, the team may miss a valuable opportunity to explore the cause and effect relationship between the headers.

▶ **Using an Assignment from a Team or an Individual:** The team has been given its assignment. The assignment is clear and concise enough to move directly into an action-oriented Tree Diagram without employing any of the other tools first. It's also possible that the assignment was taken from a branch of a larger Tree Diagram.

▶ **Consensus on the Goal Statement**

Because the team will be stepping onto the implementation path using a Tree Diagram, be doubly sure all members of the team agree with the goal statement and that the statement is clearly articulated. Purposeful action is difficult to arrive at if the goal statement is vague or consensus has not been reached.

STEP 2 ASSEMBLING THE RIGHT TEAM

MJII p. 157

▶ **The Dream Team**

There are two key criteria to apply when selecting the right team:

- Are the future team members action planners?

- Do they have the detailed knowledge required to fulfill the goal statement?

The answer to both of these questions must be "yes." Otherwise, your Tree Diagram will be weak on implementation and/or limited by the team's expertise.

▶ Size of the Team

The recommended size is 4-6 members. However, the Tree Diagram will most likely be dealing with several layers of implementation complexity. Consequently, more people may be needed on the team, who together embody a diverse range of knowledge to achieve these more complex goals. As long as a larger group can be facilitated and all ideas are visible during the session, larger teams can be accommodated. Be sure to make all ideas visible by using larger Post-its™ or *The Memory Jogger Plus+®* Software with an LCD panel and overhead projector.

MJII pp. 157–158 | **STEP 3   GENERATING MAJOR HEADINGS**

The Tree Diagram is one of the most valuable management and planning tools for laying out implementation, but it can also be the most frustrating tool for a team to construct. The first level of the Tree, the major headings, is the most broad and conceptual level of detail in the diagram and often the most demanding of the team's persistence and patience.

▶ Resisting Temptation

Many teams solve problems by immediately jumping to solutions. These teams tend to run to the lowest level of detail in the Tree. *"Why go through all this bother, when we know what we have to do?"*

If team members "know" just what to do, they'll be operating from an existing knowledge base. There's a good chance that a team will wind up with the "same 'ole, same 'ole," because no new connections or team learning will have been triggered and included in their thinking. There's a rich opportunity to accomplish, with more efficiency and perhaps more creativity, potentially overwhelming projects by exploring new *paths* of implementation with the Tree.

▶ How Not to Get Stuck in a Tree

Here are two methods to get the major Tree headings. They both start with the question *"What important actions must be taken to achieve the team's purpose?"*

1. Conduct a simple brainstorming session around the problem statement, *"What are the main categories of action we must take to achieve our purpose?"* Select those actions that are at a broad conceptual level.

2. Construct an "Action Affinity" using the headers as the major Tree headings. Headers in this type of Affinity can be shorter than the typical Affinity. Make sure, however, that each header includes at least an active verb and a noun. These two methods can be used at any place in the Tree. Try to keep the Affinity smaller (fewer Post-its™) as the team advances to more detailed levels.

Using different colored Post-its™ can help team members to construct the diagram if the Tree is complex or if other teams are developing different branches of the same Tree. Different color Post-its™ can be used for the goal statement, the major headings, and the lowest level of detail (assignable tasks). Using color for any other level is unnecessarily confusing and really doesn't add value.

Remember, the major Tree headings function as the "means" for how the goal statement can be accomplished at the highest (broadest) level.

Tree Diagram

STEP 4 BREAKING INTO DETAIL

MJII p. 159

▶ **Branching Out**

Creating the lower branches of the Tree is similar to creating the major Tree headings; the team is just dealing with more detail. It's important to note that the *means* generated on any one branch become the *goals* for the next lower level of the branch. Staying focused on this simple means/goal language as the team moves from level to level eliminates the need to distinguish between goals, objectives, strategies, and so on.

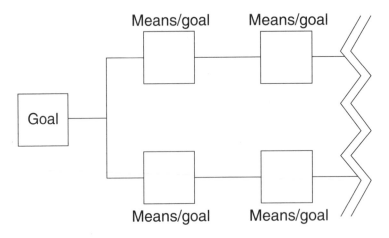

▶ **Know When to Stop**

When the means generated are in a form that can be "handed off" to another group or person, the team has reached an assignable task level. It's time to stop. Also, when the team is generating detail below or beyond its expertise, it's time to stop!

STEP 5 REVIEWING COMPLETED TREE

MJII p. 160

▶ **Did We Forget Something?**

It's hard to imagine, if the team has created an expansive Tree, that team members might have overlooked something. It's not only possible, it almost always happens. Because constructing a Tree Diagram can be exhausting, it's best to leave the flipchart papers on the wall overnight for an incubation period. A clear mind and a fresh pair of eyes can reveal quite a bit. Also, inviting people outside the team to look at the Tree can channel valuable input into the branches.

▶ **Logic and Sanity Checks: The How and the Why**

Starting at the goal statement level, the team should move down each one of the branches asking *"**How** can this goal be accomplished?"* The following branch should provide the answer and the means. For a double check, reinforce the question by asking *"If we want to accomplish these results, do we really need to do these tasks?"* This rigor ensures that you have what you need, and not "motherhood" statements that sound good, but have little to do with implementation.

Next, have the team begin at the lowest level of detail and move up the Tree asking, *"**Why** are we taking these actions?"* The next level of detail going up should provide the answer and the respective goal. To test the implementation linkage further, ask *"Will these actions actually lead to these results?"*

Now the moment the team has been waiting for . . . yes, you can draw the connecting lines!

Tree Diagram

Preparing to Run
in the Boston Marathon

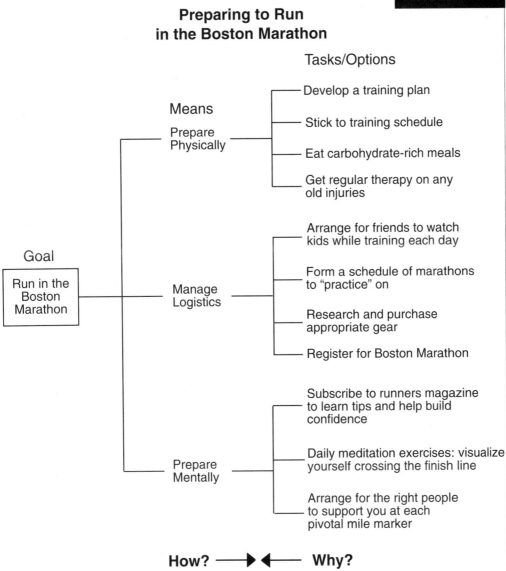

Tasks/Options

Means

Prepare Physically
— Develop a training plan
— Stick to training schedule
— Eat carbohydrate-rich meals
— Get regular therapy on any old injuries

Goal

Run in the Boston Marathon

Manage Logistics
— Arrange for friends to watch kids while training each day
— Form a schedule of marathons to "practice" on
— Research and purchase appropriate gear
— Register for Boston Marathon

Prepare Mentally
— Subscribe to runners magazine to learn tips and help build confidence
— Daily meditation exercises: visualize yourself crossing the finish line
— Arrange for the right people to support you at each pivotal mile marker

How? ━━▶ ◀━━ Why?

A widely-used variation of the Tree Diagram is the Process Decision Program Chart (PDPC). The PDPC is a valuable tool that many organizations use to map out conceivable and likely implementation problems along with appropriate and reasonable countermeasures. The result of using the PDPC is that a team prepares a *realistic* plan since they have anticipated the potential barriers to the success of a proposed project. Teams at all organizational levels have been using the PDPC when:

— Tasks are new, unique, or substantially revised

— Tasks are complex, problems are likely during implementation, and the stakes of failure are high

The PDPC is a tool that flows very naturally in most team situations. Once a team has been introduced to the PDPC, it quickly becomes part of the planning routine. This tool can present two interesting challenges to team leaders and facilitators. One, leaders and facilitators must use the tool in a way that allows a team to stretch its thinking, and at the same time, keep its feet on the ground. Leaders and facilitators should keep this in mind when the team is generating a list of potential problems, solutions, and/or preventive measures.

Tree Diagram

Another challenge in using the PDPC is that some team members may view other team members who raise potential problems as negative or unwilling people who lack the "can-do" spirit. To avoid this possible team sentiment, the leader of the PDPC process needs to create an open atmosphere from the start by actively encouraging those who identify potential problems, asking everyone else to participate as well, and then quickly moving on to potential solutions. If the team is just not moving forward, try one or two practice charts on simple (and fun) topics such as "Getting to work in the morning," "Planning a vacation," or "Painting a house."

▶ Step 1 Assembling the Right Team

More than any other tool, the PDPC requires intimate knowledge of what it really takes to get the job done. Therefore, the first choice is to go to the "doers" for the input. If this isn't practical, at the very least, involve the "doers" in the review process with the understanding that the chart will be modified if necessary. No "imaginary" involvement here!

▶ Step 2 Determining Proposed Steps

The PDPC is different from the Tree Diagram because the PDPC places the proposed broad implementation steps into a natural sequence. These tasks should be as broad as possible, i.e., 4–10 steps, to avoid "exploding" every detail of implementation. The steps that pose the highest risks will be broken into greater detail as problems are identified. It might be helpful to think of the PDPC's first level of detail as a "macro flowchart." Additional levels of implementation detail are possible, but try to limit the implementation detail to one level.

In this step, the team has the option of constructing the PDPC graphically, (as is the Tree Diagram), or in a numbered outline format. The graphical format is generally more powerful because it is easier to read, and it encourages communication among team members. The outline format is easier to draw and reproduce unless the team is using *The Memory Jogger Plus+*® Software, in which both formats are simultaneously produced. Generally, the graphical format is used most frequently.

▶ Step 3 Generating Likely Problems

From each step ask either: "What could go wrong?" or "What if ... ?" Ideally, the team should do traditional brainstorming (without filters), but the PDPC also requires the team to make judgments about the relative likelihood of each possible problem.

▶ Step 4 Generating Reasonable Solutions

Just as in Step 3, the team has to be both creative and reasonable in generating the contingencies (either preventive or reactive) for each potential problem. The team should, however, allow itself more creative latitude at this stage. This step can often generate small or large breakthroughs that turn problems into opportunities. For example, if a team is exploring the challenges in publishing a company newsletter, one of the possible problems could be that "no one will read it." The proposed solution may be to put the newsletter on-line and let individuals choose the specific features they want to print out. A customized newsletter for every person!

▶ Step 5 Choosing Countermeasures

Review and select the proposed solutions that are expected to be both the most effective and the most reasonable to carry out. Mark these solutions so they are easy to find. An "O" is often used to indicate that the countermeasure has been selected. Also mark the remaining solutions, which the team is choosing not to implement. An "X" is often used to show that the solution would be difficult or impossible to carry out, and so will not be implemented. The solutions that have been selected must be integrated with the original plan. Returning to the example of the company newsletter described in Step 4: implementing the solution of putting the newsletter on-line will eliminate the steps required in both printing and distributing the newsletter. Talk about turning a problem into a breakthrough!

For more information on the PDPC, see pages 160-161 of *The Memory Jogger™ II* or pages 171-199 of *The Memory Jogger Plus+®* or pages 42-47 of *The Educators' Companion to The Memory Jogger Plus+®.*

EXAMPLE

A: Modified Tree Diagram

Extending the School Year by Ten Days

KEY:
X = Difficult/Impossible   O = Selected Countermeasure

B: Numbered Outline

Extending the School Year by Ten Days

Implementation Steps	1.0	Determine Costs
	1.1	Allocate Budget
	1.2	Get Budget Approval
	2.0	Decide Where to Add Instructional Days
	2.1	Summer/June and August
	2.2	Vacation Days
	2.3	Saturdays
	3.0	Sell Idea to Internal and External Community
	3.1	School Staff
	3.2	Parents and Students
	3.3	Employer and Community at Large

"What If" Problems	1.1.1	Beyond Budget
	3.1.1	Staff Resists or Opposes Idea

Possible Countermeasures	X	1.1.1.1	Raise Taxes
	O	1.1.1.2	Get Foundation or Private Funding as a Pilot
	X	1.1.1.3	Get Union Concessions
	X	1.1.1.4	Cut Other Areas
	X	3.1.1.1	Hire New Staff
	O	3.1.1.2	Begin with Small Pilot and Self-Selected Staff
	X	3.1.1.3	Staff Extra Days with Volunteers
	O	3.1.1.4	Visit Schools that Have Implemented Extended School Year

KEY:
X = Difficult/Impossible   O = Selected Countermeasure

Data Points
Turning data into information

▶ Does the team need to think about how to collect data?

▶ Is the data not showing any patterns or problems and yet the team knows there is something wrong or different about the process they are studying?

▶ Does the team need to describe a graphic with numbers?

CHOOSING THE RIGHT TOOL

Choose the tool to use, based on the type of data you have or plan to collect.

Number Data (Count or attribute)	Tool to Use
• Show frequency of events	• Check Sheet • Pareto
• Show process performance over time	• Run Chart • Control Chart
• Show capability of process to meet customer requirements	• Process Capability

Number Data (Measure or variable)	Tool to Use
• Show relationships among multiple data sets over time	• Radar Chart • Run Chart
• Show centering and variation of a process	• Histogram
• Show correlations between two or more data sets	• Scatter
• Show process performance over time	• Run Chart • Control Chart
• Show capability of process to meet customer requirements	• Process Capability

Word Data	Tool to Use
• Show process flow	• AND • Gantt • Flowchart
• Generate ideas • Narrow Ideas	• Brainstorming • NGT/Multivoting
• Sort ideas	• Affinity • Cause & Effect • Force Field
• Show relationships	• Cause & Effect • Interrelationship
• Show greater level of detail	• Cause & Effect • Tree Diagram
• Show correlations	• Cause & Effect • Force Field • Interrelationship • Prioritization • Radar Chart
• Develop consensus	• Matrix Diagram • Prioritization
• Plan contingencies	• PDPC

Data Points

217

DATA POINTS

Q. **Why collect data?**

A. Data is collected for several reasons:

To reveal a problem. A team can't fix something they don't know about.

To analyze a problem. If a team can understand the root cause of a problem, then they can fix the problem, rather than the symptom.

To monitor and control a problem. A team will want to make sure that what they fix, stays fixed.

To prevent a problem. It's always better to prevent a problem than to have to deal with it. Preventing problems allows teams to produce products and services that have significantly higher quality, higher productivity, lower cost, and better competitive position.

Q. **How much data should be collected?**

A. It depends. The frequency with which a team collects data depends on each situation. What data does the team already have? How much data does the team think will be necessary to detect cycles or patterns? What are the resource constraints, e.g., cost, time, people, measurement devices? Three general rules are:

1) If the team is collecting word data, they should get as much as they can.

2) If the team is collecting individual data points, they should get between 50 and 100 observations.

3) If the team is collecting paired data, (e.g., to plot in a Scatter Diagram or Control Chart), they should collect at least 20–25 paired data sets.

Q. **Who is responsible for collecting the data?**

A. Review the responsibilities and assign them as appropriate. Should one of the team members collect the data or can you use people on the job? If so, remember to assure them that the data will reflect the performance of the process, not their performance. Otherwise the data may not truly reflect what's happening in the process.

Q. **How will the data be recorded?**

A. Use a Check Sheet, and keep it simple. Remember to record the elements of the data: Who collected it? An operator, recorder? When was it collected? Every hour, day, week, month, year? What problem or defect was observed? How often? Any special notes about the current circumstances? In designing the form, involve the people who will use it. For more specific information, see the Check Sheet chapter in this book.

If: **A team is uneasy about selecting a tool, analyzing and interpreting data or a graphic, or doing a calculation . . .**

Then: Don't be afraid to seek help from an expert, or first use a tool that the team is comfortable with, such as a Run Chart if the Control Chart is daunting, or the Affinity Diagram if the Cause & Effect Diagram is too confusing.

If: **The team has trouble deciding what type of data to collect or measure . . .**

Then: Encourage them to think about the process and think about how the customer would measure the performance of the process. You might also use the table of measures below to help team members get their thoughts flowing.

Category	Measures
Quality	Mistakes, failures, complaints, returned items, repairs
People	Grade level, age, experience, skill, individual
Equipment	Machines (computers, copiers, TVs, typewriters), phones, buses, trucks, ovens, tools, instruments—by kind, manufacturer, lot, etc.
Material	Resins, paints, medications, thermometers, books, paper, curricula, videos, software, pens
Procedure/Policy	Conditions, orders, arrangements, methods
Environment	Building, room, temperature, humidity, lightness and darkness
Cost	Time, expense
Delivery	Shortages, instruction, defaults in payments, delays, time spent waiting
Safety	Accidents, mistakes, breakdowns

Data Points

CLASSIFYING DATA

MJII p. 52

▶ **What Type of Data Do You Have?**

Here are a few reasons why it matters:

– The type of data you have will often dictate the tool you use. Keep it simple and go with what feels comfortable for the team.

– Selecting the right tool is a key step toward solving a problem or improving a process.

– Sometimes the choice of which tool(s) to use is clear, sometimes there are options. Keep in mind what you are trying to accomplish.

COLLECTING DATA

MJII p. 52

▶ **Do You Need to Collect Data?**

Whether the answer is yes, or no, the team should do the following:

– Clarify the problem. Make sure the team members understand what process is being studied.

– Make sure the data is appropriate and represents the process. Know what type of data you have or want to have. Words? Numbers? Countable, discrete numbers? Variable numbers?

– Be aware that the data may need to be stratified. For example, data may need to be separated out by days, or machines, or types, or whichever category fits your situation.

▶ **Tips for Setting Up A Data Collection Form (Check Sheet)**

– Keep the purpose in mind. This will help the team focus on what data they need and how to lay it out on a form. Remember, keep it simple.

– Collect only relevant data and set a time limit. Use a Flowchart to determine where in the process you can go to gather the information you need. Don't collect everything, just because it's there. There is a price to collect data, both in time and money. Don't overburden the person collecting the data by asking for information you might never need.

– Use historical data first, if it is available. This will set a baseline of past performance.

– Organizationally plan the data collection effort. Clear it with supervisors to go in and collect data or to use someone on the job. Assign roles: Who will collect the data? Who will analyze and interpret it? Who will graph it?

– Refer to the Check Sheet chapter for more information on setting up a data collection form.

STRATIFYING DATA

MJII p. 53

▶ **Can You Categorize Your Data Into Subgroups?**

– Variation exists! No two things are exactly alike. We use process improvement to identify excessive variation in our processes. Sources of variation can be found in people, policies and procedures, equipment, materials, environment, and so on. Sometimes, teams must divide the sources of variation into sub-sources, to measure the different levels at which they are operating. For example, two identical machines may be producing product at different levels, or two people may be providing a service differently, thus each resulting in different levels of performance. Identifying these differences and working to reduce or eliminate them is what process improvement is all about.

— Stratification of data may be useful when interpreting many of the graphic tools, such as the Pareto Chart, Histogram, Run Chart, Scatter Diagram, and Control Chart. If you see no discernable pattern to show you something about the process, then look to see if you have groupings of data that should be stratified. (MJII page 53 for example.)

MJII pp. 53–55

DESCRIBING DATA

▶ **What Patterns Are Important in Your Data?**

Before your team begins to collect and compile data, they should have a basic understanding of terms such as population, sample, mean, median, range, and standard deviation. These definitions are listed below.

▶ **Data:** Data are numerical measures that provide teams with information which will help them understand how the process is performing and what action needs to be taken to fix or improve it. Using the Check Sheet, Pareto Chart, Run Chart, Histogram, or Control Chart, the team will be able to visualize the process, make inferences about the process, and go about implementing actions to correct or improve the process.

▶ **Measures of Location:** Measures of location show the centering of the values of a group of data points. These measures are the mean, median, and mode.

▶ **Measures of Variation:** Measures of variation show how the values of a group of data points vary from one another or from the centering. These measures are the range, standard deviation, and shape of the distribution.

▶ **Population:** The total number of products or services that can be, are, or will be provided, constitute a *population*.

▶ **Sample:** Restraints such as time, money, and destroyed product prevent us from measuring every product or service produced. Therefore, a subset, or *sample*, of the population is drawn and measurements taken to provide information on the population.

▶ **Statistic:** Sometimes, when samples get extremely large, or samples must be taken periodically over time, numbers are more useful than visuals. A value calculated from a sample, such as the mean or standard deviation, is a *statistic*. Statistics help to summarize a group of data points down to a few numbers. Statistics from a sample help estimate the larger population.

EXAMPLE

▶ **Measures of Location: Mean, Median, & Mode**

For the data below, calculate the mean, median, and mode.

10	63	32	21	30	2	13	19
9	15	50	24	30	21	15	35
52	8	33	27	22	40	28	42

The total number of data points in this sample is n = 24

To find the Mean: Take the sum of the values of the sample and divide it by n, or in this case, 24.

$$\overline{X} = \frac{(2 + 8 + 9 + 10 + 13 \ldots 50 + 52 + 63)}{24}$$

$$= \frac{641}{24}$$

$$= \mathbf{26.708}$$

To find the Median: When sampled data are rank ordered, lowest to highest, the median is the middle number.

When the data points (shown above) are ranked, they look like this:

2, 8, 9, 10, 13, 15, 15, 19, 21, 21, 22, **24**, **27**, 28, 30, 30, 32, 33, 35, 40, 42, 50, 52, 63

Since there is an even number of values, n = 24, take the average of the two middle numbers (the 12th and 13th).

$$\frac{24 + 27}{2}$$

$$= \frac{51}{2}$$

$$= \mathbf{25.5}$$

To find the Mode: Find the most frequently occurring value(s) in the sample. There are three modes in this example:

15 occurs twice

21 occurs twice

30 occurs twice

▶ Measures of Variation: Range and Standard Deviation

For both data sets below, calculate the range, mean, (since it is necessary in the standard deviation calculation), and sample standard deviation.

A	10	8	12	9	11
B	6	14	5	15	10

Range = $X_{max} - X_{min}$

Range for A:
$12 - 8 = \textbf{4}$

Range for B:
$15 - 5 = \textbf{10}$

Mean = $\bar{X}$

$$= \frac{(X_1 + X_2 + X_3 \ldots X_n)}{n}$$

Mean for A:

$$\frac{(10 + 8 + 12 + 9 + 11)}{5} = \frac{50}{5} = \textbf{10}$$

Mean for B:

$$\frac{(6 + 14 + 5 + 15 + 10)}{5} = \frac{50}{5} = \textbf{10}$$

The mean for both A and B is the same: 10.

Sometimes, as in this example, the measure of centering is not enough to understand the process performance. The measure of variation then becomes key to discerning differences between two or more groups. The limitation of the range as a measure of variation is that it compares only the two extreme data points in a set. The standard deviation, however, takes every data point into account.

Standard Deviation

The general formula for finding the standard deviation, s, is:

$$s = \sqrt{\frac{\Sigma(X_i - \bar{X})^2}{n-1}}$$

Note: $X_i = (X_1 + X_2 + X_3 \ldots X_n)$

Standard deviation for A:

$$s = \sqrt{\frac{(10-10)^2 + (8-10)^2 + (12-10)^2 + (9-10)^2 + (11-10)^2}{5-1}}$$

$$= \sqrt{\frac{(0)^2 + (-2)^2 + (2)^2 + (-1)^2 + (1)^2}{4}}$$

$$= \sqrt{\frac{(0 + 4 + 4 + 1 + 1)}{4}}$$

$$= \sqrt{\frac{10}{4}}$$

$$= \sqrt{2.5}$$

$$= \mathbf{1.581}$$

Standard deviation for B:

$$s = \sqrt{\frac{(6-10)^2 + (14-10)^2 + (5-10)^2 + (15-10)^2 + (10-10)^2}{5-1}}$$

$$= \sqrt{\frac{(-4)^2 + (4)^2 + (-5)^2 + (5)^2 + (0)^2}{4}}$$

$$= \sqrt{\frac{(16 + 16 + 25 + 25 + 0)}{4}}$$

$$= \sqrt{\frac{82}{4}}$$

$$= \sqrt{20.5}$$

$$= \mathbf{4.527}$$

While the mean for both A and B is the same, the sample standard deviation shows us that sample B is much more variable than A.

	5	6	7	8	9	10	11	12	13	14	15
A				■	■	■	■	■			
B	■	■				■				■	■

▶ **A Few Words on Standard Deviation:** As you've seen above, two groups of data may have the same centering but are vastly different in how they vary about that centering. For example: Take these two groups of data:

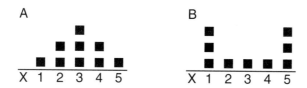

Obviously, both groups of data have the same centering, $\overline{X} = 3$, and both have the same range, $R = 4$. However, Group A is clustered tighter around 3 than Group B. If standard deviation measures the average amount each individual point varies about the mean, then the closer to the mean each point is, the less variation. Therefore, the standard deviation will approach zero as the variation lessens. Likewise, the more variation about the mean, the greater the measured variation and the larger the standard deviation.

▶ **The Bell Curve and Normal Distribution**

The *normal or Gaussian distribution* is a bell-shaped curve that describes the distribution of many natural processes: heights of people, hardness, density, wait times, and so on.

The normal distribution is based on the assumption that most of the output of a process will be close to the mean value with fewer and fewer observations occurring as you move away from that mean. The *mean* identifies location of the center of the distribution and the sample *standard deviation, s,* describes the variation from that mean.

What are the three characteristics of a normal distribution?

– The mean = median = mode.

– The curve is symmetrical, that is, the curve is a mirror image along the vertical axis at the mean value.

– The area under the curve is equal to 1 (or 100%).

What does a bell curve tell you?

▶ **Curve Height:** The height of the curve at any point is related to the probability of occurrence for a particular value.

▶ **Curve Width:** If the sample standard deviation is large, the bell curve will be wide. If the sample standard deviation is small (approaching zero), then the bell curve will be narrow. Regardless of whether the curve is narrow or wide, the relationship between the sample standard deviation and the total area under the curve remains the same.

▶ **Area Under Curve:** The percentage of normally distributed data that fall under the curve can be predicted as follows:

±1s	=	0.6826 or approximately	68% of the total area
±2s	=	0.9544 or approximately	95% of the total area
±3s	=	0.9974 or approximately	99.7% of the total area

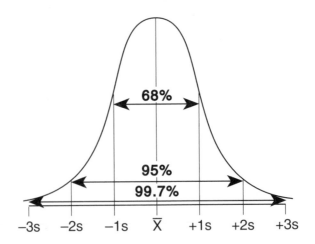

▶ **Skewness:** Some processes are naturally skewed; don't expect every distribution to follow a bell-shaped curve. There are also other curves such as binomial and Poisson. Consult other statistical books for more information.

INCIDENTALLY

I often say that when you can measure what you are speaking about, and express it in numbers, you know something about it; but when you cannot measure it, you cannot express it in numbers, your knowledge is of a meager and unsatisfactory kind.

— Lord Kelvin

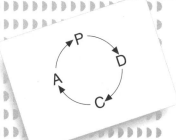

Problem-Solving/
Process-Improvement Model

Improvement Storyboard

IS THIS THE RIGHT TOOL? ASK . . .

▶ Have there been repeated attempts to "take a shot" at a persistent problem with minimal or temporary results?

▶ Is there a need to move away from "gut-feel" to "fact-based" decision making?

▶ Are you attempting to get more people involved in both diagnosing and solving the root causes of important problems?

▶ Does the team need to better understand and improve its basic processes that produce the problems that arise day to day?

STEPS AT A GLANCE

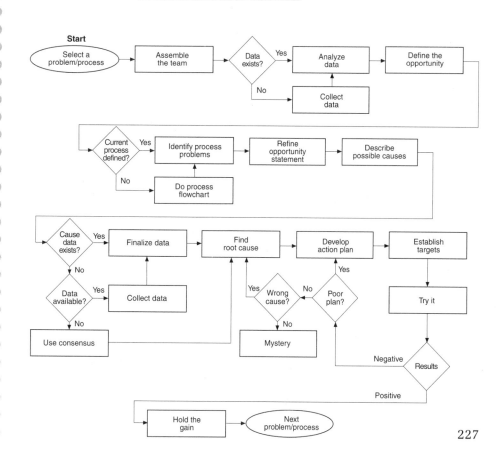

227

PS/PI Model

PS/PI MODEL

Q. Doesn't this systematic method slow down the process of improvement?

A. The process may *appear* slower than the traditional shotgun approach to solving problems, but this observation is often deceiving. As is traditionally the case, solutions are produced quickly *and* they are frequently off the mark. A great deal of time is spent in making poor plans workable or "selling" the solution. However, when more time is spent up front to define the real problem, measures of success, and an effective plan, the *total* time to real solutions is generally shorter.

Q. Aren't there ever just obvious problems and great solutions?

A. Sure, but the advantage of this process is that you can go through it as quickly as is necessary. When the facts are very clear, this process becomes more of a "check" to make sure that all the questions have been considered in the proposed solution. Remember that each step is simply a way to ensure that the Plan-Do-Check-Act (PDCA) Cycle is being followed. There is nothing inherently slow in the PDCA Cycle. It is up to the team not to get stuck in a never-ending planning step.

Q. There are so many problem-solving/process-improvement models—which one is the best?

A. The "best" is relative to which method people can and will use daily to produce results. There are so many variations on models . . . 7 steps, 9 steps, 12 steps, and so on. The one commonality is that they all represent systematic ways to move through the PDCA Cycle. The steps that are used in *The Memory Jogger*™ *II* represent a combination of many models. If your organization has its own version, don't get hung up on the subtle differences. Feel free to combine models as needed. The important thing is to agree on one that works in your environment and use it to create a common language of improvement.

Q. How does a team prevent itself from getting stuck in the "Plan" part of the PDCA Cycle?

A. Recognize and accept that everything a team does to improve a process or solve a problem is an experiment. A team will probably never have "enough" information to make the "perfect" solution. However, a PDCA process "done well" will get people asking the right questions at the right time to ensure that the team learns from the experiment and either holds the improvement, if the plan is successful, or narrows the choices for the next round of "trial and learning."

If: **A person insists on choosing a particular solution and won't let go . . .**

Then: Determine which steps in the process have been completed. If some of the steps have been completed, review your agreements. For example, *"At the last meeting we agreed that the problem statement was _____. How does this proposed solution match up to it?"* Continue this review and comparison until you encounter a step that was skipped. For example, the team may not have looked for root causes, so ask, *"What are the possible root causes of this problem and how does this solution address them?"* This review and questioning process keeps the focus on the proposed solution, (which may be a great one), while using the model as a check against random action. It also supports the ego of the person who feels so strongly about the solution. That person just might be your boss!

If: **The solution "fails" . . .**

Then: Reconvene the team and use the process to stay positive. Review each step of the process and ask *"Do we agree that this is accurate? Did we miss anything? Did anything change that we didn't expect? Did we implement the plan as it was designed?"* The focus needs to be on why the test was negative and *NOT* on the reasons for a "failure." The team's purpose is to decide whether or not there could be an improvement in the diagnosis, the solution, or the execution of the plan.

LEARNING ACTIVITY

To practice the Problem-Solving/Process-Improvement Model:

1. Break into groups of 4–6 people.

2. The challenge before each group is to "improve the process of buying a car."

3. Ask each group to agree on a specific part of the car-buying process that they would like to improve. For example: how to decide what car to get, how to get the best deal, and so on. Write a brief statement that describes the problem. (Plan)

4. Ask each group to produce a simple flowchart, (with no more than 10 steps), or written description of the process of buying a car. Advise the groups to *begin* the flowchart with the decision to buy a car, not at the auto dealership. (Plan)

5. Ask the groups to do a simple Cause & Effect Diagram focusing on both the initial problem statement and where problems arise in the flowchart that they produced in the previous step. Agree on the most concrete root cause. (Plan)

6. Develop an action plan with no more than six steps, along with three measures of success. For example, one of the action steps may be to use a consumer rating magazine to compare options. A related measure may be that the buyer would go to the dealership with a list of features that the car *Must Have* and *Must Not Have*. (Plan)

7. Have the groups briefly brainstorm some problems that they could anticipate in carrying out their plan. (Do)

8. Discuss as a large group how the car-buying process could be evaluated and improved for the next time around. (Check & Act)

STEP 1 SELECTING A PROBLEM/PROCESS

MJII pp. 116–118

▶ Linking Problem Solving and Process Improvement

The seven-step model in *The Memory Jogger™ II* is designed to combine both a problem-solving and process-improvement approach. The model assumes that problem solving is a process *within* process improvement. The ideal way to manage is to continually try to understand and improve the way people do work (processes) based on the demands of customers and the organization. As managers, coaches, team leaders, and team members are reaching for this understanding, they are going to find ways and places where the process is falling short. These are *problems.* Therefore, a process improvement model should naturally provide the focus for a problem-solving process. People need to find a way to do problem solving *AND* process improvement.

▶ Improve What Matters to Customers AND the Organization

If continuous improvement is to become a permanent part of an organization's culture, teams need to be asked to address problems that will have an impact on the factors affecting the overall success of the enterprise. For example, let's say that Stop 'N Go Pizza produces the highest quality pizzas and delivers them on time, every time, and customers are calling their friends to tell them about it. But unless Stop 'N Go Pizza figures out how to make a profit on its booming sales, the company will go out of business. The point is that each process or problem a team is asked to improve should be based on data that balances the needs of the customers and those of the organization. Notice that the Run Chart and Pareto Chart (MJII page 117) address the concerns of both the company (sales volume decline) and those of the customer (increasing complaints). In this case, the increasing complaints seemed to have a direct relationship with lower sales.

▶ Data: The Great Equalizer

Whenever possible, start with data. The discovery and definition of a problem through data collection and analysis reduces the power of opinions. It's not that opinions are bad, but when used as a basis for making choices about processes or problems, there is often a lack of consensus about the nature of the problem or even if there is a problem. Don't let the person with the loudest voice, nor most persistent nature, nor official leader in title, lead the team's decision making. Let the relevant data lead the team's decision making!

▶ Stratify, Classify, and Clarify

When the data points to a problem area, test it. For example, at Stop 'N Go Pizza, the Pareto Chart answered the questions: Are late delivery complaints occurring in equal numbers in all of the shops? Are the complaints happening on only a few days of the week? The data shows that the problem is not significantly *stratified* by location, but it is by day of the week. The problem can now be *classified* as a company-wide issue that occurs mainly on the weekend. By going this extra step, (using the Pareto Chart to get a visual picture of the data collected), the nature of the problem is *clarified* before the question "Why are there so many complaints from customers?" is asked.

STEP 2 DEFINING CURRENT PROCESS

▶ What's The Big Deal About Flowcharts?

Drawing process flowcharts is a form of team data gathering. It gathers the knowledge of the people closest to the process and creates a consensus view of how work actually gets done. Flowcharting often reveals very different ways of doing work and unnecessary steps in the process. Just as importantly, it focuses the entire team on finding the sources of the problem in the process and not on finding the person who may be responsible for creating, monitoring, or avoiding the problem. This takes some of the emotion out of both the diagnosis and the solution.

Macro or micro—at what level of detail should a team start?

Start with the highest (simplest) level of detail and create a macro-flowchart (MJII pages 57 and 119 and also page 71 in this book). This deceptively simple tool is a great way to focus the team's discussion on where the problem occurs. At the very least it can help the team identify locations at which initial data collection should occur. For example, the team at Stop 'N Go Pizza asked two questions as they looked at the macro-flowchart: 1) Which step in the overall process *might* contribute to the problem of customer complaints due to late deliveries? and 2) What is the *actual* average time that it takes to complete each step of the process? Clearly, each step in the process had a potential to affect the total time it took to receive and fulfill an order. Data from the process would either identify a consistent bottleneck or one that moved around, depending on who was working at the time. The Stop 'N Go Pizza team found there were delays throughout the process. If the problem had been addressed at only one point in the process, the overall problem would not have decreased since the product or service could not have moved any faster than the slowest step in the process.

STEP 3 FINDING ROOT CAUSES

▶ Standard vs. Customized Cause Categories

There are standard cause categories that are used in Cause & Effect/Fishbone Diagrams (MJII page 25 or page 28 of this book). These are often referred to as the Four M's: Machinery/Equipment, Manpower/People, Methods, and Materials. These categories can be helpful as a starting point, but they can be limiting as well. A very effective way to generate customized categories is to use an Affinity Diagram (MJII pages 12–18).

Ask the team: *"What are all the possible causes for _____?"* The Affinity process will allow the team to organize the causes, which may create groupings that are more meaningful. Use the header cards from the Affinity as the titles for the cause categories in the C & E Diagram. Shorten the titles if they seem too long. Use the detailed Post-its™ from the Affinity as the initial input for the remainder of the C & E Diagram. Add more causes as needed.

▶ Confirm Causes With Data

Consensus is the most frequently used method for selecting the root problem on a Cause & Effect/Fishbone Diagram. Consensus can be reached by open discussion or a rating method such as Nominal Group Technique or Multivoting. These can be effective methods to gain commitment from team members, but remember that the results represent a collective opinion. For example, in the Stop 'N Go Pizza case, there were *opinions* that employee turnover and training were at the heart of the "late delivery" problem. After the managers reviewed the data, they found that the time spent training new employees had indeed declined and that employee turnover had increased dramatically over the same period. It in fact appeared that there was a *possible* cause/effect relationship between these two factors. Employee turnover could have increased as a result of new employees receiving little training, OR, training could have decreased as a result of the increase in employee turnover, as this turnover created too much demand on the system. If there were more data points, i.e., 50 or more, a Scatter Diagram (MJII pages 145–149) could have been used to test the strength of the relationship between these two factors. In either case, the data made employee training an important business issue for everyone from the president to the newest delivery driver.

STEP 4 DEVELOPING ACTION PLANS

MJII pp. 122–125

▶ Think Small and Learn Fast

A natural tendency is to want to arrive at the "perfect solution" and implement it everywhere as quickly as possible. Pilot implementations have a number of advantages:

– The risk is small. If the solution is not the right one there will be less of a tendency to try to make a poor solution work because of "sunk costs."

– More careful "measurement" can be done. This includes the more subtle effects of a solution that can only be picked up through conversations with the participants. This is usually as revealing as the "hard" measures that we generally take.

– PDCA can be done much faster on a smaller project.

– Innovative solutions are more likely because the cost of "failing " is manageable.

▶ Arbitrary Goals or Helpful Measures?

Dr. W. Edwards Deming warned companies repeatedly about the dangers of arbitrary numerical goals being used as substitutes for good management. His real concern, however, was with goals that were not accompanied by plans of how the system was going to change to support that goal. The targets used in the Stop 'N Go Pizza example (MJII pages 122–123) were milestones to measure the impact of improved training and reduced turnover.

▶ Criteria-Based Solutions

"Best" is a relative term. Team members often come into a discussion with a predetermined picture of what the "best" solution would look like. However, these assumptions are usually not discussed as a group. Instead, they are invisibly applied by each person during the discussion and decision making. These factors often become "hidden agendas." The Prioritization Matrices, or many other criteria-based methods, force the team to make these decision factors visible. The Prioritization Matrices tool goes several steps further by determining the relative importance of each criterion and then applying each weighted criterion to each option. The example for Stop 'N Go Pizza (MJII page 124) is a modified matrix. Notice that the criteria weightings at the top of the matrix have been determined by using a criterion vs. criterion matrix (MJII page 108). However, the Stop 'N Go Pizza team did not continue using the Full Analytical Method. Instead, they arrived at consensus as to how well each option met each criterion using the symbols to show the relative merits of each option. This rating was done through an open discussion. This is an example of mixing and matching methods so that the important decisions are supported by the most helpful tools.

STEP 5 TRYING IT

MJII p. 126

▶ **Just Do It, But . . .**

While an improvement activity is happening there are three things that should be occurring:

1. Follow the plan as it was designed.

2. Document any changes to the plan along with the reasons why the change happened.

3. Take the measurements to measure progress.

These may seem obvious, but if these steps are not done *while* the plan is being implemented, it is very difficult to learn from the process.

STEP 6 REVIEWING RESULTS

MJII p. 127–129

▶ **Connect Real Causes With Real Effects**

The purpose of the PDCA Cycle is to learn from experience which root causes can be eliminated and which activities should continue as they are. The team then must ask this fundamental question: *"Did we do what we said we were going to do and did it have the positive effect that we said it would have?"* At Stop 'N Go Pizza it was clear that the results were very positive and the plan was well executed. The team should feel great about their accomplishments as shown in the Pareto and Run Charts (MJII pages 127–129). However, just as in any experiment, the team needs to look for any other possible explanations for the positive change. For example, if during the time that training time was increased and delivery times were improved, everyone was given a substantial raise and pizza prices were slashed, these changes would tend to have a big impact on both employee turnover and sales volume.

STEP 7 MAKING CHANGES/HOLDING GAINS

MJII pp. 130–131

▶ **Focus On Both the Process and the Results**

When the team is wrapping up the improvement process, members should take the time to examine how well everyone worked together. Regardless of whether this specific team will work as a unit again, everyone can take away lessons learned that will help them be more effective in the next project.

▶ **Work Yourself Out of a Job**

The legacy of an effective improvement team is when another team doesn't have to solve the same problem six months later. This requires the solution to be standardized and for process improvement to become the way that business is done. In the Stop 'N Go Pizza example, the improved training, methods, and measurements would have to be made part of someone's ongoing job responsibilities, or otherwise the improvement will be buried by the day-to-day tasks of running the business. This doesn't mean that improvement in these areas will stop. It only means that the solution will be implemented until circumstances change or a new level of performance is required.

Team Guidelines
From "me" to "we"

IS THIS THE RIGHT TOOL? ASK . . .

▶ Does your team need to develop a common understanding of how it will operate?

▶ Do you want to prevent your team from losing its focus during the life of the project?

▶ Does your team need to develop a common language for discussing issues and developing effective solutions?

▶ Do you want to keep *everyone* on the team involved and enthusiastic at every phase of the project?

▶ Do you want every meeting to be as effective and efficient as possible?

▶ Do you want to end the project in a way that leaves everyone feeling that it was a positive experience with an effective solution?

STEPS AT A GLANCE

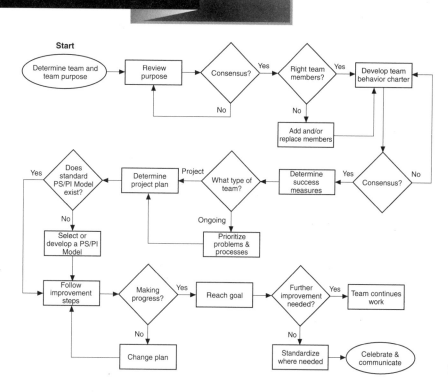

235

TEAM GUIDELINES

Team Guidelines

Q. **Should we form a team at all? When should something simply be an individual assignment?**

A. Teams often fail because they were formed unintentionally and automatically. In fact, people often joke about "forming a committee" as the easiest way to kill an unpopular idea. In order to form intentional teams that are set up to succeed, the following conditions should be met:

– No one person has the necessary knowledge about all of the dimensions of the issue.

– The knowledge of each person should build on that of the other people involved, building a synergy that no one person working alone could create.

– The acceptability of the solution by those people who will implement it should be critical to the success of the project.

An individual assignment is often the most effective option when there is a person that is truly an acknowledged "expert" (not self-proclaimed), who is required to come up with a "technical" solution. Even when others have a piece of the solution, an individual assignment may still be the best option if an individual is simply gathering data rather than truly combining and blending ideas.

Q. **What kind of leadership roles should exist in a team for it to be successful?**

A. Start from the assumption that any team activity has two components: task and process. *Task* refers to all of the things that relate to the **content** of the issue being addressed and the **conduct** of the team meeting itself. This would include such things as the quality of the ideas generated, the degree to which the agenda is being followed, how decisions are made, how much progress is being made on the project topics, how assignments are being assigned and fulfilled, and so on. *Process* refers to how well (or poorly) all of the team members are interacting while forming the team and performing their tasks. This would include such things as the degree to which everyone is participating, the existence of interpersonal conflict among team members, the causes for the team getting "stuck," and so on. These two key areas of *task* and *process* should be handled by someone on the team. Some team leaders are skilled enough to handle both areas. However, most of the time at least two people are required. The person responsible for the task areas is generally called the *team leader* while the person who monitors and helps with the process areas is referred to as a *facilitator*. Depending on the size of the team and the complexity of the project, the team leader can delegate even further by assigning roles such as recorder/scribe, timekeeper, and other roles.

Q. **What makes a team great?**

A. Respectful leadership, a focused purpose that everyone agrees is important, clear and fulfilled assignments, members that hold each other accountable, open communication, respectful conflict, and an atmosphere of energy and fun!

Unlike the chapters in Part II of the *Coach's Guide*, which are dedicated to a specific method, this entire chapter focuses on the essentials of facilitation at every stage of a team's life. Look for these essentials throughout the chapter.

LEARNING ACTIVITY

The purpose of this learning activity is to experience two team styles of operation: unstructured and structured.

Unstructured

1. Break into groups of 4–6 people.

2. Give each group the following assignment: *Plan the next, (or first, depending on the organization), organization-wide "state-of-the-state" meeting.*

3. Give the groups 20 minutes to come up with the design for that meeting.

4. Spend 10 minutes to review the team's impression of the meeting in the following areas: What is the quality of the plans that were produced by the groups? What leadership roles were taken on by whom? How did everyone feel about their own participation and contribution to the process?

Structured

1. Stay in the same groups as in the unstructured portion of the exercise.

2. Give each group the following assignment: *Improve the quality of staff meetings.*

3. Ask each of the groups to complete the four steps listed below. (Allow about 35 minutes for the groups to complete all of the steps.)

   – Write and post a purpose statement for the meeting. (5 minutes.)

   – Select a meeting leader, recorder, and timekeeper. (2 minutes.)

   – Identify and post five items for the agenda, along with times for each item. Allow 20 minutes for the total agenda. (5 minutes.)

   – Follow the agenda.

4. Evaluate the meeting process using the same review questions as in the unstructured example above. Add the question, *"What value was added by introducing the meeting structure?"*

The best way to achieve a common goal is to *intentionally* start a team. Teams often fail when people "fall" into them out of habit or because it is the preferred operating style of progressive organizations. Team because you want to. Team because you need to. Just don't team for the sake of teaming!

▶ **Write A Team Behavior Charter: Develop Your Own or Buy One "Off the Shelf"?**

On page 150 of *The Memory Jogger™ II* there is a list of typical items in a behavior charter. It's a good list, but should a team simply reproduce it and swear allegiance to it? No, and here's why. The purpose of a team is to create a process for the right people to collaborate effectively toward a common purpose. Especially among people who don't generally work together, the first real challenge is to commit to working and supporting each other as well as to the team's goal. What better way to start than to state and agree on the things that will help you succeed. Even among people who have worked together on other projects, it's a great way to remind them to build on those things that helped them in the past and to avoid the things that have hindered their performance. In either the case of a new team and a new purpose, or an old team and a new purpose, spend no more than 20 minutes of the first meeting creating and posting this list.

▶ **Why Post the Behavior Charter at Every Meeting?**

Posting the behavior charter on a flipchart at each meeting can be a visible reminder to keep the process in focus while the team "gets the job done." It can also serve as a simple device to stop whatever craziness team members are involved in outside of the meeting.

▶ **Decision Making: What are the Options?**

There are two major dimensions of decision making that any team needs to clarify if it is to be successful: Process and Authority. *Process* refers to how the team is going to make decisions. *Authority* refers to the extent that the team can make things happen as a result of its work. Both are important because they affect the expectations of team members. If these expectations are not consistent, someone is bound to be either confused or disappointed. Listed below are three options for teams to use in deciding how they will make decisions *as a team*.

▶ **Consensus (Option 1):** Consensus is: "Finding a proposal acceptable enough that all members can support it; no member opposes it." (*The Team Handbook*, Joiner Associates, Inc., page 2-40.) Consensus is not unanimity, which is generally not a feasible goal. Rather, consensus is based on the assumption that solutions are more likely to succeed if all of the key participants are "comfortable enough" with the outcome to move forward. This willingness to support a decision comes largely from a process in which everyone feels that they (and their ideas) have been treated fairly and that all of the relevant factors have been taken into account.

When should you use consensus?

– When support by all team members of the team is vital to the success of the plan created by the team.

– When both circumstances and the team members will allow the time necessary to get all the ideas on the table and discuss them thoroughly.

– When building the cohesiveness of the team is as important as the quality of the team's solution.

What are the strengths and weaknesses of consensus?

Strengths
- Consensus creates support and likelihood of success.
- Consensus respects the contribution of all team members.
- Consensus increases the chances of creative solutions.
- Consensus does not create winners and losers.

Weaknesses
- Consensus appears to be time consuming (sometimes a reality and sometimes a perception).
- It's hard to know when you have "it."
- Consensus requires good team facilitation skills to get everyone to contribute consistently.

▶ **Majority Rule (Option 2):** This simply states that 51% of the team members determine the fate of the process and the solution. This is by far the simplest option since it only requires that team members know how to count.

When should you use majority rule?

- When a decision has to be made quickly.
- When the team has had a thorough discussion, failed to reach consensus and must move quickly to a decision.
- When an established team agrees that it's an acceptable way to proceed.

What are the strengths and weaknesses of majority rule?

Strengths
- Majority rule is fast.
- Sometimes majority rule is the only way to move the team forward if they have been unable to achieve consensus.
- Majority rule is familiar and requires minimal facilitation.

Weaknesses
- Majority rule creates winners and losers.
- Majority rule makes it possible (and likely) that conflict and true disagreement is avoided rather than being dealt with productively.
- Majority rule is too convenient and comfortable. At the first sign of "trouble," a team may say, "Let's take a vote."

▶ **Anarchy (Option 3):** Sometimes anarchy is the rule rather than the exception in many team meetings. The consistent popularity of anarchy is that it draws upon a basic law of nature: "survival of the fittest."

When should you use anarchy?

- When team members threaten you with expulsion, (or worse), if you say "Can we do a process check . . . one more time?"
- When half of the team is doing expense reports during the meeting.
- When machine operators knock on the door to ask you to keep the noise down because they can't hear themselves think.

What are the strengths and weaknesses of anarchy?

Strengths
- Everyone knows what anarchy feels like.

- It is never dull.

- It will sharpen your survival skills.

Weaknesses
- Somebody could get hurt.

- PDCA is often interpreted as **P**lease **D**on't **C**ome **A**rmed!

- Victories are celebrated at the expense of the rest of the team.

▶ Each Person Has a Part to Play: Meeting Roles and Responsibilities

The phrase "conducting" a meeting is very appropriate. Compare the success of an orchestra's performance during a show with a team's performance during a meeting: both performances require synchronized activities; and the performance of a team can lead to either celestial harmony or "the meeting from hell." A good meeting, as a good performance from an orchestra, depends on balanced participation. An orchestra, (contrary to appearances), has different people playing different kinds of leadership roles. For example, the first violin plays a key role in keeping the tone and pace consistent.

The same is true for "conducting" team meetings.

What are the equivalent roles involved in conducting an effective meeting?

▶ **Leader:** The leader keeps everyone on track by making sure the team is making progress on achieving their purpose. The leader handles the logistics of arranging for the meeting space, gathering supplies for the meeting, setting and publishing the agenda, and making sure that the meeting minutes are produced and distributed.

▶ **Facilitator:** The facilitator monitors the health and quality of the teamwork and participation and intervenes as necessary. Facilitators need to be aware at all times of how well the team is functioning as a team.

▶ **Recorder:** This person records the major points of the meeting on a flipchart or board. The person records at the level of detail requested by the group and then captures major summary points, decisions, action steps, and assignments in the meeting minutes. For an excellent example of various alternatives to recording meetings, see pages 4-9 through 4-14 of *The Team Handbook*, published by Joiner Associates, Inc.

▶ **Timekeeper:** The timekeeper monitors and intervenes as necessary the time allocations that the team members have agreed on for the agenda items, and announces the time remaining until the end of the meeting.

In unusual cases, the team leader is skilled enough to perform both the task-oriented role as well as that of the process-oriented facilitator's role. It is much more common for a team to combine the role of the timekeeper and the recorder. While it is always desirable to "spread the wealth" by rotating roles, team leaders generally stay in place for the life of the project. Team facilitators can be rotated as long as there is a strong set of skills present. If not, leave an effective facilitator in place. The easiest roles to rotate are the timekeeper and the recorder. This is particularly recommended for the recorder role since the production of the minutes can be quite time consuming.

▶ Develop a Purpose Charter

Watch out for this step, it will kill you! During the team process, achieving consensus ranges in importance from helpful to absolutely critical. Gaining full consensus on the purpose of a team project goes off the critical scale. Time and again the failure to slug it out at the beginning of the process has led to project inefficiency, if not outright failure. A helpful way to clarify this statement is: *"What would success look like in this project?"* This not only creates focus, but it often uncovers a deeper purpose than was originally envisioned.

Once the consensus on the purpose is achieved, post it at the beginning of each meeting, alongside the team's behavior charter. This is a simple and absolutely powerful way to keep the team on track. In fact, it is a close to foolproof facilitation device when members want to roam into parts unknown. Simply point to the purpose statement and ask, *"How does that move us closer toward our stated purpose?"* If this doesn't work ask, *"Has our purpose changed?"* The beauty of both these approaches is that they place the burden for making progress squarely on the shoulders of those responsible for it: the entire team, not just the leader.

▶ Develop Measures of Team Progress

Assess both the process and the project. The team needs to set benchmarks for itself at all times if it hopes to practice the Plan, Do, Check, Act Cycle during the life of the project.

▶ **Team Process:**
At the end of each meeting it's helpful to take five minutes to ask and record: *"What were the positives and negatives (opportunities) of this meeting?"* *"What should we work on improving at our next meeting?"* *"How did we do in following our own team charter?"* These comments and suggestions should be included in the meeting records. In addition, on a regular basis, every six weeks or six meetings, ask everyone to either rate the effectiveness of the team within the meeting or as individuals using standard categories and scales. The illustration shown on the next page is a typical self-assessment form. (The source is *Growing Teams: A Down-to-Earth Approach*, GOAL/QPC, 1993, pages 67–69.)

How Do the Members of Your Team Participate on the Team?

Review the 10 key factors of effective teams listed below. Draw a circle around the number that most accurately describes your team. A "1" is the lowest rating and indicates that many problems exist. A "5" is the highest rating and indicates that the team is strong and effective.

1 Purpose and objectives

1	2	3	4	5
Not clear and not understood by everyone				Clearly understood by everyone

2 Involvement/Participation

1	2	3	4	5
Some members are silent and contribute very little				All members are encouraged to participate

3 Conflict

1	2	3	4	5
Occurs continuously and is not dealt with properly				When it occurs, it is dealt with openly

4 Communication/Listening

1	2	3	4	5
Guarded: feelings are not freely expressed				Members feel free to say what is on their minds

5 Leadership

1	2	3	4	5
Team leader plays a strong dominant role				Members share leadership role

6 Problem Solving

1	2	3	4	5
Tools have not been identified and agreed on for this purpose				Team members share knowledge of the tools

7 Meeting Climate

1	2	3	4	5
Formal, rigid, with many signs of tension				Members are relaxed and think meetings are fun

8 Roles and Assignments

1	2	3	4	5
Assignments are vague and not distributed evenly				Assignments are clear and involve all members

9 Creativity

1	2	3	4	5
No premium for "wild" ideas: they are in fact discouraged				Members use brainstorming often to seek fresh approaches

10 Self-Assessment

1	2	3	4	5
There is never enough time for the team to evaluate its effectiveness				Team members frequently assess their progress

▶ **Project Progress:** The easiest things to assess in a project are the tasks completed and the adherence to the projected project schedule. For the task completion review, look at the tools such as the Affinity Diagram (MJII pages 12–18), Matrix Diagram (MJII pages 85–90), Prioritization Matrices (MJII pages 105–114), Tree Diagram (MJII pages 156–160), and the Process Decision Program Chart (MJII pages 160–161). For the schedule review, use tools such as the Activity Network Diagram (MJII pages 3–11), and the Gantt Chart (MJII page 9).

All of these assessments relate to the team and project *process*. The *product* of the team should always be assessed using the fact-based tools whenever possible. Once there has been significant progress in completing the tasks of the project, gather the original data again using tools such as the Check Sheet (MJII pages 31–35), Control Chart (MJII pages 36–51), Histogram (MJII pages 66–75), Pareto Chart (MJII pages 95–104), Run Chart (MJII pages 141–144), and the Scatter Diagram (MJII pages 145–149).

MAINTAINING MOMENTUM (PHASE 2)

MJII pp. 151–153

Starting teams is in many ways the easy part. Many of the steps in the formation of teams (reviewed above) are crucial for helping a team to keep on track and improve itself during the course of the project. However, it takes a combination of leadership and discipline to build on these beginning structures and maintain the energy and focus among team members with very busy schedules and varied agendas. What can mere mortals do to keep the enthusiasm constant from the beginning to the end of a project?

▶ **Follow a Common Roadmap: The Power of a Standard Process**

Much of a team's inertia is due to either a genuine lack of knowledge about the next thing to do or an overabundance of opinions of same. The end result is this: the team spins its wheels! Team members often unfairly look to the leader or coach to "get us out of this." A common Problem-Solving/Process Improvement Model has a number of advantages:

– The steps have been agreed to up front by the entire team, so that there is positive pressure to follow the model.

– The model can be kept visible, just as is the behavior charter and the team purpose.

– The model helps creates a common language to talk about tough problems. A common language will take some of the negative emotion out of the discussion.

– The model provides a proven path because thousands of companies have adopted such models with tremendous results.

▶ **Agree on the Improvement Model to Use**

There are many different common improvement models. In fact, it is very likely that your organization has adopted one as its own. If not, *do not paralyze your team or organization in the selection of the "perfect" model.* The most important thing to do is to choose one and follow it faithfully. Ideally, the entire organization or location should choose one common model so that team members can move easily from one team to another with this common framework and language.

The model shown in the Problem-Solving/Process Improvement Model chapter of *The Memory Jogger™ II*, pages 115–131, was created as a hybrid from many different sources. The model comes from proven sources and would be very appropriate for most situations. Regardless of whether your team chooses this particular model, ANY model should meet the following criteria:

— It should be as simple as possible. Additional steps do not always equate to added-value.

— It should build on both available data *and* the knowledge of the team members (and outside resources).

— It should reflect the complete Plan, Do, Check, Act (PDCA) Cycle within its steps.

— It should encourage discipline but also allow necessary flexibility.

▶ Master Methods: Don't Let Methods Master You

There is only one proven way to prevent leaders and teams from becoming "tool addicts": ask *"What are we trying to discover and how will this tool help us?"* Without a clear picture of the *purpose* of any method, using a tool can easily become an end unto itself. There is such a thing as a problem that is best resolved by team members who *talk* about the facts and their feelings, and then decide as a team the most effective, acceptable solution. Some teams, however, may need or desire more structure and feel more comfortable using an established method (a tool) in support of team discussion.

The only cautionary note is that the team should always ask what *the data* is revealing about the issue under discussion before turning to personal judgments. If there is a need to enhance the team's understanding of either opinions or the facts (or both), *only then* turn to the excellent toolkit of methods that have evolved over the last 35 years. The two Tool Selector Charts shown at the beginning of this book can be very helpful in making a wise choice.

▶ Harness the Power of Team Dynamics: Get Skilled or Get Resources

Good people working in teams on important topics can self-destruct simply because they are unaware of what's really going on. The team gets so immersed in trying to "take care of business" that they miss most of the trouble signs. By thorough training, the team can become skilled at healing itself. The same can be done for any leader. However, sometimes it is advisable to bring in a "pro" on either a full- or part-time basis to help the team assess its own process. If the team does not have the luxury of a full-time facilitator, at least a regular check-up every fourth meeting would help the team stay or get back on track. As always, a balance must be struck between a healthy attention to the "vital signs" of a team and becoming obsessed with "process."

Sometimes teams and projects are like relatives that come for a little visit and then just stay . . . and stay . . . and stay. Sometimes teams have become so effective that the team members simply don't want the experience to end (even when it should). Other times, the team is afraid to finish because there is a feeling that they have failed. If the team never "wraps it up," then the team doesn't have to confront its own problems.

In the end, there are only two questions that help a team bring closure to its work:

- "Did we do what we said we were going to do, using the plan that we said we were going to follow?" (See "Develop a Purpose Charter" under Phase I, Starting Teams.)

- "Did we behave in the way that our 'team behavior charter' stated?"

Both questions relate to the concept of "synthesis." What did team members learn from their experience? What actions had a given reaction? The more that the team members can know about what worked, the easier it will be for them to function on another team again, and perhaps apply to other situations the knowledge of a process that led to a solution.

▶ **Standardize or Be Doomed to the "Curse of the Never-Ending Team"**

One of the least appreciated contributions of the continuous improvement revolution is the Standardize, Do, Check, Act (SDCA) Cycle. Any team that ends a project with proven solutions should also be building in a process for reviewing whether a solution that is being implemented is consistently addressing the problem. (The SDCA Cycle is often linked with the phrase "holding the gains.") "Holding the gains" includes changes in procedures and process documentation as needed, as well as providing additional training. In brief, "holding the gains" requires careful planning that makes the solution a part of daily life, and which will not "slip back" when other issues arise as priorities.

Take heed: don't change the way you or your coworkers do something unless there is a reason and capability to improve the situation or process. This state of "business as usual" requires a team to constantly maintain a delicate balance between the discipline of performing a process as it was designed and the creativity to look for new ways of improving process performance.

Team Guidelines

▶ Books

Amsden, Davida M., Robert T. Amsden, and Howard E. Butler. *SPC Simplified: Practical Steps to Quality.* White Plains, NY: Quality Resources, 1989.
This hands-on manual describes the basics of statistical process control. It simplifies the essentials for monitoring, analyzing, and improving quality. Numerous practice problems and real-life examples are provided.

_____. *SPC Simplified for Services: Practical Tools for Continuous Quality Improvement.* White Plains, NY: Quality Resources, 1991.
This book provides a source for service personnel to learn and apply the tools and techniques of statistical process control. Numerous practice problems and real-life examples are provided.

Automotive Industry Action Group. *Fundamental Statistical Process Control Reference Manual.* Southfield, MI: Automotive Industry Action Group, 1992.
This manual was prepared by the quality and supplier assessment staffs at Chrysler, Ford, and General Motors, working under the auspices of the Automotive Division of the American Society for Quality Control Supplier Quality Requirements Task Force, in collaboration with the Automotive Industry Action Group (A.I.A.G.). For more information, call A.I.A.G. at 810-358-3570.

Brassard, Michael, Francine Oddo, and Susan Tucker, eds. *The Educators' Companion to The Memory Jogger Plus+®.* Methuen, MA: GOAL/QPC, 1993.
A complete resource guide for learning, teaching, and facilitating the 7 MP Tools in grades K–12.

Brassard, Michael, ed. *The Memory Jogger™.* Methuen, MA: GOAL/QPC, 1988.
This pocket-size booklet consists of practical descriptions and examples of some of the tools and techniques used in problem solving, problem identification, and problem analysis. Includes: Brainstorming, Cause & Effect Diagram, Check Sheet, Control Chart, Flowchart, Force Field Analysis, Histogram, Nominal Group Technique, Pareto Chart, Process Capability, Run Chart, Scatter Diagram, and Stratification.

Brassard, Michael and Diane Ritter. *The Memory Jogger™ II.* Methuen, MA: GOAL/QPC, 1994.
This pocket-size booklet consists of practical descriptions and examples of the quality control (QC) tools, management and planning (MP) tools, a tool selector chart, guidelines for teams, and a full case study.

Brassard, Michael. *The Memory Jogger Plus+®.* Methuen, MA: GOAL/QPC, 1989.
Describes in-depth the 7 MP Tools, and provides numerous tool illustrations and examples. Includes a complete case study, glossary of terms, and 10 removable, pocket-sized cards. The tools are: Activity Network Diagram, Affinity Diagram, Interrelationship Digraph, Matrix Diagram, Prioritization Matrices, Process Decision Program Chart (PDPC), and Tree Diagram.

Chambers, David and Donald Wheeler. *Understanding Statistical Process Control.* Knoxville, TN: Statistical Process Controls, 1992.
Industrial practitioners who have little or no formal statistical training will find that this straightforward book takes the mystique out of understanding the statistical techniques used in process control.

Collett, Dennis and Larry McClosky. *TQM: A Basic Text.* Methuen, MA: GOAL/QPC, 1993.
The first basic comprehensive book that describes the elements and tools of TQM.

Harper, Ann and Bob Harper. *Team Barriers: Actions for Overcoming the Blocks to Empowerment, Involvement, and High-Performance.* Mohegan Lake, NY: MW Corporation, 1994.
Examines the planning, implementation, maintenance, and renewal "skills" that high-performance teams must have if they are to succeed. This book/workbook is an action plan for succeeding at empowerment, involvement, and high performance.

Howard, Jennifer M. and Lawrence M. Miller. *Team Management: Creating Systems & Skills for a Team-Based Organization.* Atlanta: Miller Consulting Group, Inc., 1994.
This workbook provides team leaders and team members with the necessary skills for total involvement in continuous improvement.

Ishikawa, Kaoru. *Guide to Quality Control.* Tokyo: Asian Productivity Organization, 1982.
Considered the indispensible basic text on statistical quality control. Includes information on the QC tools, data collection and analysis, sampling, sampling inspection, practice problems, and other topics.

Kume, Hitoshi. *Statistical Methods for Quality Improvement.* Tokyo: The Association for Overseas Technical Scholarship, 1991.
This book will help you analyze and control processes to improve quality, reduce costs, and increase productivity. It illustrates how statistics methods may be applied to solve real-world problems.

Michalko, Michael. *Thinkertoys: A Handbook of Business Creativity for the 90s.* Berkeley, CA: Ten Speed Press, 1991.
More than 30 meticulously outlined techniques, and hundreds of hints, tricks, tips, and tales to turn anyone into a startlingly creative thinker.

Montgomery, William. *Power Up Teams and Tools: For Process Improvement and Problem Solving.* Pittstown, NJ: Montgomery Group, 1994.
Provides specific guidance on the potentials and pitfalls in using problem-solving and process-improvement tools. For facilitators, trainers, team leaders, process sponsors, and team members.

Scholtes, Peter. *The Team Handbook.* Madison, WI: Joiner Associates Inc., 1988.
A practical guide to working in or with project teams. It is packed with step-by-step instructions, illustrations, and worksheets that demonstrate how to implement many quality improvement principles.

Western Electric Company. *Statistical Quality Control Handbook.* Indianapolis, IN: Western Electric Company, 1982.

Wycoff, Joyce. *Mindmapping: Your Personal Guide to Exploring Creativity and Problem Solving.* New York: Berkley Books, 1991.
A no-nonsense, practical, extremely readable guide to help you put your creative powers to work.

Other Resources

▶ Job Aid

Problem-Solving Machine for The Memory Jogger™ II. GOAL/QPC and Compact Training Company, 1994.

> A portable and reusable tool that guides individuals and teams, step-by-step, through the Problem-Solving/Process-Improvement Model in *The Memory Jogger™ II.* This convenient reference to the seven steps in the model, with cross-references to support pages in *The Memory Jogger™ II,* helps teams spend time on solving problems, not on deciding what to do next.

▶ Software

The Memory Jogger™ Software. Methuen, MA: GOAL/QPC, 1993.

> Written for Windows™ and based on *The Memory Jogger™* and the basic quality control tools. (Cause & Effect Diagram, Check Sheet with Pareto Analysis, Control Chart, Flowchart, Histogram with Capability Analysis, Pareto Chart, Run Chart, Scatter Diagram with Regression Analysis.)

The Memory Jogger Plus+® Software. Methuen, MA: GOAL/QPC, 1994.

> Written for Windows™ and based on *The Memory Jogger Plus+®* and the management and planning tools. (Activity Network Diagram, Affinity Diagram, Interrelationship Digraph, Matrix Diagram, Prioritization Matrices, Process Decision Program Chart, Tree Diagram.)

Tools of Total Quality. Cambridge, MA: MicroMentor, Inc., 1994.

> An engaging CD-ROM desktop learning module that enables teams and individuals to learn, practice, or refresh their understanding of a variety of TQM analytical tools on a just-in-time basis.

▶ Videotapes

Basic Tools for Quality & Process Improvement Videotape Series. Cincinnati, OH: Amatulli & Associates, 1994.

> This series of 4 tapes includes the most commonly used of the basic quality control tools: Cause & Effect Diagram, Check Sheet, Flowchart, Pareto Diagram, and Run Chart. Supporting materials included.

Integrated Management & Planning Tools: A Company Case Study Videotape. Methuen, MA: GOAL/QPC, 1994.

> This tape presents a business situation that is based on an actual case study of a company who uses the 7 MP Tools as an integral part of their project planning. Supporting materials included.

The Memory Jogger Plus+® Videotape Series. Methuen, MA: GOAL/QPC, 1992.

> This series of 8 tapes is designed to educate your employees in the use of the 7 MP Tools. (Activity Network Diagram, Affinity Diagram, Interrelationship Digraph, Matrix Diagram, Prioritization Matrices, Process Decision Program Chart, Tree Diagram.) Supporting materials included.

Total Quality Management in Education Videotape Series. Methuen, MA: GOAL/QPC, 1994.

> This is a comprehensive, two-part series that will help education leaders implement TQM in their K–12 school systems. Package includes 14 tapes and supporting materials.

Index

Index